The Best Of
Alex
2011

Charles Peattie & Russell Taylor

Masterley Publishing

The Best Of
Alex
2011

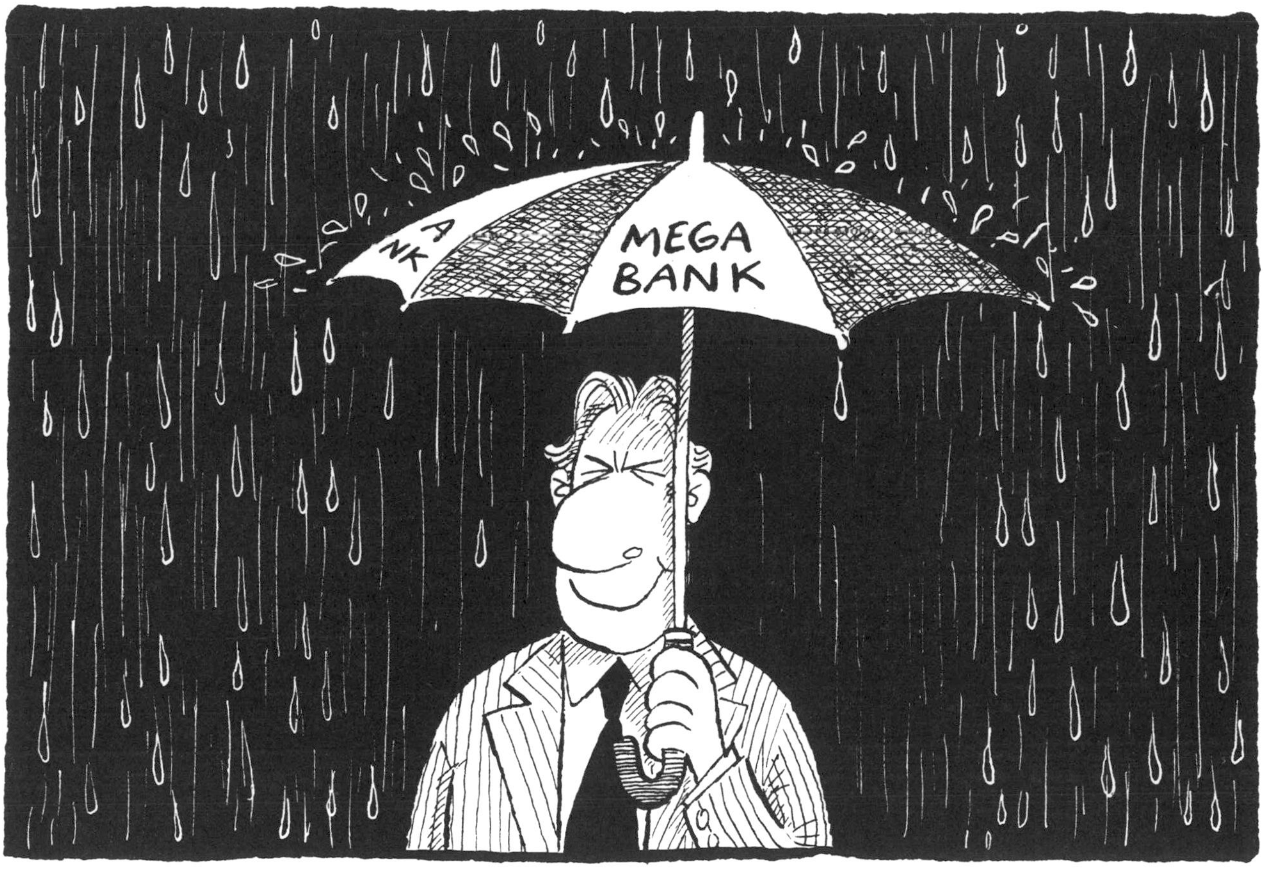
MEGA
BANK

Copyright © 2010 - 2011 Charles Peattie and Russell Taylor

The right of Charles Peattie and Russell Taylor to be identified as the Authors of the Work has been asserted by them in accordance with the Copyright, Designs and Patents Act 1988.

First Published in 2011 by MASTERLEY PUBLISHING

All rights reserved. No part of this publication may be reproduced, stored in a retrieval system, or transmitted, in any form or by any means without the prior written permission of the publisher, nor be otherwise circulated in any form of binding or cover other than that in which it is published and without a similar condition being imposed on the subsequent purchaser.

Layout and Artwork: Suzette Field

ISBN: 978 1 85375 827 0

Printed and bound by CPI Group (UK) Ltd, Croydon, CR0 4YY

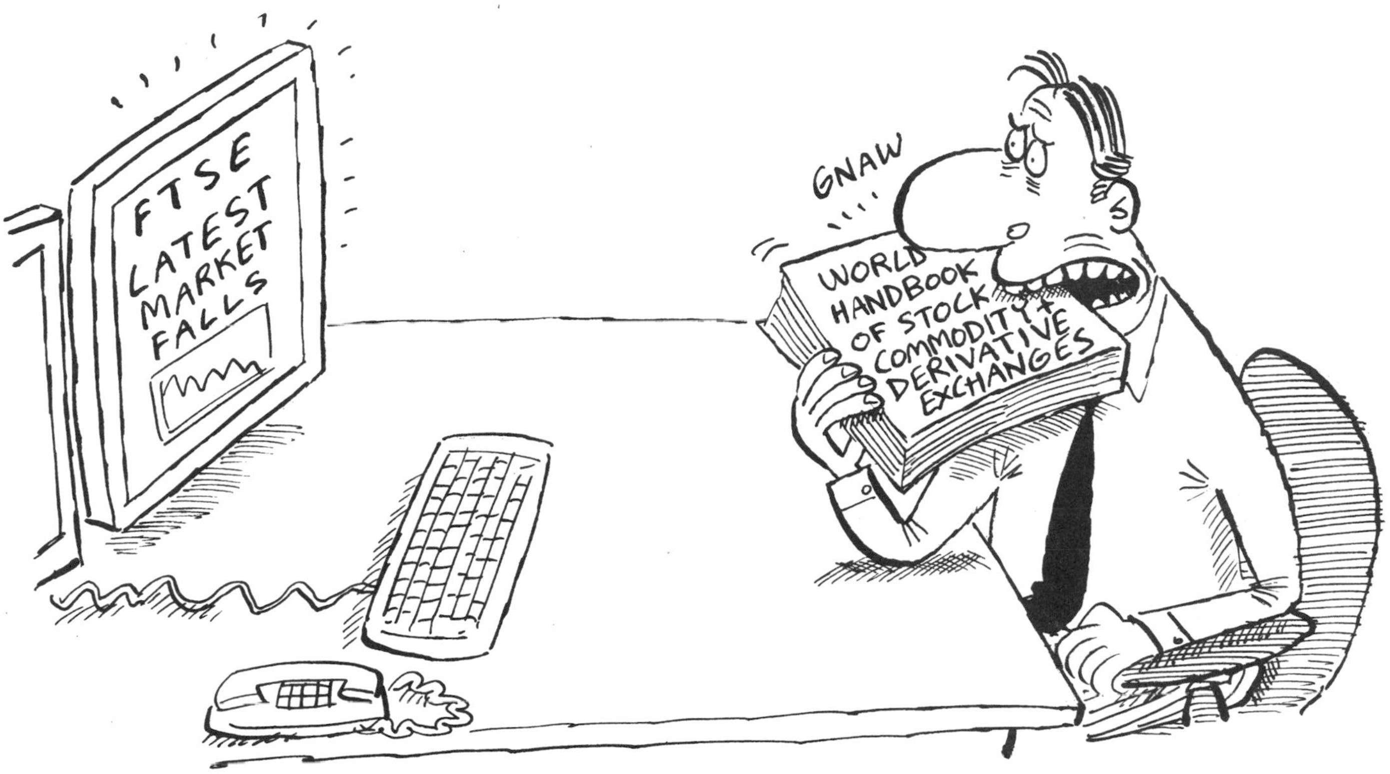
FTSE
LATEST
MARKET
FALLS
GNAW
WORLD
HANDBOOK
OF STOCK
COMMODITY +
DERIVATIVE
EXCHANGES

Our usual gratitude goes to our generous sponsors.

FTSE Group (FTSE) is the world-leader in the creation and management of index solutions.

Mondo Visione provides vital knowledge about the world's exchanges and trading venues.

FOREWORD

A question that we are often asked by readers is: what comes first in creating an Alex cartoon: the words or the pictures? The answer is neither. What comes first is the lunch. Lunch is an integral part of our job. In the same way that Alex will ply a CFO with wine to get him to blurt out some price sensitive information about his company, we dine with the real life Alexes who tell us all about the arcane world they work in.

You see we don't need to make up much stuff. A lot of what you'll read in this book comes straight from the horse's mouth. In fact our job is frequently to tone down the stories we're told, so that our non-City readership (and there are quite a few of them) won't conclude that we are taking too many liberties with our satirical licence.

Sometimes we wonder what's in it for the guys who find themselves (or rather their banks) picking up the tab for these lunches with us. Perhaps it's a sort of confessional for them. In a world of corporate conformity it gives them the chance to divulge their real opinion about the people that blight their lives: bosses, clients, compliance officers etc.

Or maybe it's that it allows them to unburden themselves of a mindset that is as taboo as sexism or ageism in the financial workplace, namely: pessimism. Whatever their private opinions may be, in the City everyone has to be unremittingly bullish in public: about their bonuses, about their business, about the state of the economy..

But for the last three years we have been hearing pretty much the same message from nearly all the bankers, brokers, traders and financial PR people who we lunch with. It's usually expressed along the lines of "Well, I don't know.. This market looks like pants to me and there's a load more bad stuff in the pipeline. But everyone else seems to think it's going to be okay"

This is what they tell us in private. In public they remain as unremittingly upbeat as ever. That's because a general mood of confidence sustains markets and stops the economy going down the tubes.

It's all very worrying.

Do they think that as satirists and social commentators we have so little influence on public opinion that it's safe for them to tell us this stuff? Or are we expected to respect the sanctity of the upmarket French restaurant and not reveal anything said in it?

Sometimes we wonder what would happen if all those people found out that everyone else was (like them) seemingly merely putting on a macho display of bullishness in public while inwardly quaking..

No, it's probably best not to go there.. In fact it's probably best to go to a restaurant, while you still have a job and expense account, and have a nice lunch. And if you need someone to come with you we're always available.

Charles Peattie   Russell Taylor

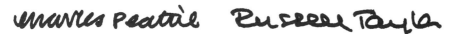

Charles Peattie and Russell Taylor

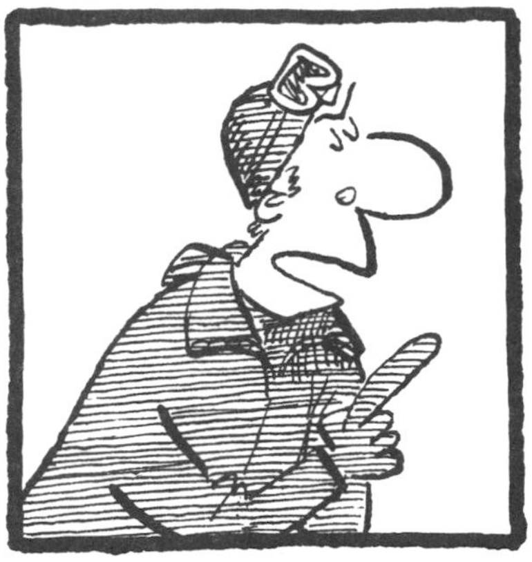

Alex - investment banker

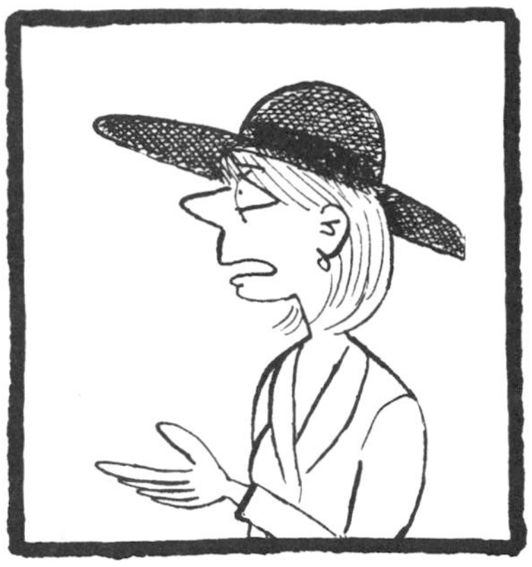

Penny - Alex's wife

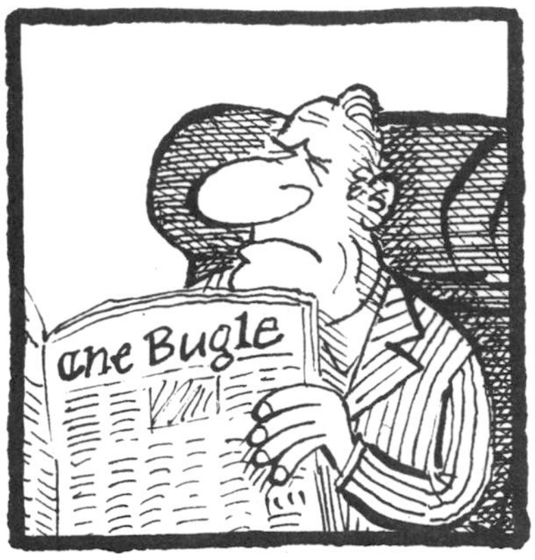
the Bugle

Rupert - senior banker

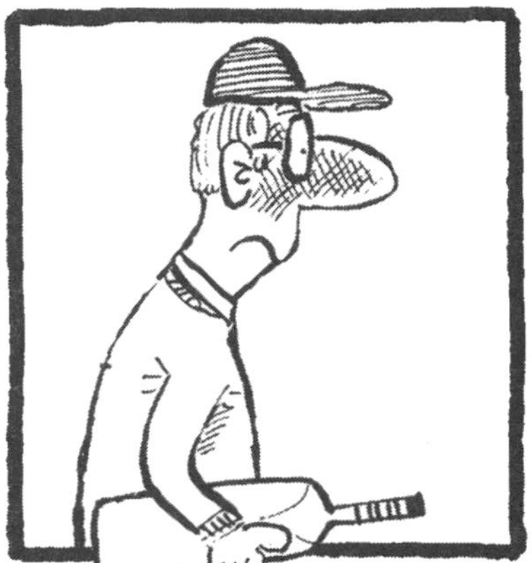

Clive - Alex's colleague

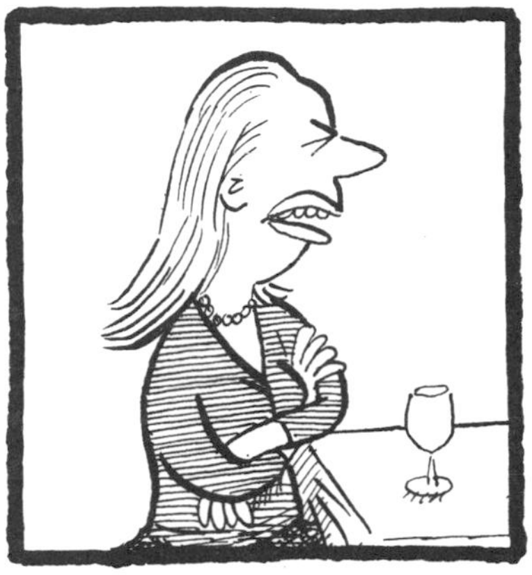

Bridget - Clive's wife

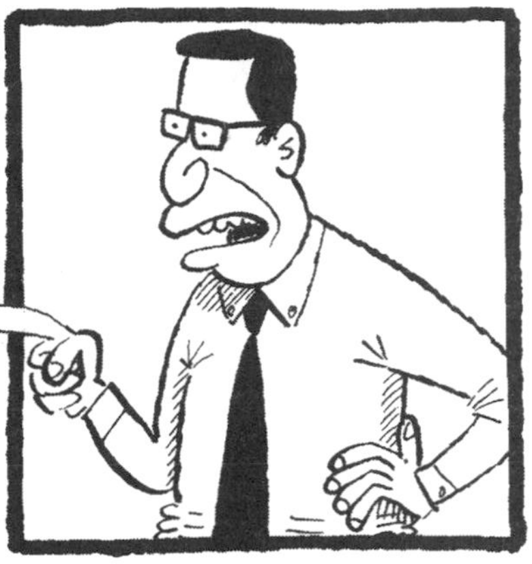

Cyrus - Alex's boss

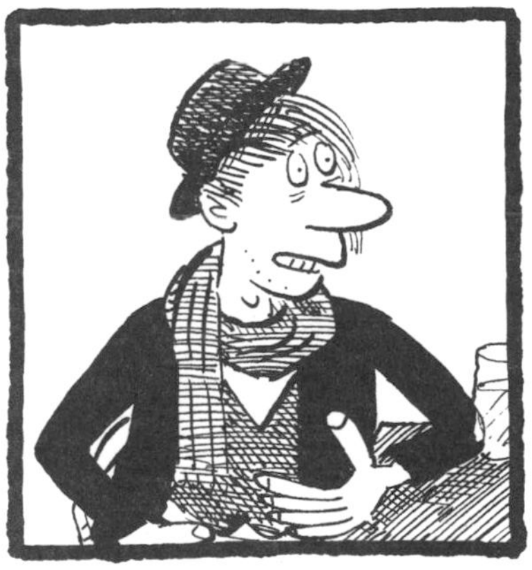

Christopher - Alex's son

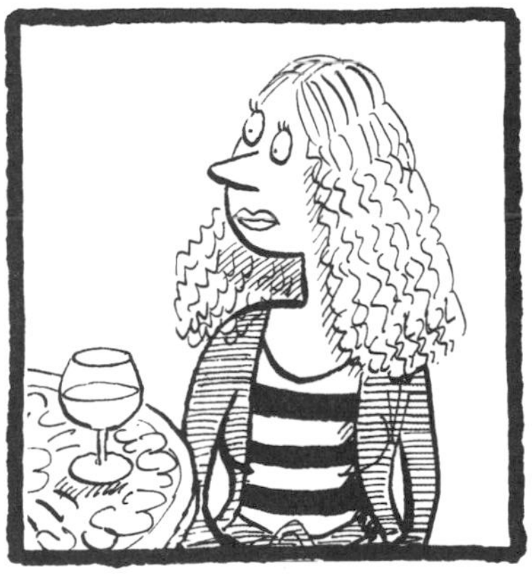

Sophie - Christopher's girlfriend

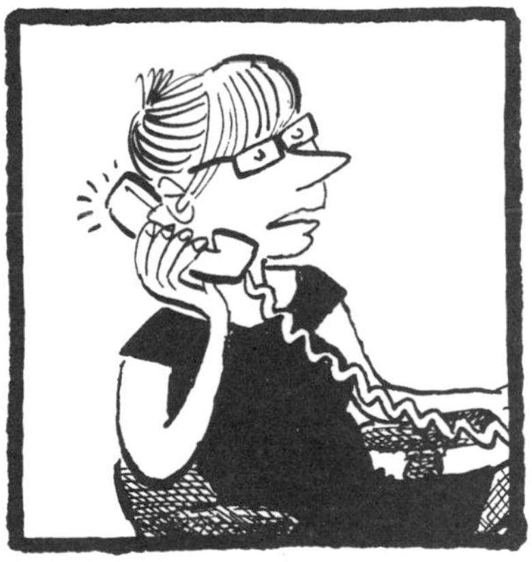

Sara - headhunter

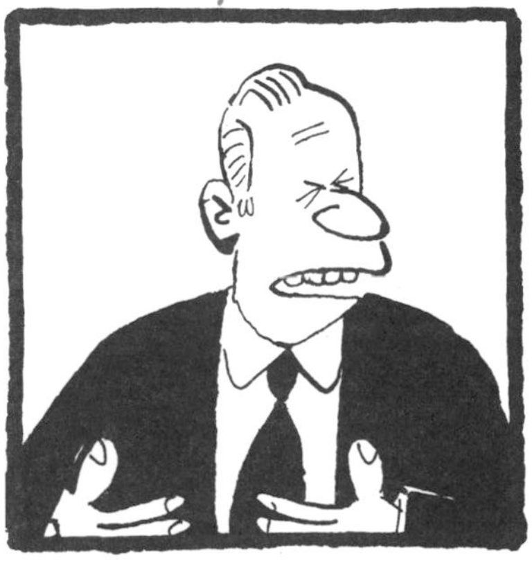

Justin - ex-banker MP

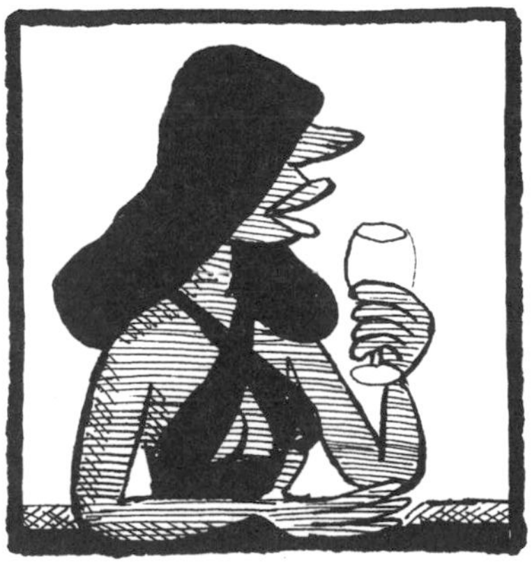

Fabergé - lapdancer

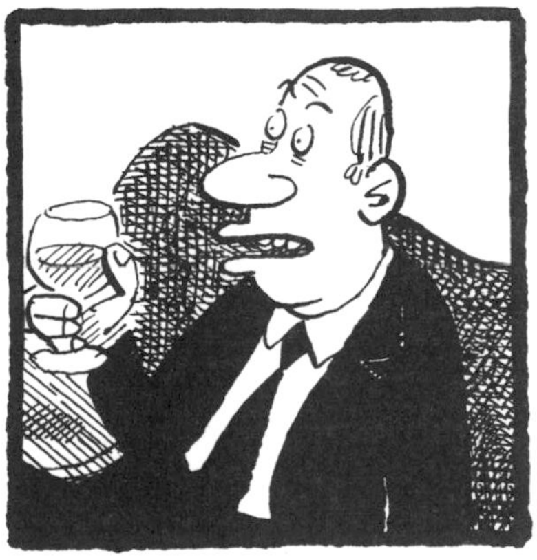

William - wealth manager

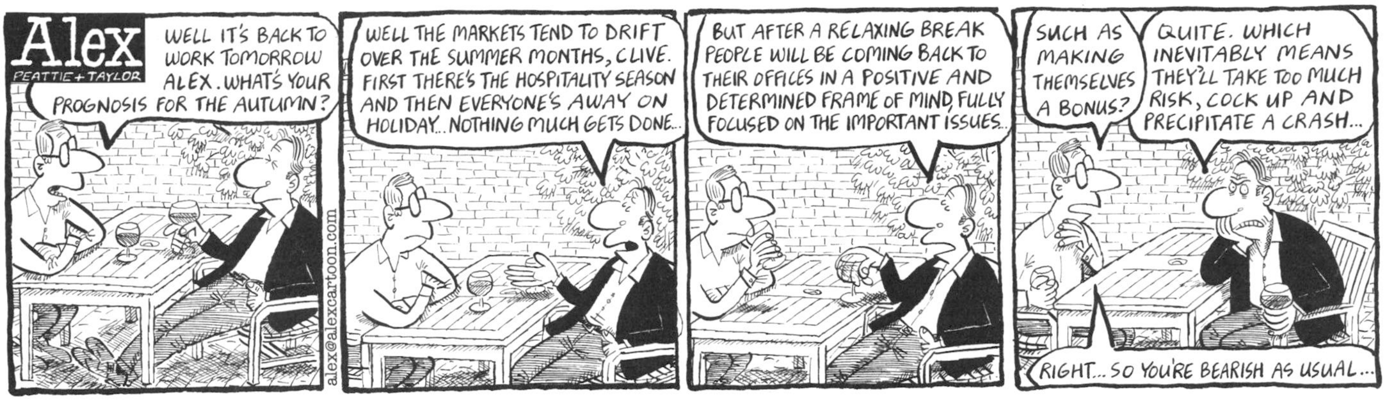
Alex
PEATTIE + TAYLOR
WELL IT'S BACK TO WORK TOMORROW ALEX. WHAT'S YOUR PROGNOSIS FOR THE AUTUMN?
WELL THE MARKETS TEND TO DRIFT OVER THE SUMMER MONTHS, CLIVE. FIRST THERE'S THE HOSPITALITY SEASON AND THEN EVERYONE'S AWAY ON HOLIDAY... NOTHING MUCH GETS DONE...
alex@alexcartoon.com
BUT AFTER A RELAXING BREAK PEOPLE WILL BE COMING BACK TO THEIR OFFICES IN A POSITIVE AND DETERMINED FRAME OF MIND, FULLY FOCUSED ON THE IMPORTANT ISSUES...
SUCH AS MAKING THEMSELVES A BONUS?
QUITE. WHICH INEVITABLY MEANS THEY'LL TAKE TOO MUCH RISK, COCK UP AND PRECIPITATE A CRASH...
RIGHT... SO YOU'RE BEARISH AS USUAL...

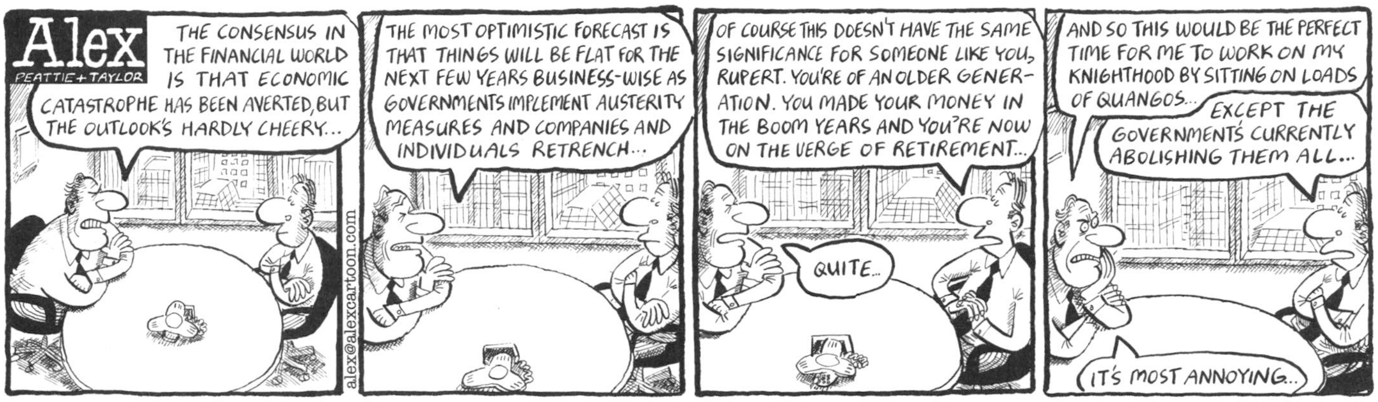
Alex
PEATTIE + TAYLOR
THE CONSENSUS IN THE FINANCIAL WORLD IS THAT ECONOMIC CATASTROPHE HAS BEEN AVERTED, BUT THE OUTLOOK'S HARDLY CHEERY...
THE MOST OPTIMISTIC FORECAST IS THAT THINGS WILL BE FLAT FOR THE NEXT FEW YEARS BUSINESS-WISE AS GOVERNMENTS IMPLEMENT AUSTERITY MEASURES AND COMPANIES AND INDIVIDUALS RETRENCH...
alex@alexcartoon.com
OF COURSE THIS DOESN'T HAVE THE SAME SIGNIFICANCE FOR SOMEONE LIKE YOU, RUPERT. YOU'RE OF AN OLDER GENERATION. YOU MADE YOUR MONEY IN THE BOOM YEARS AND YOU'RE NOW ON THE VERGE OF RETIREMENT...
QUITE...
AND SO THIS WOULD BE THE PERFECT TIME FOR ME TO WORK ON MY KNIGHTHOOD BY SITTING ON LOADS OF QUANGOS...
EXCEPT THE GOVERNMENT'S CURRENTLY ABOLISHING THEM ALL...
IT'S MOST ANNOYING...

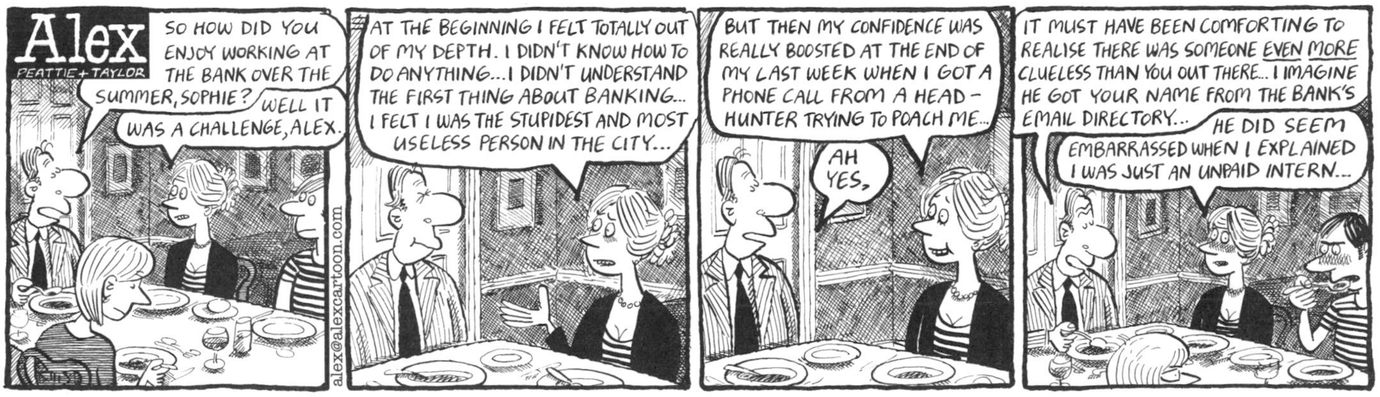
Alex
PEATTIE + TAYLOR
SO HOW DID YOU ENJOY WORKING AT THE BANK OVER THE SUMMER, SOPHIE?
WELL IT WAS A CHALLENGE, ALEX.
alex@alexcartoon.com
AT THE BEGINNING I FELT TOTALLY OUT OF MY DEPTH. I DIDN'T KNOW HOW TO DO ANYTHING... I DIDN'T UNDERSTAND THE FIRST THING ABOUT BANKING... I FELT I WAS THE STUPIDEST AND MOST USELESS PERSON IN THE CITY...
BUT THEN MY CONFIDENCE WAS REALLY BOOSTED AT THE END OF MY LAST WEEK WHEN I GOT A PHONE CALL FROM A HEAD-HUNTER TRYING TO POACH ME...
AH YES,
IT MUST HAVE BEEN COMFORTING TO REALISE THERE WAS SOMEONE EVEN MORE CLUELESS THAN YOU OUT THERE... I IMAGINE HE GOT YOUR NAME FROM THE BANK'S EMAIL DIRECTORY...
HE DID SEEM EMBARRASSED WHEN I EXPLAINED I WAS JUST AN UNPAID INTERN...

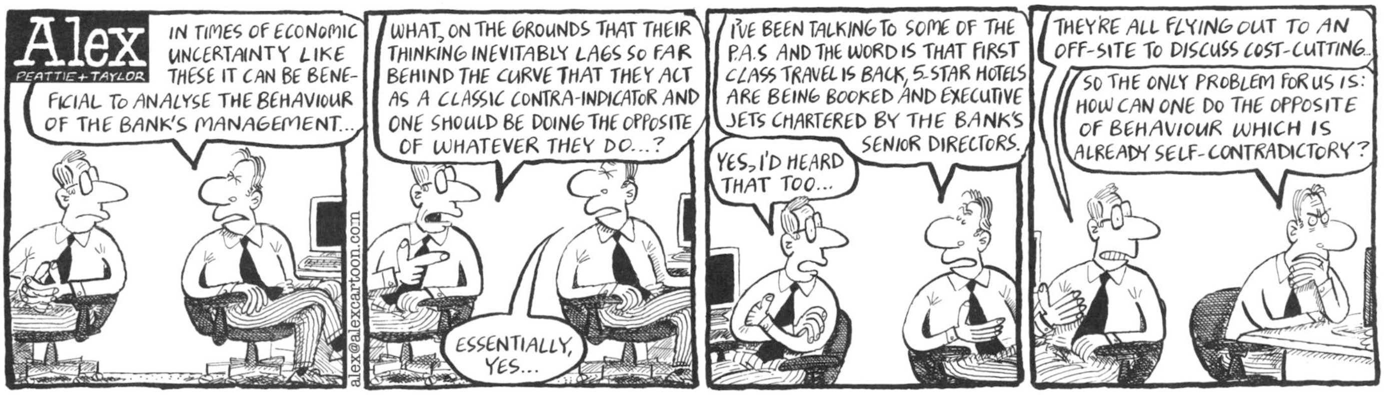
Alex
PEATTIE + TAYLOR
IN TIMES OF ECONOMIC UNCERTAINTY LIKE THESE IT CAN BE BENEFICIAL TO ANALYSE THE BEHAVIOUR OF THE BANK'S MANAGEMENT...
WHAT, ON THE GROUNDS THAT THEIR THINKING INEVITABLY LAGS SO FAR BEHIND THE CURVE THAT THEY ACT AS A CLASSIC CONTRA-INDICATOR AND ONE SHOULD BE DOING THE OPPOSITE OF WHATEVER THEY DO...?
ESSENTIALLY, YES...
alex@alexcartoon.com
I'VE BEEN TALKING TO SOME OF THE P.A.S AND THE WORD IS THAT FIRST CLASS TRAVEL IS BACK, 5-STAR HOTELS ARE BEING BOOKED AND EXECUTIVE JETS CHARTERED BY THE BANK'S SENIOR DIRECTORS.
YES, I'D HEARD THAT TOO...
THEY'RE ALL FLYING OUT TO AN OFF-SITE TO DISCUSS COST-CUTTING...
SO THE ONLY PROBLEM FOR US IS: HOW CAN ONE DO THE OPPOSITE OF BEHAVIOUR WHICH IS ALREADY SELF-CONTRADICTORY?

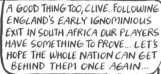

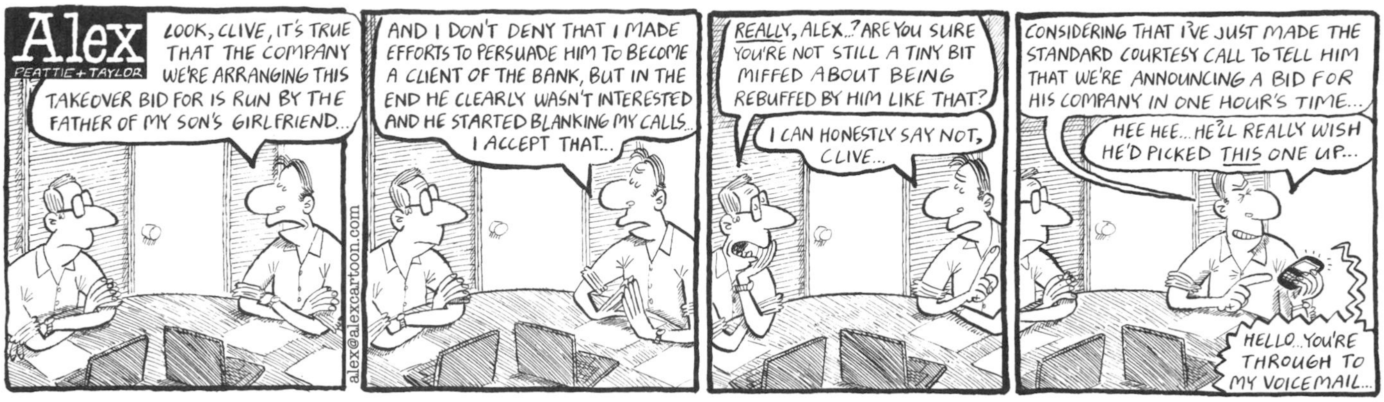
Alex
PEATTIE+TAYLOR
LOOK, CLIVE, IT'S TRUE THAT THE COMPANY WE'RE ARRANGING THIS TAKEOVER BID FOR IS RUN BY THE FATHER OF MY SON'S GIRLFRIEND...
alex@alexcartoon.com
AND I DON'T DENY THAT I MADE EFFORTS TO PERSUADE HIM TO BECOME A CLIENT OF THE BANK, BUT IN THE END HE CLEARLY WASN'T INTERESTED AND HE STARTED BLANKING MY CALLS...
I ACCEPT THAT...
REALLY, ALEX..? ARE YOU SURE YOU'RE NOT STILL A TINY BIT MIFFED ABOUT BEING REBUFFED BY HIM LIKE THAT?
I CAN HONESTLY SAY NOT, CLIVE...
CONSIDERING THAT I'VE JUST MADE THE STANDARD COURTESY CALL TO TELL HIM THAT WE'RE ANNOUNCING A BID FOR HIS COMPANY IN ONE HOUR'S TIME...
HEE HEE... HE'LL REALLY WISH HE'D PICKED THIS ONE UP...
HELLO... YOU'RE THROUGH TO MY VOICEMAIL...

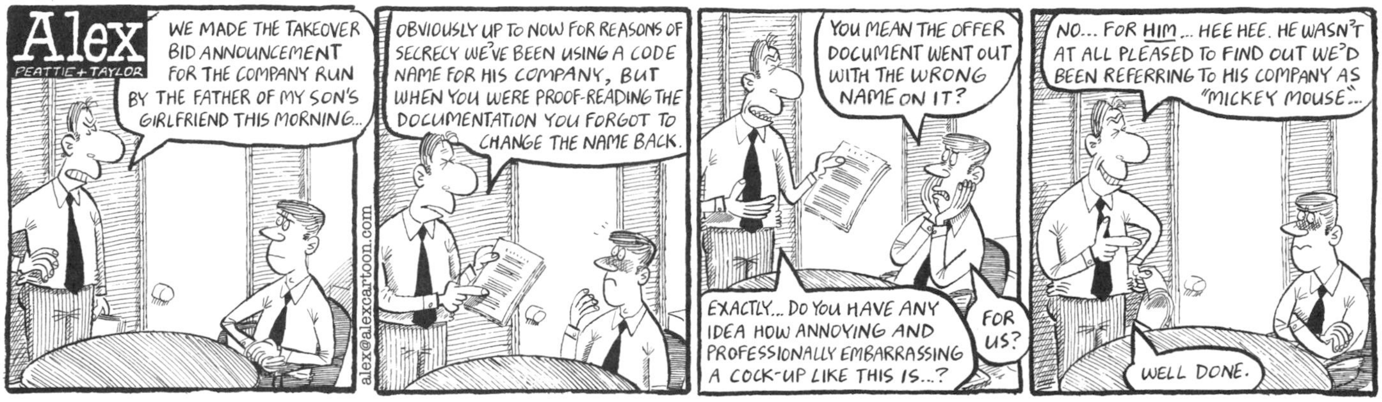
Alex
PEATTIE+TAYLOR
WE MADE THE TAKEOVER BID ANNOUNCEMENT FOR THE COMPANY RUN BY THE FATHER OF MY SON'S GIRLFRIEND THIS MORNING...
alex@alexcartoon.com
OBVIOUSLY UP TO NOW FOR REASONS OF SECRECY WE'VE BEEN USING A CODE NAME FOR HIS COMPANY, BUT WHEN YOU WERE PROOF-READING THE DOCUMENTATION YOU FORGOT TO CHANGE THE NAME BACK.
YOU MEAN THE OFFER DOCUMENT WENT OUT WITH THE WRONG NAME ON IT?
EXACTLY... DO YOU HAVE ANY IDEA HOW ANNOYING AND PROFESSIONALLY EMBARRASSING A COCK-UP LIKE THIS IS...?
FOR US?
NO... FOR HIM... HEE HEE. HE WASN'T AT ALL PLEASED TO FIND OUT WE'D BEEN REFERRING TO HIS COMPANY AS "MICKEY MOUSE"...
WELL DONE.

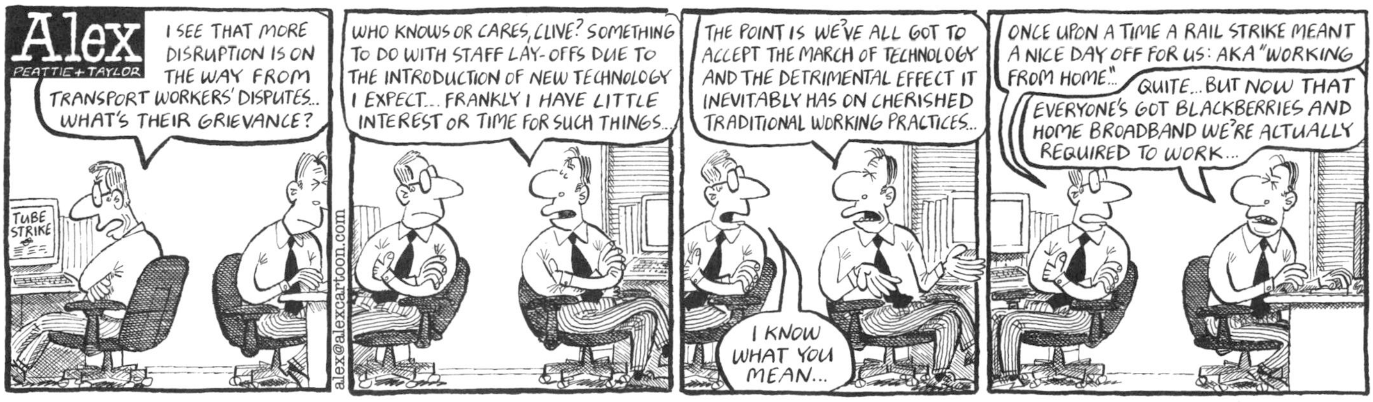
Alex
PEATTIE+TAYLOR
I SEE THAT MORE DISRUPTION IS ON THE WAY FROM TRANSPORT WORKERS' DISPUTES... WHAT'S THEIR GRIEVANCE?
TUBE STRIKE
alex@alexcartoon.com
WHO KNOWS OR CARES, CLIVE? SOMETHING TO DO WITH STAFF LAY-OFFS DUE TO THE INTRODUCTION OF NEW TECHNOLOGY I EXPECT... FRANKLY I HAVE LITTLE INTEREST OR TIME FOR SUCH THINGS...
THE POINT IS WE'VE ALL GOT TO ACCEPT THE MARCH OF TECHNOLOGY AND THE DETRIMENTAL EFFECT IT INEVITABLY HAS ON CHERISHED TRADITIONAL WORKING PRACTICES...
I KNOW WHAT YOU MEAN...
ONCE UPON A TIME A RAIL STRIKE MEANT A NICE DAY OFF FOR US: AKA "WORKING FROM HOME".
QUITE... BUT NOW THAT EVERYONE'S GOT BLACKBERRIES AND HOME BROADBAND WE'RE ACTUALLY REQUIRED TO WORK...

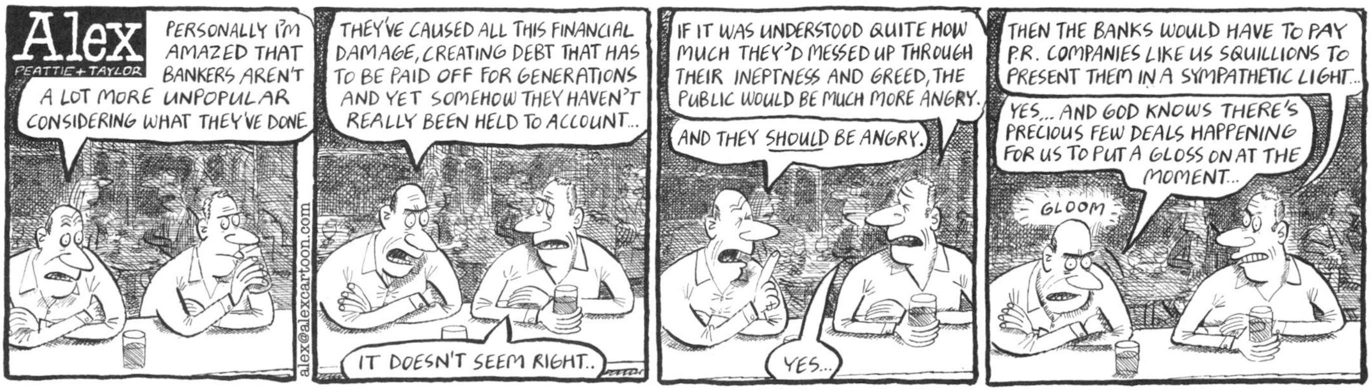
Alex
PEATTIE+TAYLOR
PERSONALLY I'M AMAZED THAT BANKERS AREN'T A LOT MORE UNPOPULAR CONSIDERING WHAT THEY'VE DONE
alex@alexcartoon.com
THEY'VE CAUSED ALL THIS FINANCIAL DAMAGE, CREATING DEBT THAT HAS TO BE PAID OFF FOR GENERATIONS AND YET SOMEHOW THEY HAVEN'T REALLY BEEN HELD TO ACCOUNT...
IT DOESN'T SEEM RIGHT...
IF IT WAS UNDERSTOOD QUITE HOW MUCH THEY'D MESSED UP THROUGH THEIR INEPTNESS AND GREED, THE PUBLIC WOULD BE MUCH MORE ANGRY.
AND THEY SHOULD BE ANGRY.
YES...
THEN THE BANKS WOULD HAVE TO PAY P.R. COMPANIES LIKE US SQUILLIONS TO PRESENT THEM IN A SYMPATHETIC LIGHT...
YES... AND GOD KNOWS THERE'S PRECIOUS FEW DEALS HAPPENING FOR US TO PUT A GLOSS ON AT THE MOMENT...
GLOOM

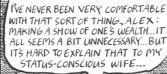

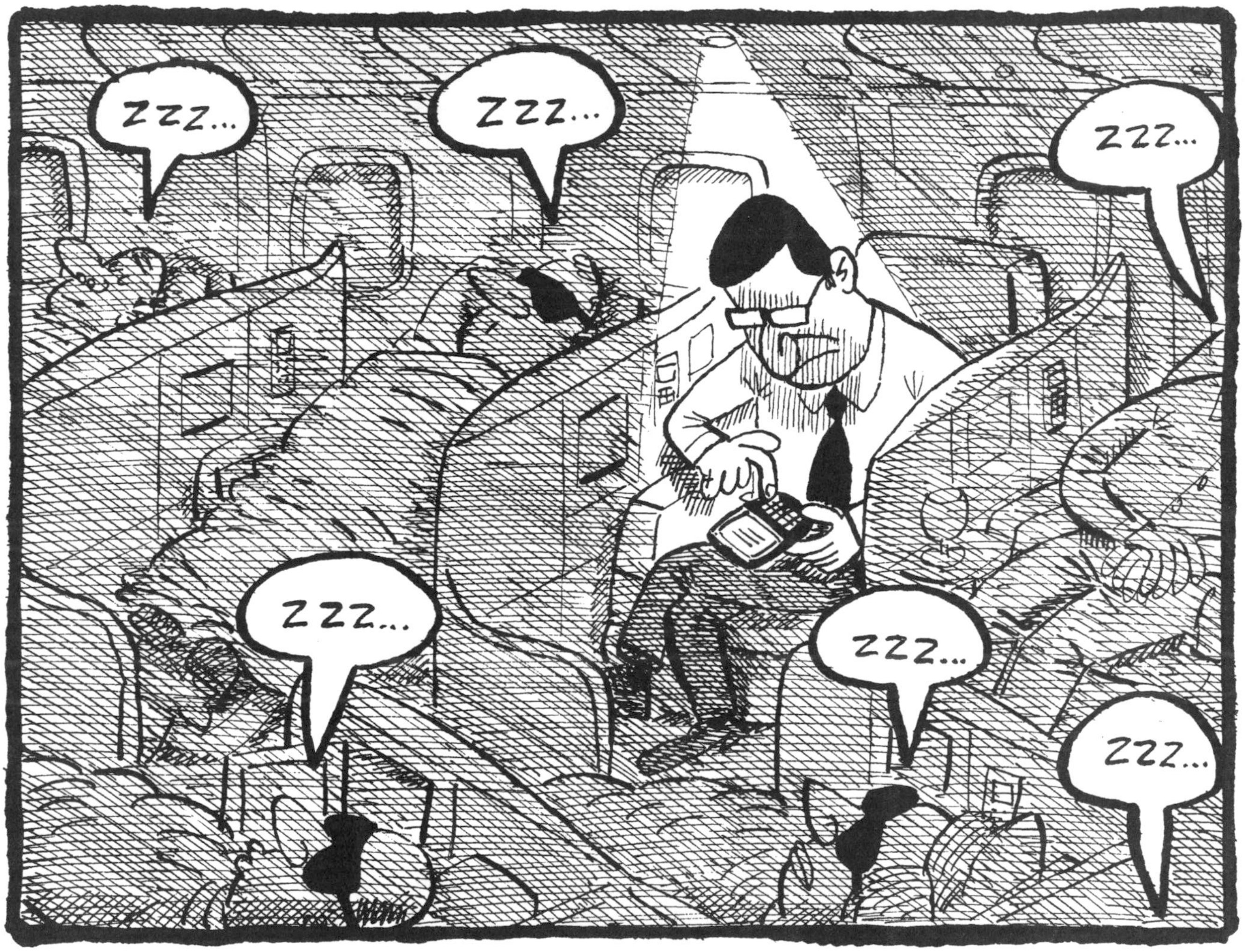
ZZZ...
ZZZ...
ZZZ...
ZZZ...
ZZZ...
ZZZ...

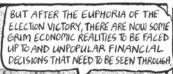

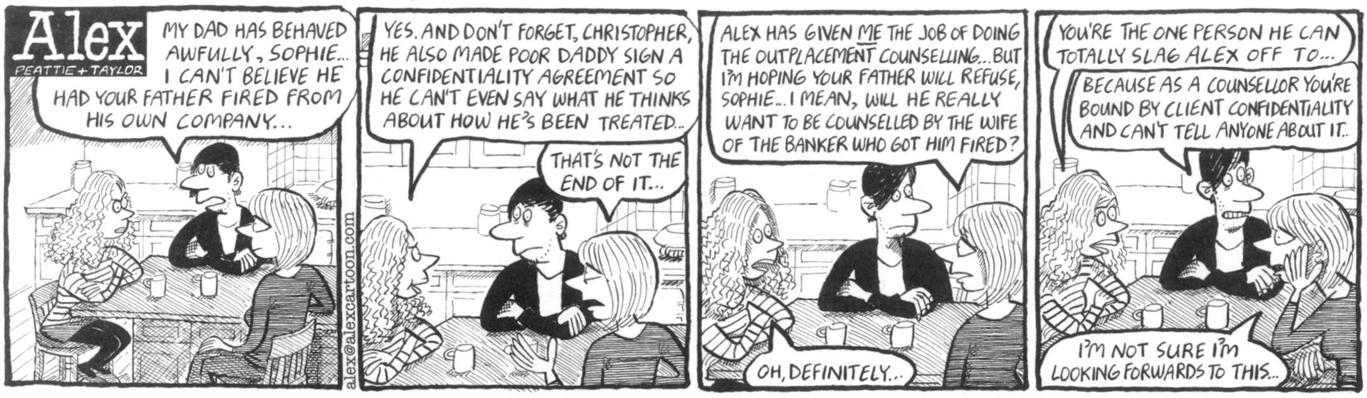
Alex
PEATTIE + TAYLOR
MY DAD HAS BEHAVED AWFULLY, SOPHIE... I CAN'T BELIEVE HE HAD YOUR FATHER FIRED FROM HIS OWN COMPANY...
YES. AND DON'T FORGET, CHRISTOPHER, HE ALSO MADE POOR DADDY SIGN A CONFIDENTIALITY AGREEMENT SO HE CAN'T EVEN SAY WHAT HE THINKS ABOUT HOW HE'S BEEN TREATED...
THAT'S NOT THE END OF IT...
alex@alexcartoon.com
ALEX HAS GIVEN ME THE JOB OF DOING THE OUTPLACEMENT COUNSELLING... BUT I'M HOPING YOUR FATHER WILL REFUSE, SOPHIE... I MEAN, WILL HE REALLY WANT TO BE COUNSELLED BY THE WIFE OF THE BANKER WHO GOT HIM FIRED?
OH, DEFINITELY...
YOU'RE THE ONE PERSON HE CAN TOTALLY SLAG ALEX OFF TO...
BECAUSE AS A COUNSELLOR YOU'RE BOUND BY CLIENT CONFIDENTIALITY AND CAN'T TELL ANYONE ABOUT IT...
I'M NOT SURE I'M LOOKING FORWARDS TO THIS...

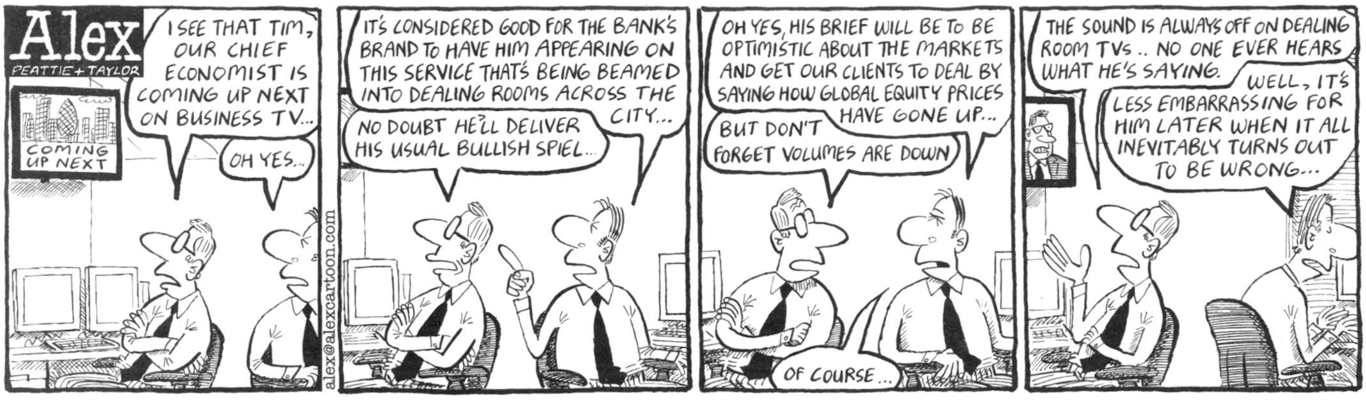
Alex
PEATTIE + TAYLOR
I SEE THAT TIM, OUR CHIEF ECONOMIST IS COMING UP NEXT ON BUSINESS TV...
COMING UP NEXT
OH YES...
alex@alexcartoon.com
IT'S CONSIDERED GOOD FOR THE BANK'S BRAND TO HAVE HIM APPEARING ON THIS SERVICE THAT'S BEING BEAMED INTO DEALING ROOMS ACROSS THE CITY...
NO DOUBT HE'LL DELIVER HIS USUAL BULLISH SPIEL...
OH YES, HIS BRIEF WILL BE TO BE OPTIMISTIC ABOUT THE MARKETS AND GET OUR CLIENTS TO DEAL BY SAYING HOW GLOBAL EQUITY PRICES HAVE GONE UP...
BUT DON'T FORGET VOLUMES ARE DOWN
OF COURSE...
THE SOUND IS ALWAYS OFF ON DEALING ROOM TVs .. NO ONE EVER HEARS WHAT HE'S SAYING.
WELL, IT'S LESS EMBARRASSING FOR HIM LATER WHEN IT ALL INEVITABLY TURNS OUT TO BE WRONG...

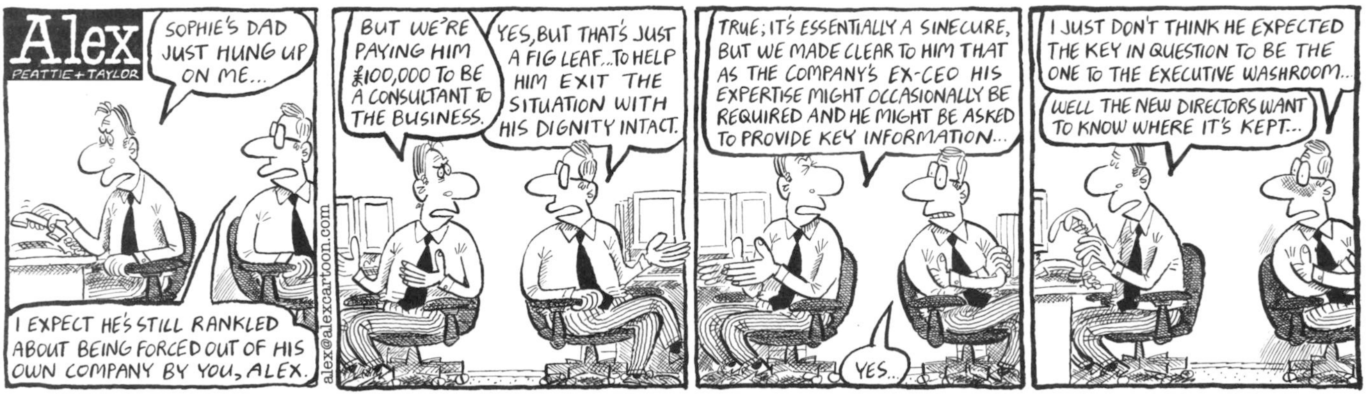
Alex
PEATTIE + TAYLOR
SOPHIE'S DAD JUST HUNG UP ON ME...
I EXPECT HE'S STILL RANKLED ABOUT BEING FORCED OUT OF HIS OWN COMPANY BY YOU, ALEX.
alex@alexcartoon.com
BUT WE'RE PAYING HIM £100,000 TO BE A CONSULTANT TO THE BUSINESS.
YES, BUT THAT'S JUST A FIG LEAF... TO HELP HIM EXIT THE SITUATION WITH HIS DIGNITY INTACT.
TRUE; IT'S ESSENTIALLY A SINECURE, BUT WE MADE CLEAR TO HIM THAT AS THE COMPANY'S EX-CEO HIS EXPERTISE MIGHT OCCASIONALLY BE REQUIRED AND HE MIGHT BE ASKED TO PROVIDE KEY INFORMATION...
YES...
I JUST DON'T THINK HE EXPECTED THE KEY IN QUESTION TO BE THE ONE TO THE EXECUTIVE WASHROOM...
WELL THE NEW DIRECTORS WANT TO KNOW WHERE IT'S KEPT...

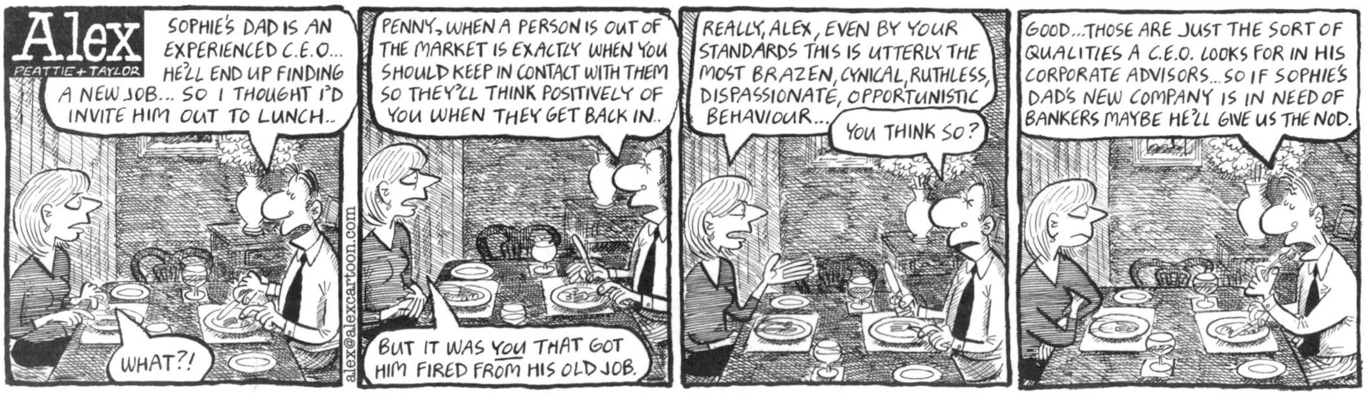
Alex
PEATTIE + TAYLOR
SOPHIE'S DAD IS AN EXPERIENCED C.E.O... HE'LL END UP FINDING A NEW JOB... SO I THOUGHT I'D INVITE HIM OUT TO LUNCH...
WHAT?!
alex@alexcartoon.com
PENNY, WHEN A PERSON IS OUT OF THE MARKET IS EXACTLY WHEN YOU SHOULD KEEP IN CONTACT WITH THEM SO THEY'LL THINK POSITIVELY OF YOU WHEN THEY GET BACK IN..
BUT IT WAS YOU THAT GOT HIM FIRED FROM HIS OLD JOB.
REALLY, ALEX, EVEN BY YOUR STANDARDS THIS IS UTTERLY THE MOST BRAZEN, CYNICAL, RUTHLESS, DISPASSIONATE, OPPORTUNISTIC BEHAVIOUR...
YOU THINK SO?
GOOD... THOSE ARE JUST THE SORT OF QUALITIES A C.E.O. LOOKS FOR IN HIS CORPORATE ADVISORS... SO IF SOPHIE'S DAD'S NEW COMPANY IS IN NEED OF BANKERS MAYBE HE'LL GIVE US THE NOD.

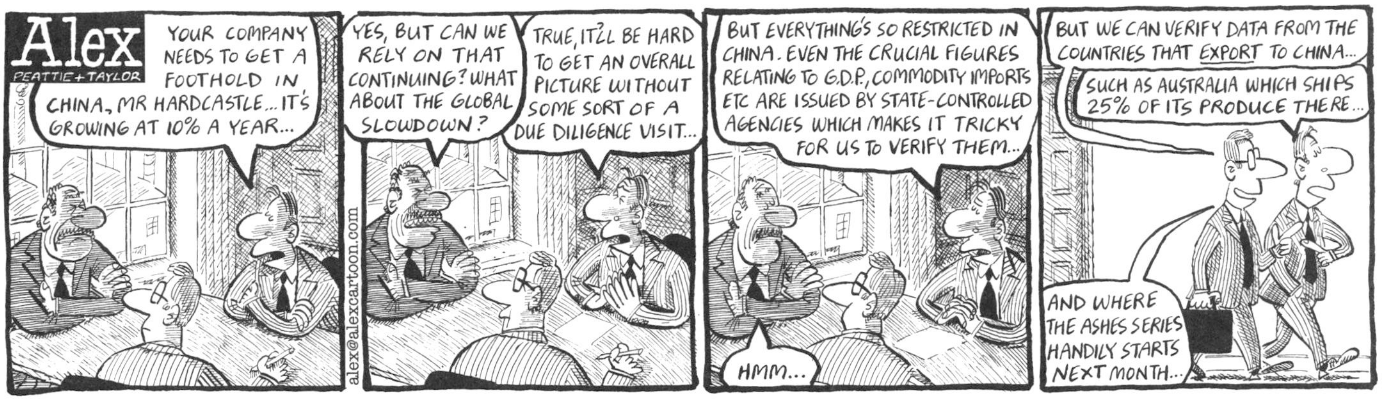
Alex
PEATTIE + TAYLOR
YOUR COMPANY NEEDS TO GET A FOOTHOLD IN CHINA, MR HARDCASTLE... IT'S GROWING AT 10% A YEAR...
YES, BUT CAN WE RELY ON THAT CONTINUING? WHAT ABOUT THE GLOBAL SLOWDOWN?
TRUE, IT'LL BE HARD TO GET AN OVERALL PICTURE WITHOUT SOME SORT OF A DUE DILIGENCE VISIT...
alex@alexcartoon.com
BUT EVERYTHING'S SO RESTRICTED IN CHINA. EVEN THE CRUCIAL FIGURES RELATING TO G.D.P., COMMODITY IMPORTS ETC ARE ISSUED BY STATE-CONTROLLED AGENCIES WHICH MAKES IT TRICKY FOR US TO VERIFY THEM...
HMM...
BUT WE CAN VERIFY DATA FROM THE COUNTRIES THAT EXPORT TO CHINA...
SUCH AS AUSTRALIA WHICH SHIPS 25% OF ITS PRODUCE THERE...
AND WHERE THE ASHES SERIES HANDILY STARTS NEXT MONTH...

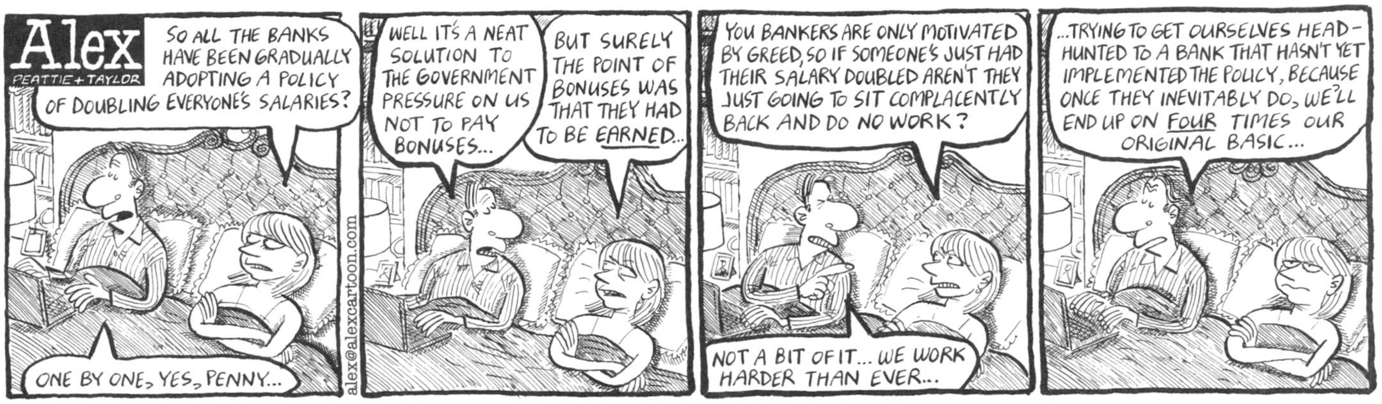
Alex
PEATTIE + TAYLOR
SO ALL THE BANKS HAVE BEEN GRADUALLY ADOPTING A POLICY OF DOUBLING EVERYONE'S SALARIES?
ONE BY ONE, YES, PENNY...
WELL IT'S A NEAT SOLUTION TO THE GOVERNMENT PRESSURE ON US NOT TO PAY BONUSES...
BUT SURELY THE POINT OF BONUSES WAS THAT THEY HAD TO BE EARNED...
alex@alexcartoon.com
YOU BANKERS ARE ONLY MOTIVATED BY GREED, SO IF SOMEONE'S JUST HAD THEIR SALARY DOUBLED AREN'T THEY JUST GOING TO SIT COMPLACENTLY BACK AND DO NO WORK?
NOT A BIT OF IT... WE WORK HARDER THAN EVER...
...TRYING TO GET OURSELVES HEAD-HUNTED TO A BANK THAT HASN'T YET IMPLEMENTED THE POLICY, BECAUSE ONCE THEY INEVITABLY DO, WE'LL END UP ON FOUR TIMES OUR ORIGINAL BASIC...

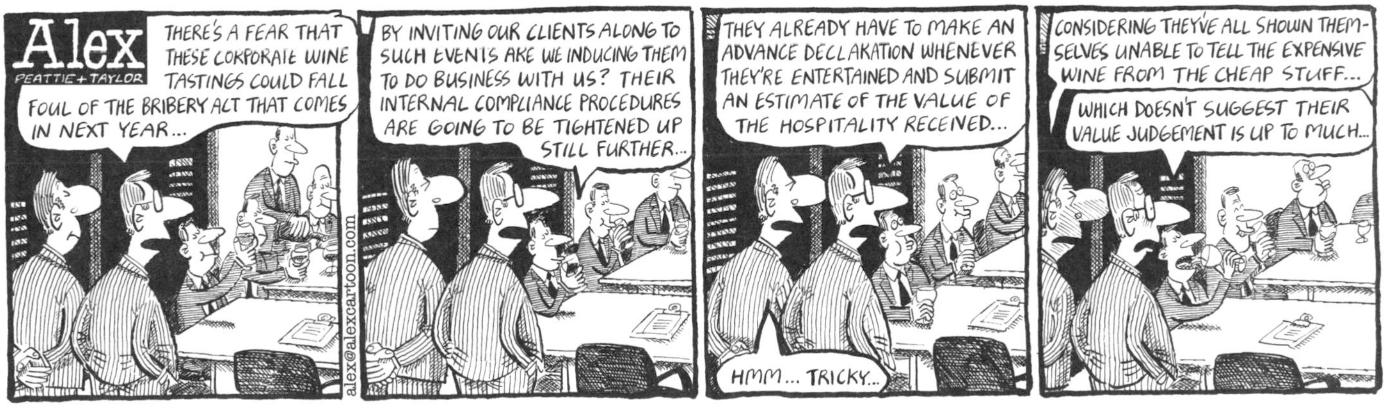
Alex
PEATTIE + TAYLOR
THERE'S A FEAR THAT THESE CORPORATE WINE TASTINGS COULD FALL FOUL OF THE BRIBERY ACT THAT COMES IN NEXT YEAR...
BY INVITING OUR CLIENTS ALONG TO SUCH EVENTS ARE WE INDUCING THEM TO DO BUSINESS WITH US? THEIR INTERNAL COMPLIANCE PROCEDURES ARE GOING TO BE TIGHTENED UP STILL FURTHER...
alex@alexcartoon.com
THEY ALREADY HAVE TO MAKE AN ADVANCE DECLARATION WHENEVER THEY'RE ENTERTAINED AND SUBMIT AN ESTIMATE OF THE VALUE OF THE HOSPITALITY RECEIVED...
HMM... TRICKY...
CONSIDERING THEY'VE ALL SHOWN THEMSELVES UNABLE TO TELL THE EXPENSIVE WINE FROM THE CHEAP STUFF...
WHICH DOESN'T SUGGEST THEIR VALUE JUDGEMENT IS UP TO MUCH...

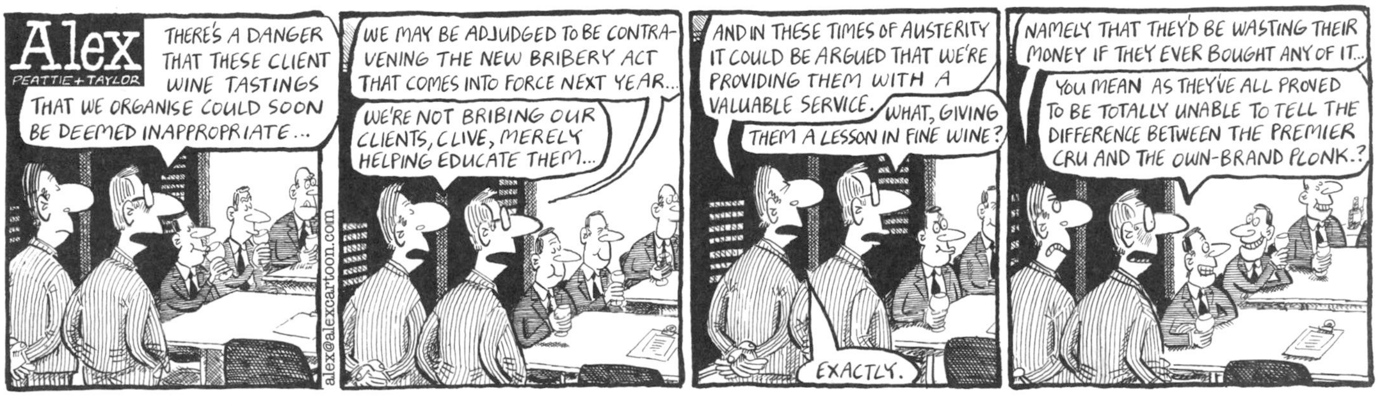
Alex
PEATTIE + TAYLOR
THERE'S A DANGER THAT THESE CLIENT WINE TASTINGS THAT WE ORGANISE COULD SOON BE DEEMED INAPPROPRIATE...
WE MAY BE ADJUDGED TO BE CONTRAVENING THE NEW BRIBERY ACT THAT COMES INTO FORCE NEXT YEAR...
WE'RE NOT BRIBING OUR CLIENTS, CLIVE, MERELY HELPING EDUCATE THEM...
alex@alexcartoon.com
AND IN THESE TIMES OF AUSTERITY IT COULD BE ARGUED THAT WE'RE PROVIDING THEM WITH A VALUABLE SERVICE.
WHAT, GIVING THEM A LESSON IN FINE WINE?
EXACTLY.
NAMELY THAT THEY'D BE WASTING THEIR MONEY IF THEY EVER BOUGHT ANY OF IT...
YOU MEAN AS THEY'VE ALL PROVED TO BE TOTALLY UNABLE TO TELL THE DIFFERENCE BETWEEN THE PREMIER CRU AND THE OWN-BRAND PLONK.?

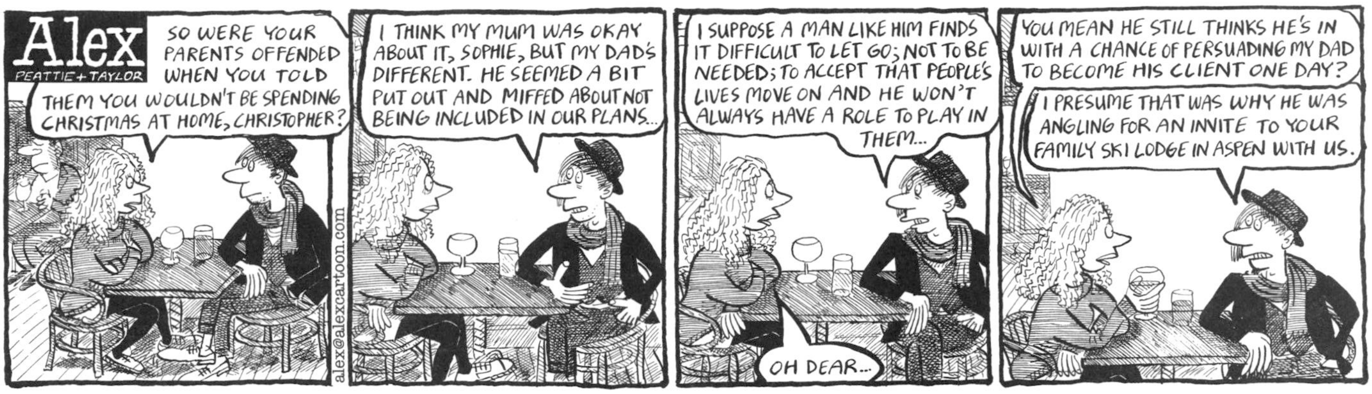
Alex
PEATTIE + TAYLOR
SO WERE YOUR PARENTS OFFENDED WHEN YOU TOLD THEM YOU WOULDN'T BE SPENDING CHRISTMAS AT HOME, CHRISTOPHER?
I THINK MY MUM WAS OKAY ABOUT IT, SOPHIE, BUT MY DAD'S DIFFERENT. HE SEEMED A BIT PUT OUT AND MIFFED ABOUT NOT BEING INCLUDED IN OUR PLANS...
I SUPPOSE A MAN LIKE HIM FINDS IT DIFFICULT TO LET GO; NOT TO BE NEEDED; TO ACCEPT THAT PEOPLE'S LIVES MOVE ON AND HE WON'T ALWAYS HAVE A ROLE TO PLAY IN THEM...
OH DEAR...
YOU MEAN HE STILL THINKS HE'S IN WITH A CHANCE OF PERSUADING MY DAD TO BECOME HIS CLIENT ONE DAY?
I PRESUME THAT WAS WHY HE WAS ANGLING FOR AN INVITE TO YOUR FAMILY SKI LODGE IN ASPEN WITH US.
alex@alexcartoon.com

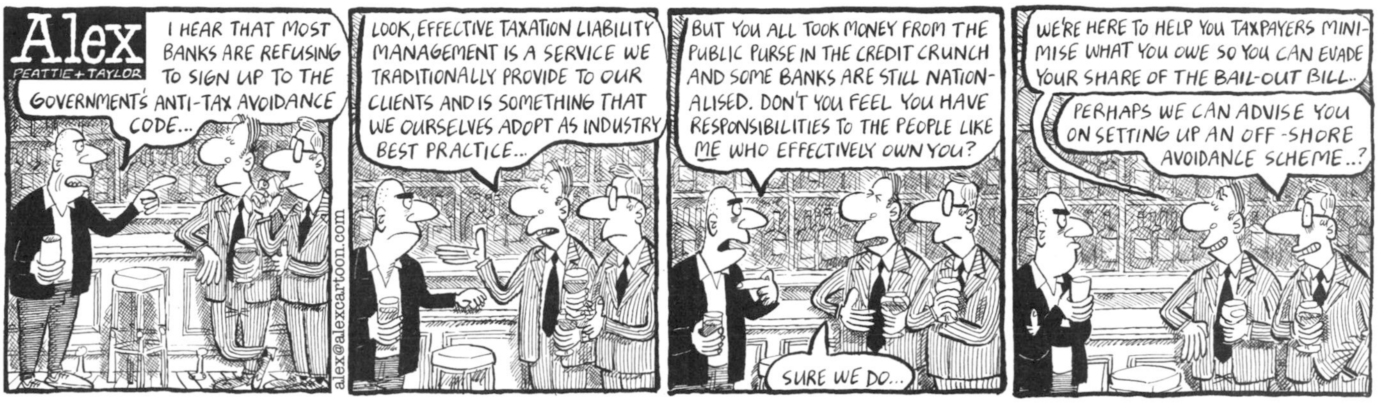
Alex
PEATTIE + TAYLOR
I HEAR THAT MOST BANKS ARE REFUSING TO SIGN UP TO THE GOVERNMENT'S ANTI-TAX AVOIDANCE CODE...
LOOK, EFFECTIVE TAXATION LIABILITY MANAGEMENT IS A SERVICE WE TRADITIONALLY PROVIDE TO OUR CLIENTS AND IS SOMETHING THAT WE OURSELVES ADOPT AS INDUSTRY BEST PRACTICE...
BUT YOU ALL TOOK MONEY FROM THE PUBLIC PURSE IN THE CREDIT CRUNCH AND SOME BANKS ARE STILL NATIONALISED. DON'T YOU FEEL YOU HAVE RESPONSIBILITIES TO THE PEOPLE LIKE ME WHO EFFECTIVELY OWN YOU?
SURE WE DO...
WE'RE HERE TO HELP YOU TAXPAYERS MINIMISE WHAT YOU OWE SO YOU CAN EVADE YOUR SHARE OF THE BAIL-OUT BILL...
PERHAPS WE CAN ADVISE YOU ON SETTING UP AN OFF-SHORE AVOIDANCE SCHEME..?
alex@alexcartoon.com

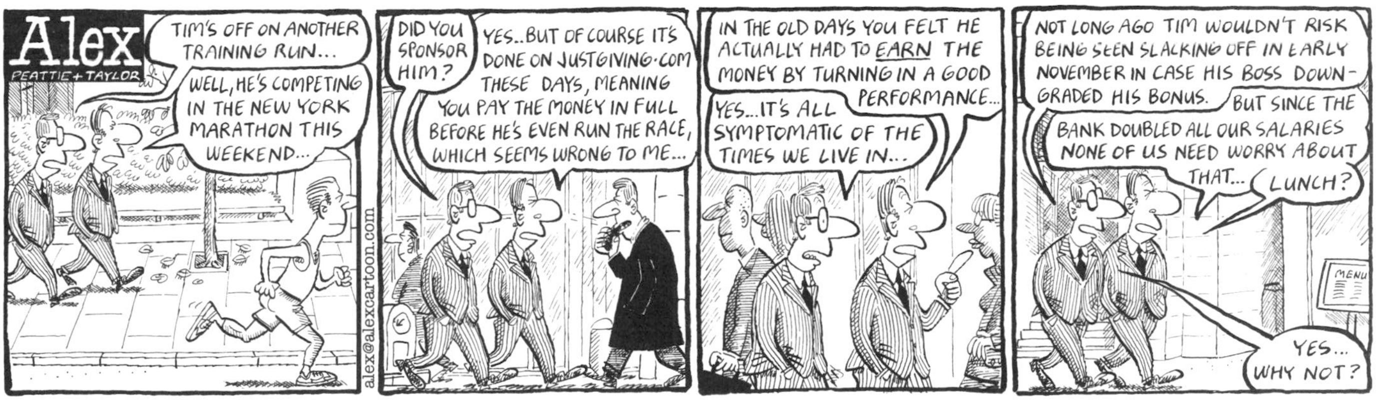
Alex
PEATTIE + TAYLOR
TIM'S OFF ON ANOTHER TRAINING RUN...
WELL, HE'S COMPETING IN THE NEW YORK MARATHON THIS WEEKEND...
DID YOU SPONSOR HIM?
YES..BUT OF COURSE IT'S DONE ON JUSTGIVING.COM THESE DAYS, MEANING YOU PAY THE MONEY IN FULL BEFORE HE'S EVEN RUN THE RACE, WHICH SEEMS WRONG TO ME...
IN THE OLD DAYS YOU FELT HE ACTUALLY HAD TO EARN THE MONEY BY TURNING IN A GOOD PERFORMANCE...
YES...IT'S ALL SYMPTOMATIC OF THE TIMES WE LIVE IN...
NOT LONG AGO TIM WOULDN'T RISK BEING SEEN SLACKING OFF IN EARLY NOVEMBER IN CASE HIS BOSS DOWNGRADED HIS BONUS.
BUT SINCE THE BANK DOUBLED ALL OUR SALARIES NONE OF US NEED WORRY ABOUT THAT...
LUNCH?
MENU
YES... WHY NOT?
alex@alexcartoon.com

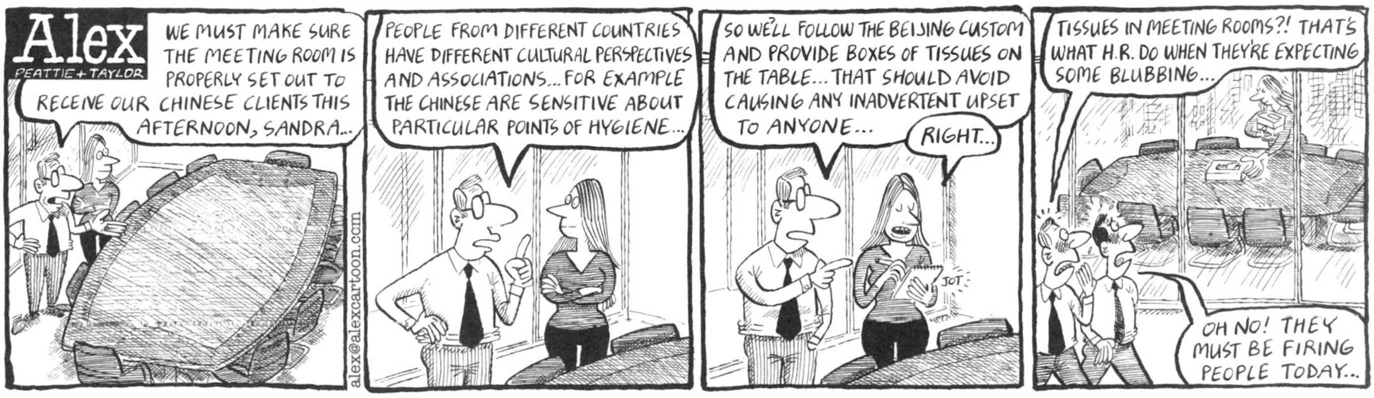
Alex
PEATTIE + TAYLOR
WE MUST MAKE SURE THE MEETING ROOM IS PROPERLY SET OUT TO RECEIVE OUR CHINESE CLIENTS THIS AFTERNOON, SANDRA...
PEOPLE FROM DIFFERENT COUNTRIES HAVE DIFFERENT CULTURAL PERSPECTIVES AND ASSOCIATIONS... FOR EXAMPLE THE CHINESE ARE SENSITIVE ABOUT PARTICULAR POINTS OF HYGIENE...
SO WE'LL FOLLOW THE BEIJING CUSTOM AND PROVIDE BOXES OF TISSUES ON THE TABLE... THAT SHOULD AVOID CAUSING ANY INADVERTENT UPSET TO ANYONE...
RIGHT...
JOT
TISSUES IN MEETING ROOMS?! THAT'S WHAT H.R. DO WHEN THEY'RE EXPECTING SOME BLUBBING...
OH NO! THEY MUST BE FIRING PEOPLE TODAY...
alex@alexcartoon.com

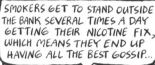

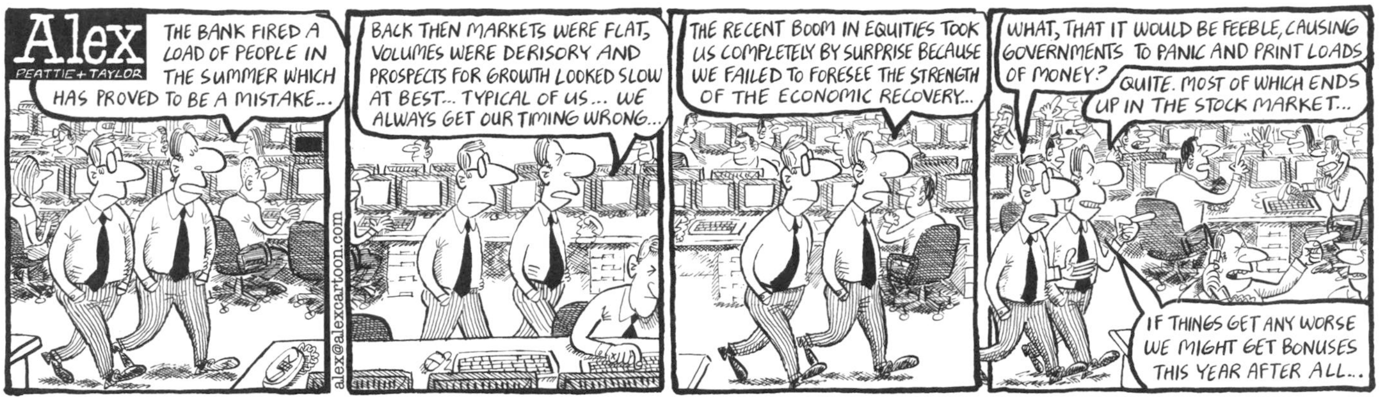
Alex
PEATTIE + TAYLOR
THE BANK FIRED A LOAD OF PEOPLE IN THE SUMMER WHICH HAS PROVED TO BE A MISTAKE...
alex@alexcartoon.com
BACK THEN MARKETS WERE FLAT, VOLUMES WERE DERISORY AND PROSPECTS FOR GROWTH LOOKED SLOW AT BEST... TYPICAL OF US... WE ALWAYS GET OUR TIMING WRONG...
THE RECENT BOOM IN EQUITIES TOOK US COMPLETELY BY SURPRISE BECAUSE WE FAILED TO FORESEE THE STRENGTH OF THE ECONOMIC RECOVERY...
WHAT, THAT IT WOULD BE FEEBLE, CAUSING GOVERNMENTS TO PANIC AND PRINT LOADS OF MONEY?
QUITE. MOST OF WHICH ENDS UP IN THE STOCK MARKET...
IF THINGS GET ANY WORSE WE MIGHT GET BONUSES THIS YEAR AFTER ALL...

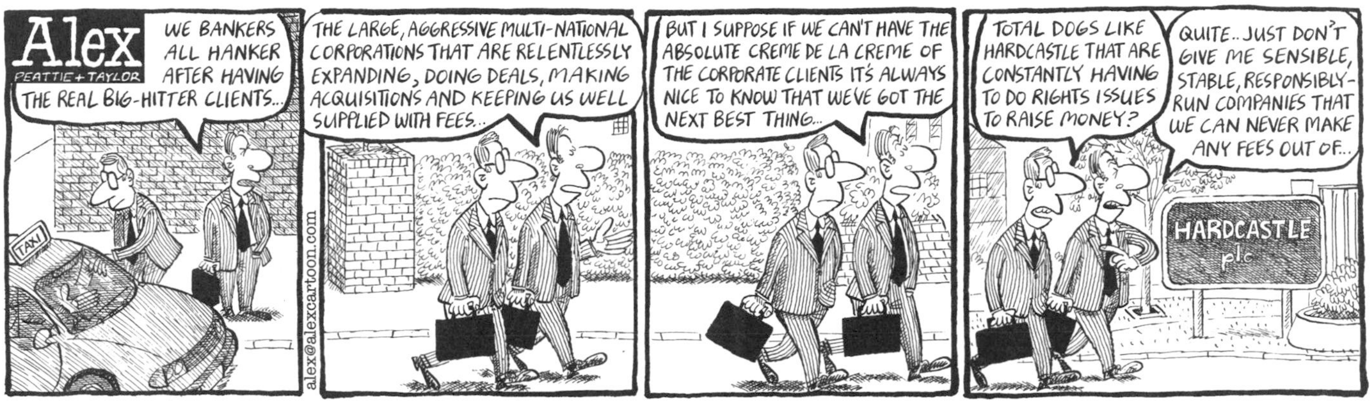
Alex
PEATTIE + TAYLOR
WE BANKERS ALL HANKER AFTER HAVING THE REAL BIG-HITTER CLIENTS...
TAXI
alex@alexcartoon.com
THE LARGE, AGGRESSIVE MULTI-NATIONAL CORPORATIONS THAT ARE RELENTLESSLY EXPANDING, DOING DEALS, MAKING ACQUISITIONS AND KEEPING US WELL SUPPLIED WITH FEES...
BUT I SUPPOSE IF WE CAN'T HAVE THE ABSOLUTE CREME DE LA CREME OF THE CORPORATE CLIENTS IT'S ALWAYS NICE TO KNOW THAT WE'VE GOT THE NEXT BEST THING...
TOTAL DOGS LIKE HARDCASTLE THAT ARE CONSTANTLY HAVING TO DO RIGHTS ISSUES TO RAISE MONEY?
QUITE.. JUST DON'T GIVE ME SENSIBLE, STABLE, RESPONSIBLY-RUN COMPANIES THAT WE CAN NEVER MAKE ANY FEES OUT OF...
HARDCASTLE plc

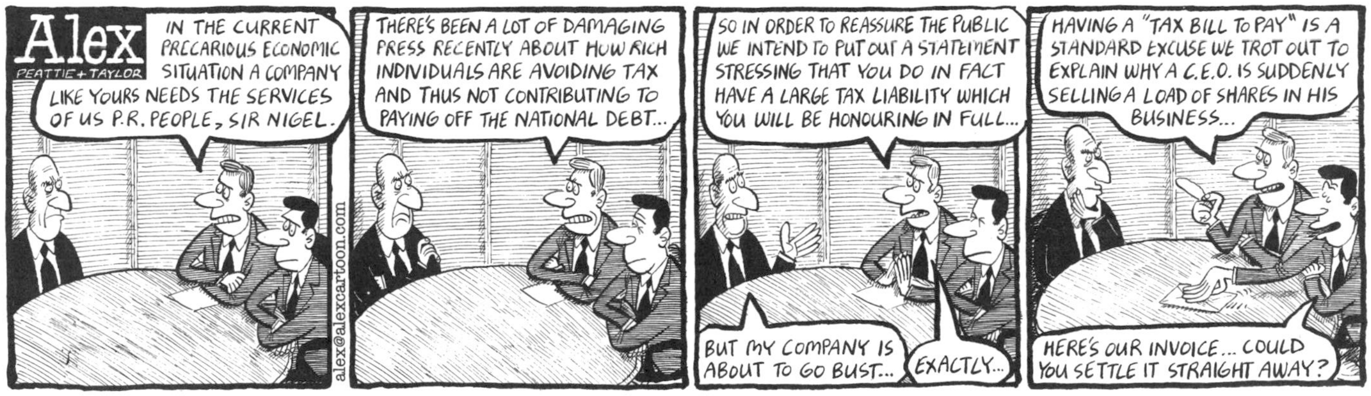
Alex
PEATTIE + TAYLOR
IN THE CURRENT PRECARIOUS ECONOMIC SITUATION A COMPANY LIKE YOURS NEEDS THE SERVICES OF US P.R. PEOPLE, SIR NIGEL.
alex@alexcartoon.com
THERE'S BEEN A LOT OF DAMAGING PRESS RECENTLY ABOUT HOW RICH INDIVIDUALS ARE AVOIDING TAX AND THUS NOT CONTRIBUTING TO PAYING OFF THE NATIONAL DEBT...
SO IN ORDER TO REASSURE THE PUBLIC WE INTEND TO PUT OUT A STATEMENT STRESSING THAT YOU DO IN FACT HAVE A LARGE TAX LIABILITY WHICH YOU WILL BE HONOURING IN FULL...
BUT MY COMPANY IS ABOUT TO GO BUST...
EXACTLY...
HAVING A "TAX BILL TO PAY" IS A STANDARD EXCUSE WE TROT OUT TO EXPLAIN WHY A C.E.O. IS SUDDENLY SELLING A LOAD OF SHARES IN HIS BUSINESS...
HERE'S OUR INVOICE... COULD YOU SETTLE IT STRAIGHT AWAY?

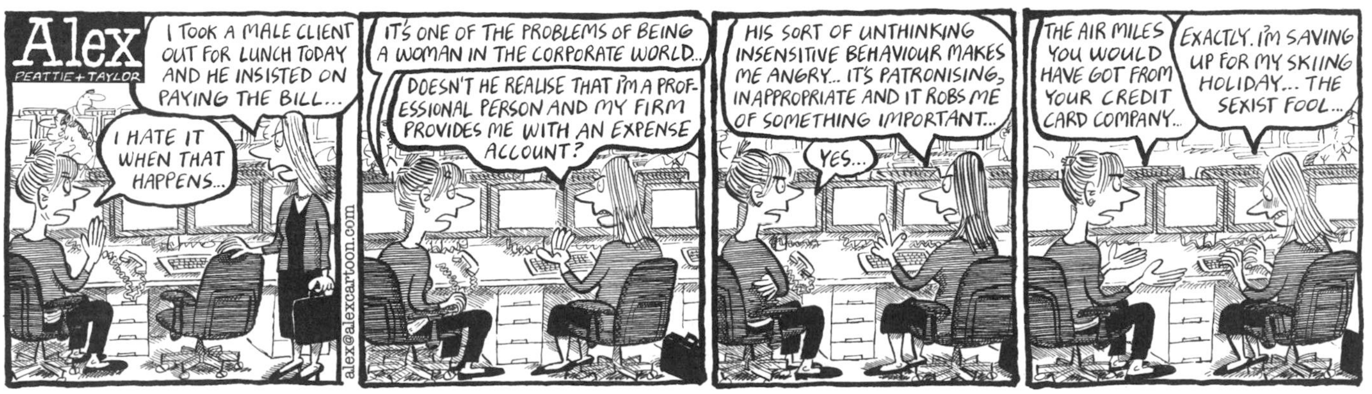
Alex
PEATTIE + TAYLOR
I TOOK A MALE CLIENT OUT FOR LUNCH TODAY AND HE INSISTED ON PAYING THE BILL...
I HATE IT WHEN THAT HAPPENS...
alex@alexcartoon.com
IT'S ONE OF THE PROBLEMS OF BEING A WOMAN IN THE CORPORATE WORLD...
DOESN'T HE REALISE THAT I'M A PROFESSIONAL PERSON AND MY FIRM PROVIDES ME WITH AN EXPENSE ACCOUNT?
HIS SORT OF UNTHINKING INSENSITIVE BEHAVIOUR MAKES ME ANGRY... IT'S PATRONISING, INAPPROPRIATE AND IT ROBS ME OF SOMETHING IMPORTANT...
YES...
THE AIR MILES YOU WOULD HAVE GOT FROM YOUR CREDIT CARD COMPANY...
EXACTLY. I'M SAVING UP FOR MY SKIING HOLIDAY... THE SEXIST FOOL...

27

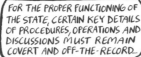

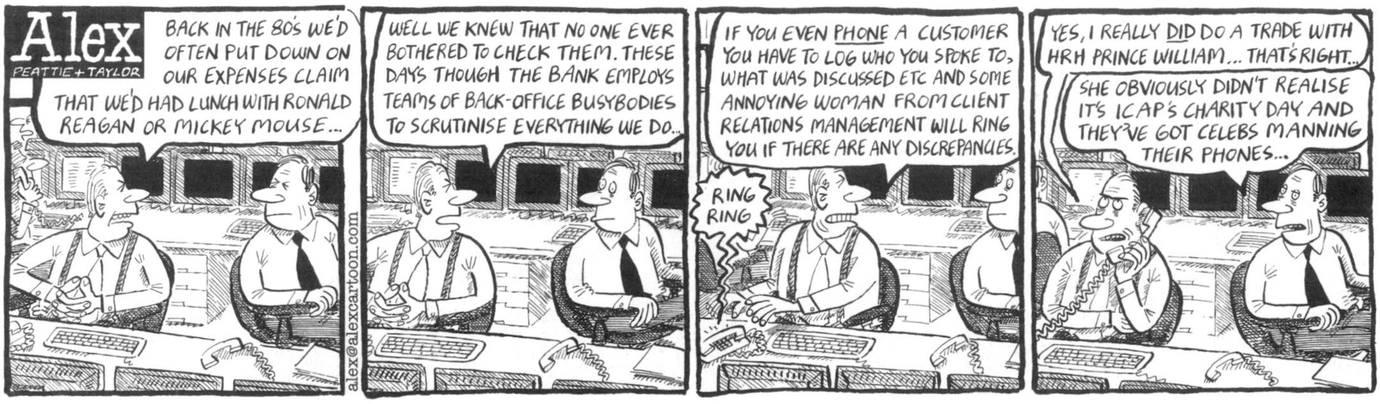
Alex
PEATTIE + TAYLOR
BACK IN THE 80'S WE'D OFTEN PUT DOWN ON OUR EXPENSES CLAIM THAT WE'D HAD LUNCH WITH RONALD REAGAN OR MICKEY MOUSE...
WELL WE KNEW THAT NO ONE EVER BOTHERED TO CHECK THEM. THESE DAYS THOUGH THE BANK EMPLOYS TEAMS OF BACK-OFFICE BUSYBODIES TO SCRUTINISE EVERYTHING WE DO...
alex@alexcartoon.com
IF YOU EVEN PHONE A CUSTOMER YOU HAVE TO LOG WHO YOU SPOKE TO, WHAT WAS DISCUSSED ETC AND SOME ANNOYING WOMAN FROM CLIENT RELATIONS MANAGEMENT WILL RING YOU IF THERE ARE ANY DISCREPANCIES.
RING RING
YES, I REALLY DID DO A TRADE WITH HRH PRINCE WILLIAM... THAT'S RIGHT...
SHE OBVIOUSLY DIDN'T REALISE IT'S ICAP'S CHARITY DAY AND THEY'VE GOT CELEBS MANNING THEIR PHONES...

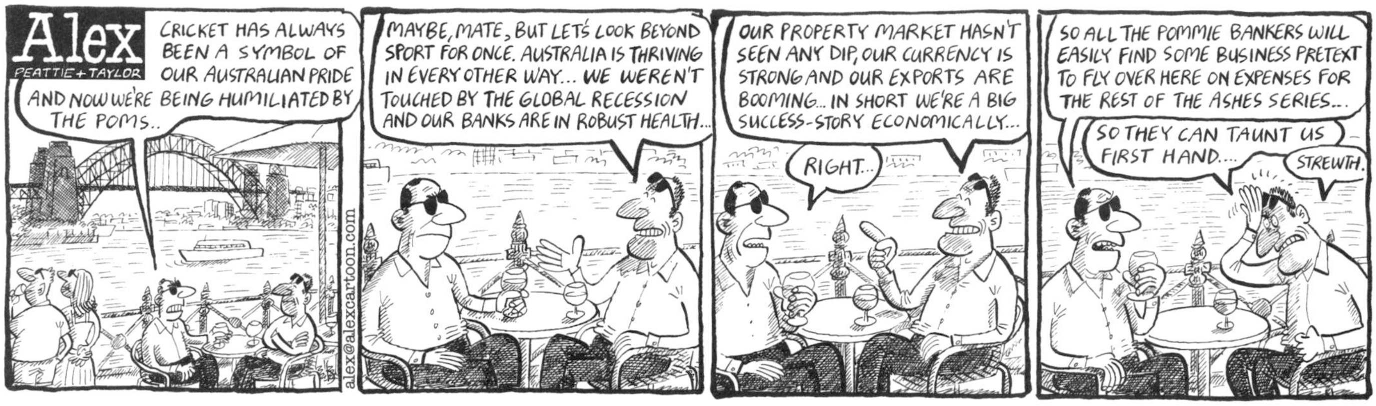
Alex
PEATTIE + TAYLOR
CRICKET HAS ALWAYS BEEN A SYMBOL OF OUR AUSTRALIAN PRIDE AND NOW WE'RE BEING HUMILIATED BY THE POMS..
MAYBE, MATE, BUT LET'S LOOK BEYOND SPORT FOR ONCE. AUSTRALIA IS THRIVING IN EVERY OTHER WAY... WE WEREN'T TOUCHED BY THE GLOBAL RECESSION AND OUR BANKS ARE IN ROBUST HEALTH...
alex@alexcartoon.com
OUR PROPERTY MARKET HASN'T SEEN ANY DIP, OUR CURRENCY IS STRONG AND OUR EXPORTS ARE BOOMING... IN SHORT WE'RE A BIG SUCCESS-STORY ECONOMICALLY...
RIGHT...
SO ALL THE POMMIE BANKERS WILL EASILY FIND SOME BUSINESS PRETEXT TO FLY OVER HERE ON EXPENSES FOR THE REST OF THE ASHES SERIES...
SO THEY CAN TAUNT US FIRST HAND....
STREWTH.

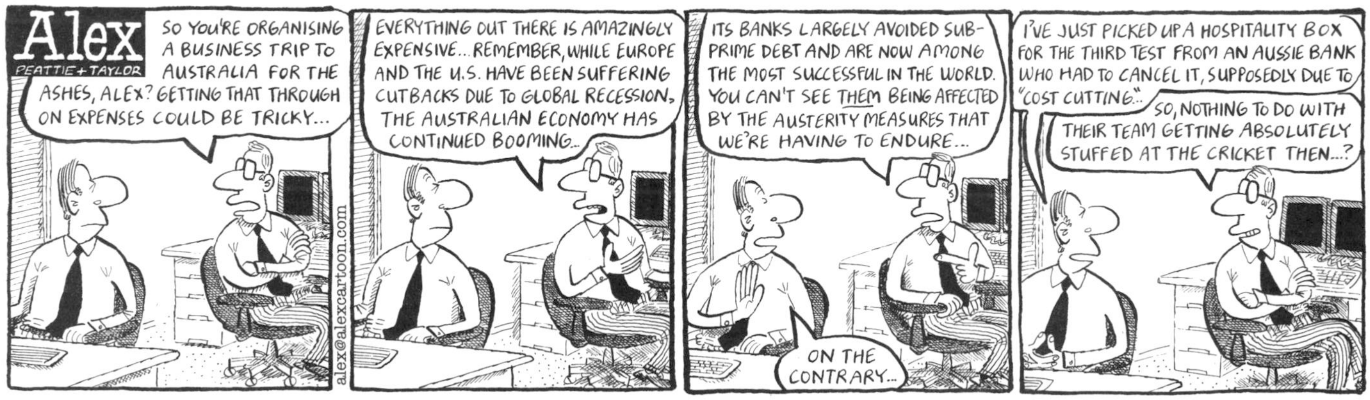
Alex
PEATTIE + TAYLOR
SO YOU'RE ORGANISING A BUSINESS TRIP TO AUSTRALIA FOR THE ASHES, ALEX? GETTING THAT THROUGH ON EXPENSES COULD BE TRICKY...
EVERYTHING OUT THERE IS AMAZINGLY EXPENSIVE... REMEMBER, WHILE EUROPE AND THE U.S. HAVE BEEN SUFFERING CUTBACKS DUE TO GLOBAL RECESSION, THE AUSTRALIAN ECONOMY HAS CONTINUED BOOMING...
alex@alexcartoon.com
ITS BANKS LARGELY AVOIDED SUB-PRIME DEBT AND ARE NOW AMONG THE MOST SUCCESSFUL IN THE WORLD. YOU CAN'T SEE THEM BEING AFFECTED BY THE AUSTERITY MEASURES THAT WE'RE HAVING TO ENDURE...
ON THE CONTRARY...
I'VE JUST PICKED UP A HOSPITALITY BOX FOR THE THIRD TEST FROM AN AUSSIE BANK WHO HAD TO CANCEL IT, SUPPOSEDLY DUE TO "COST CUTTING".
SO, NOTHING TO DO WITH THEIR TEAM GETTING ABSOLUTELY STUFFED AT THE CRICKET THEN...?

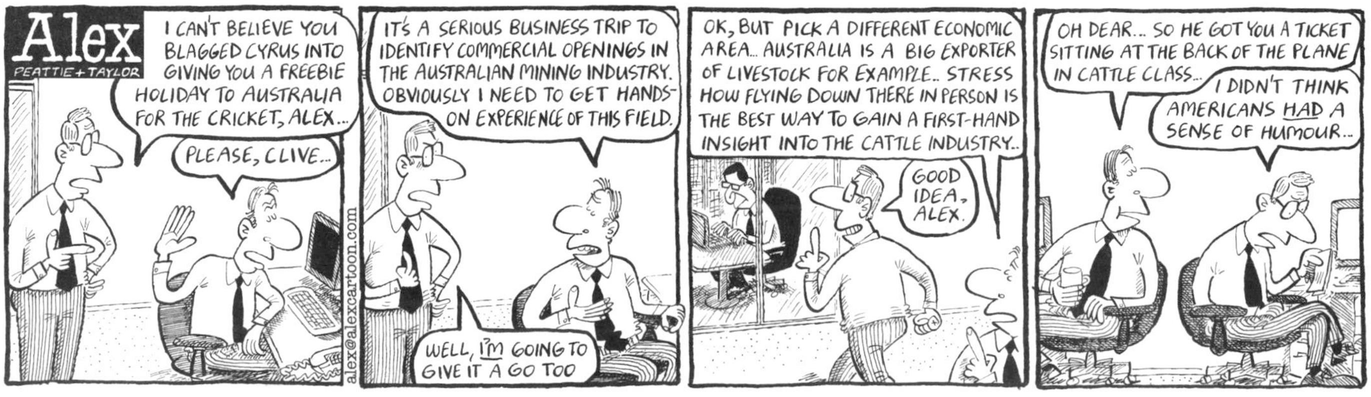
Alex
PEATTIE + TAYLOR
I CAN'T BELIEVE YOU BLAGGED CYRUS INTO GIVING YOU A FREEBIE HOLIDAY TO AUSTRALIA FOR THE CRICKET, ALEX...
PLEASE, CLIVE...
IT'S A SERIOUS BUSINESS TRIP TO IDENTIFY COMMERCIAL OPENINGS IN THE AUSTRALIAN MINING INDUSTRY. OBVIOUSLY I NEED TO GET HANDS-ON EXPERIENCE OF THIS FIELD.
WELL, I'M GOING TO GIVE IT A GO TOO
alex@alexcartoon.com
OK, BUT PICK A DIFFERENT ECONOMIC AREA... AUSTRALIA IS A BIG EXPORTER OF LIVESTOCK FOR EXAMPLE.. STRESS HOW FLYING DOWN THERE IN PERSON IS THE BEST WAY TO GAIN A FIRST-HAND INSIGHT INTO THE CATTLE INDUSTRY..
GOOD IDEA, ALEX.
OH DEAR... SO HE GOT YOU A TICKET SITTING AT THE BACK OF THE PLANE IN CATTLE CLASS...
I DIDN'T THINK AMERICANS HAD A SENSE OF HUMOUR...

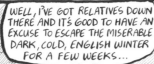

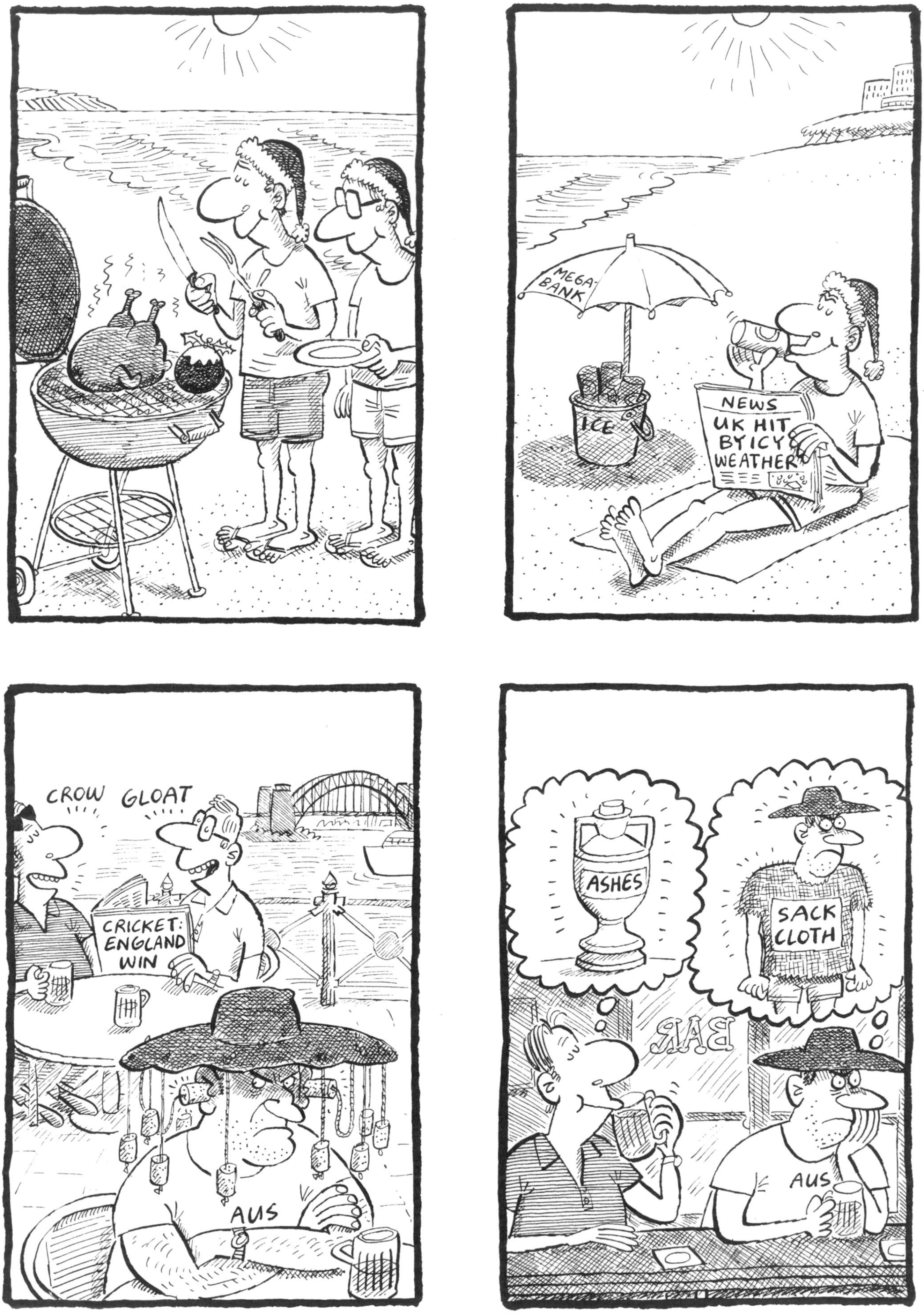
MEGA-BANK
ICE
NEWS
UK HIT BY ICY WEATHER
CROW
GLOAT
CRICKET: ENGLAND WIN
AUS
ASHES
SACK CLOTH
BAR
AUS

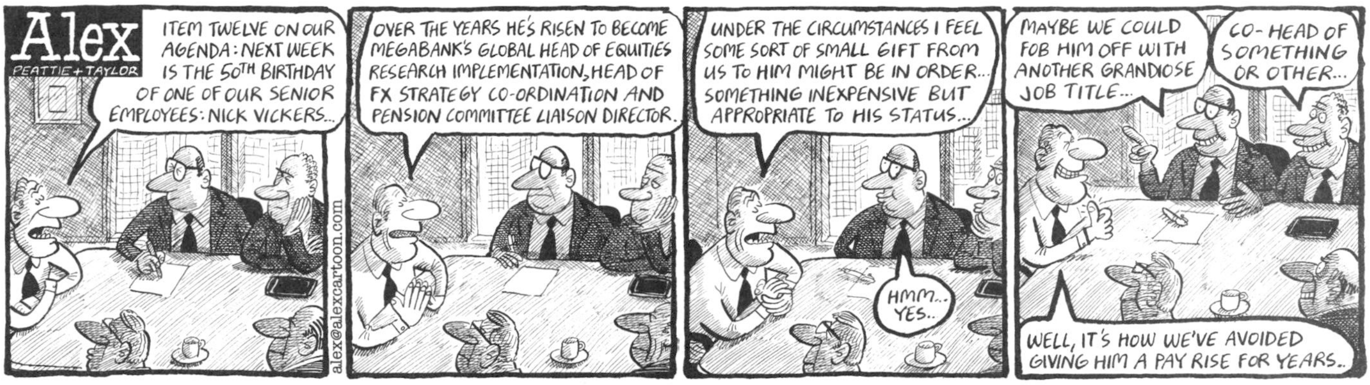
Alex
PEATTIE + TAYLOR
ITEM TWELVE ON OUR AGENDA: NEXT WEEK IS THE 50TH BIRTHDAY OF ONE OF OUR SENIOR EMPLOYEES: NICK VICKERS...
alex@alexcartoon.com
OVER THE YEARS HE'S RISEN TO BECOME MEGABANK'S GLOBAL HEAD OF EQUITIES RESEARCH IMPLEMENTATION, HEAD OF FX STRATEGY CO-ORDINATION AND PENSION COMMITTEE LIAISON DIRECTOR.
UNDER THE CIRCUMSTANCES I FEEL SOME SORT OF SMALL GIFT FROM US TO HIM MIGHT BE IN ORDER... SOMETHING INEXPENSIVE BUT APPROPRIATE TO HIS STATUS...
HMM... YES..
MAYBE WE COULD FOB HIM OFF WITH ANOTHER GRANDIOSE JOB TITLE...
CO-HEAD OF SOMETHING OR OTHER...
WELL, IT'S HOW WE'VE AVOIDED GIVING HIM A PAY RISE FOR YEARS..

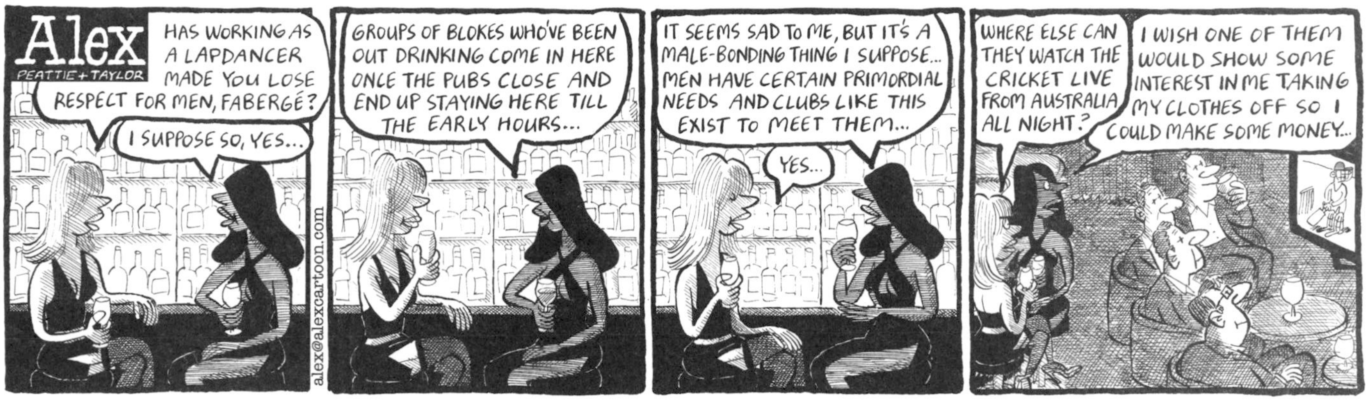
Alex
PEATTIE + TAYLOR
HAS WORKING AS A LAPDANCER MADE YOU LOSE RESPECT FOR MEN, FABERGÉ?
I SUPPOSE SO, YES...
alex@alexcartoon.com
GROUPS OF BLOKES WHO'VE BEEN OUT DRINKING COME IN HERE ONCE THE PUBS CLOSE AND END UP STAYING HERE TILL THE EARLY HOURS...
IT SEEMS SAD TO ME, BUT IT'S A MALE-BONDING THING I SUPPOSE... MEN HAVE CERTAIN PRIMORDIAL NEEDS AND CLUBS LIKE THIS EXIST TO MEET THEM...
YES...
WHERE ELSE CAN THEY WATCH THE CRICKET LIVE FROM AUSTRALIA ALL NIGHT?
I WISH ONE OF THEM WOULD SHOW SOME INTEREST IN ME TAKING MY CLOTHES OFF SO I COULD MAKE SOME MONEY...

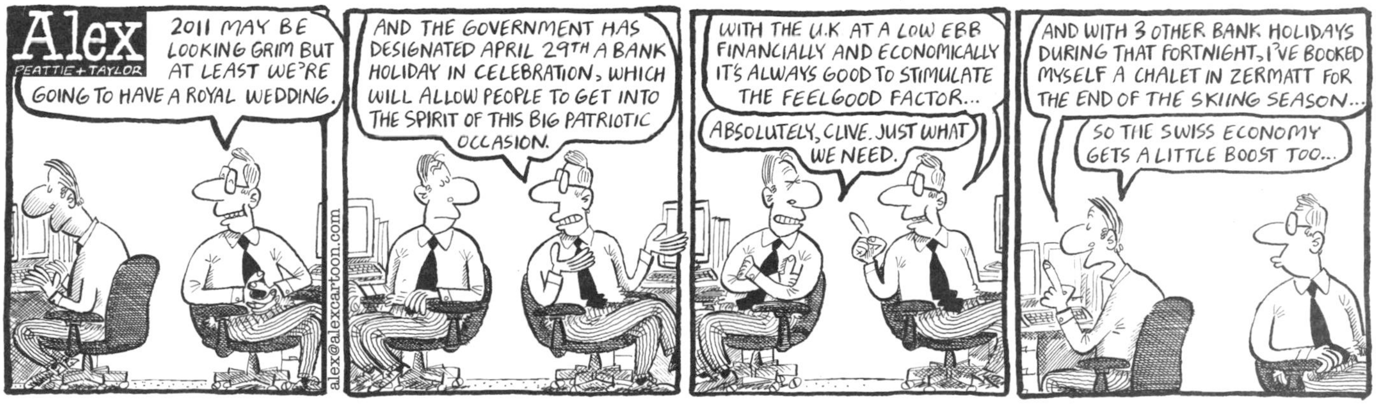
Alex
PEATTIE + TAYLOR
2011 MAY BE LOOKING GRIM BUT AT LEAST WE'RE GOING TO HAVE A ROYAL WEDDING.
alex@alexcartoon.com
AND THE GOVERNMENT HAS DESIGNATED APRIL 29TH A BANK HOLIDAY IN CELEBRATION, WHICH WILL ALLOW PEOPLE TO GET INTO THE SPIRIT OF THIS BIG PATRIOTIC OCCASION.
WITH THE U.K AT A LOW EBB FINANCIALLY AND ECONOMICALLY IT'S ALWAYS GOOD TO STIMULATE THE FEELGOOD FACTOR...
ABSOLUTELY, CLIVE. JUST WHAT WE NEED.
AND WITH 3 OTHER BANK HOLIDAYS DURING THAT FORTNIGHT, I'VE BOOKED MYSELF A CHALET IN ZERMATT FOR THE END OF THE SKIING SEASON...
SO THE SWISS ECONOMY GETS A LITTLE BOOST TOO...

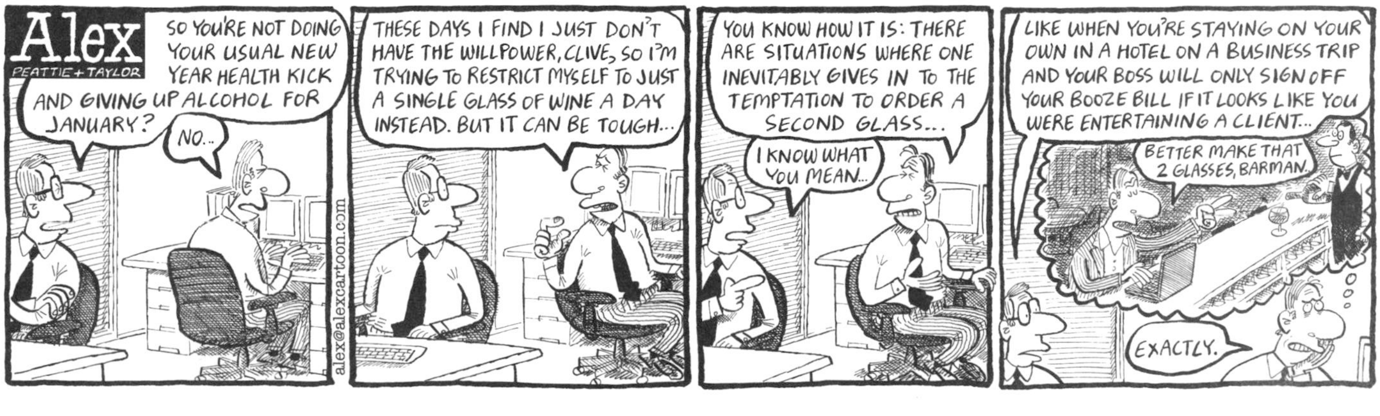
Alex
PEATTIE + TAYLOR
SO YOU'RE NOT DOING YOUR USUAL NEW YEAR HEALTH KICK AND GIVING UP ALCOHOL FOR JANUARY?
NO...
alex@alexcartoon.com
THESE DAYS I FIND I JUST DON'T HAVE THE WILLPOWER, CLIVE, SO I'M TRYING TO RESTRICT MYSELF TO JUST A SINGLE GLASS OF WINE A DAY INSTEAD. BUT IT CAN BE TOUGH...
YOU KNOW HOW IT IS: THERE ARE SITUATIONS WHERE ONE INEVITABLY GIVES IN TO THE TEMPTATION TO ORDER A SECOND GLASS...
I KNOW WHAT YOU MEAN...
LIKE WHEN YOU'RE STAYING ON YOUR OWN IN A HOTEL ON A BUSINESS TRIP AND YOUR BOSS WILL ONLY SIGN OFF YOUR BOOZE BILL IF IT LOOKS LIKE YOU WERE ENTERTAINING A CLIENT...
BETTER MAKE THAT 2 GLASSES, BARMAN.
EXACTLY.

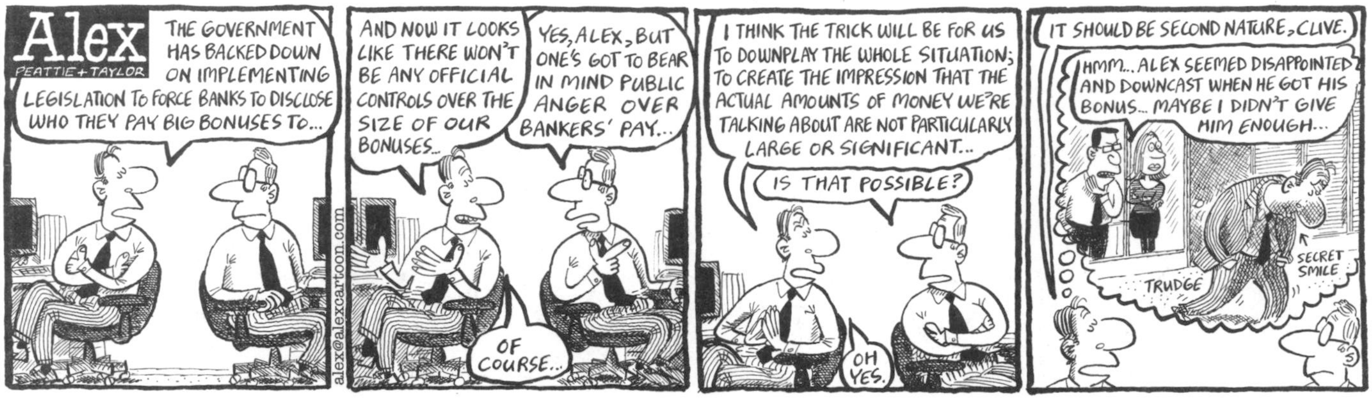
Alex
PEATTIE + TAYLOR
THE GOVERNMENT HAS BACKED DOWN ON IMPLEMENTING LEGISLATION TO FORCE BANKS TO DISCLOSE WHO THEY PAY BIG BONUSES TO...
AND NOW IT LOOKS LIKE THERE WON'T BE ANY OFFICIAL CONTROLS OVER THE SIZE OF OUR BONUSES...
YES, ALEX, BUT ONE'S GOT TO BEAR IN MIND PUBLIC ANGER OVER BANKERS' PAY...
OF COURSE...
alex@alexcartoon.com
I THINK THE TRICK WILL BE FOR US TO DOWNPLAY THE WHOLE SITUATION; TO CREATE THE IMPRESSION THAT THE ACTUAL AMOUNTS OF MONEY WE'RE TALKING ABOUT ARE NOT PARTICULARLY LARGE OR SIGNIFICANT...
IS THAT POSSIBLE?
OH YES.
IT SHOULD BE SECOND NATURE, CLIVE.
HMM... ALEX SEEMED DISAPPOINTED AND DOWNCAST WHEN HE GOT HIS BONUS... MAYBE I DIDN'T GIVE HIM ENOUGH...
TRUDGE
SECRET SMILE

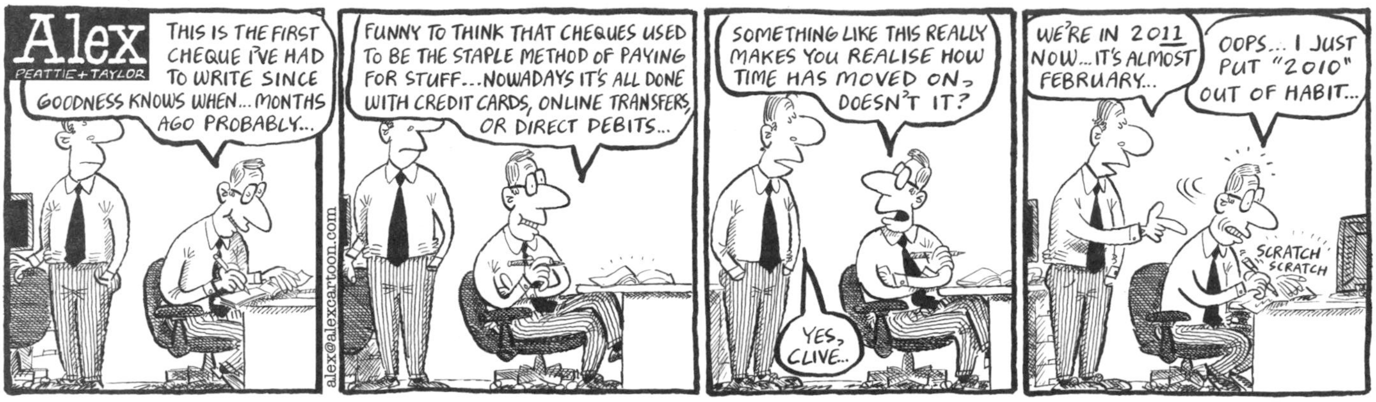
Alex
PEATTIE + TAYLOR
THIS IS THE FIRST CHEQUE I'VE HAD TO WRITE SINCE GOODNESS KNOWS WHEN... MONTHS AGO PROBABLY...
FUNNY TO THINK THAT CHEQUES USED TO BE THE STAPLE METHOD OF PAYING FOR STUFF... NOWADAYS IT'S ALL DONE WITH CREDIT CARDS, ONLINE TRANSFERS, OR DIRECT DEBITS...
alex@alexcartoon.com
SOMETHING LIKE THIS REALLY MAKES YOU REALISE HOW TIME HAS MOVED ON, DOESN'T IT?
YES, CLIVE...
WE'RE IN 2011 NOW... IT'S ALMOST FEBRUARY...
OOPS... I JUST PUT "2010" OUT OF HABIT...
SCRATCH SCRATCH

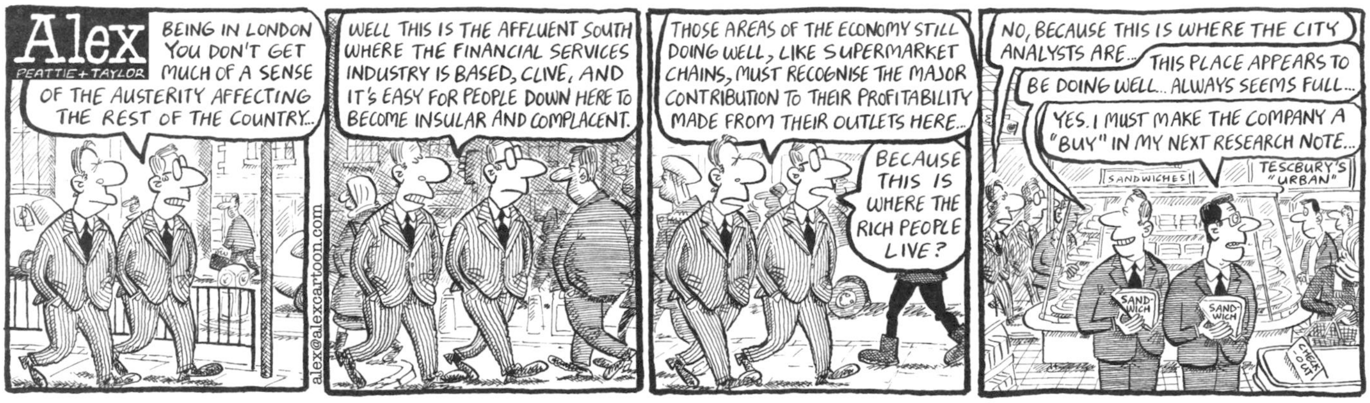
Alex
PEATTIE + TAYLOR
BEING IN LONDON YOU DON'T GET MUCH OF A SENSE OF THE AUSTERITY AFFECTING THE REST OF THE COUNTRY...
WELL THIS IS THE AFFLUENT SOUTH WHERE THE FINANCIAL SERVICES INDUSTRY IS BASED, CLIVE, AND IT'S EASY FOR PEOPLE DOWN HERE TO BECOME INSULAR AND COMPLACENT.
alex@alexcartoon.com
THOSE AREAS OF THE ECONOMY STILL DOING WELL, LIKE SUPERMARKET CHAINS, MUST RECOGNISE THE MAJOR CONTRIBUTION TO THEIR PROFITABILITY MADE FROM THEIR OUTLETS HERE...
BECAUSE THIS IS WHERE THE RICH PEOPLE LIVE?
NO, BECAUSE THIS IS WHERE THE CITY ANALYSTS ARE...
THIS PLACE APPEARS TO BE DOING WELL... ALWAYS SEEMS FULL...
YES. I MUST MAKE THE COMPANY A "BUY" IN MY NEXT RESEARCH NOTE...
SANDWICHES
TESCBURY'S "URBAN"
SAND-WICH
SAND-WICH
CHECK OUT

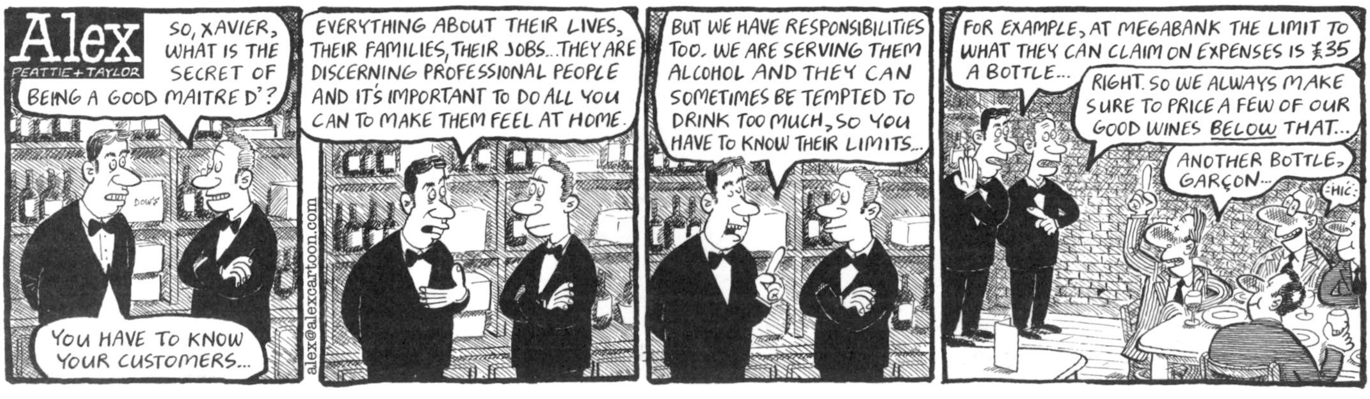
Alex
PEATTIE + TAYLOR
SO, XAVIER, WHAT IS THE SECRET OF BEING A GOOD MAITRE D'?
YOU HAVE TO KNOW YOUR CUSTOMERS...
EVERYTHING ABOUT THEIR LIVES, THEIR FAMILIES, THEIR JOBS... THEY ARE DISCERNING PROFESSIONAL PEOPLE AND IT'S IMPORTANT TO DO ALL YOU CAN TO MAKE THEM FEEL AT HOME.
alex@alexcartoon.com
BUT WE HAVE RESPONSIBILITIES TOO. WE ARE SERVING THEM ALCOHOL AND THEY CAN SOMETIMES BE TEMPTED TO DRINK TOO MUCH, SO YOU HAVE TO KNOW THEIR LIMITS...
FOR EXAMPLE, AT MEGABANK THE LIMIT TO WHAT THEY CAN CLAIM ON EXPENSES IS £35 A BOTTLE...
RIGHT. SO WE ALWAYS MAKE SURE TO PRICE A FEW OF OUR GOOD WINES BELOW THAT...
ANOTHER BOTTLE, GARÇON...
HIC

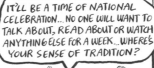

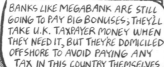

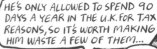

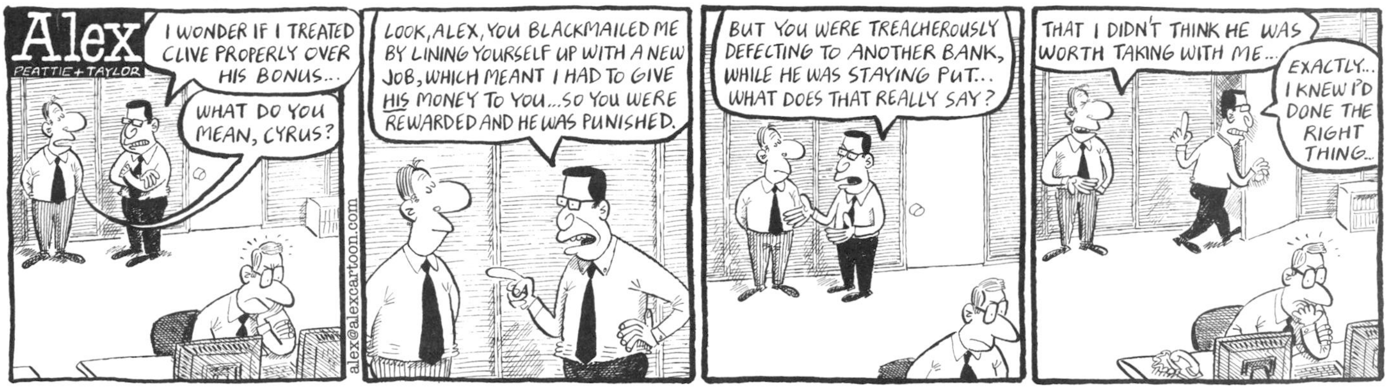
Alex
PEATTIE + TAYLOR
I WONDER IF I TREATED CLIVE PROPERLY OVER HIS BONUS...
WHAT DO YOU MEAN, CYRUS?
LOOK, ALEX, YOU BLACKMAILED ME BY LINING YOURSELF UP WITH A NEW JOB, WHICH MEANT I HAD TO GIVE HIS MONEY TO YOU... SO YOU WERE REWARDED AND HE WAS PUNISHED.
alex@alexcartoon.com
BUT YOU WERE TREACHEROUSLY DEFECTING TO ANOTHER BANK, WHILE HE WAS STAYING PUT... WHAT DOES THAT REALLY SAY?
THAT I DIDN'T THINK HE WAS WORTH TAKING WITH ME...
EXACTLY... I KNEW I'D DONE THE RIGHT THING...

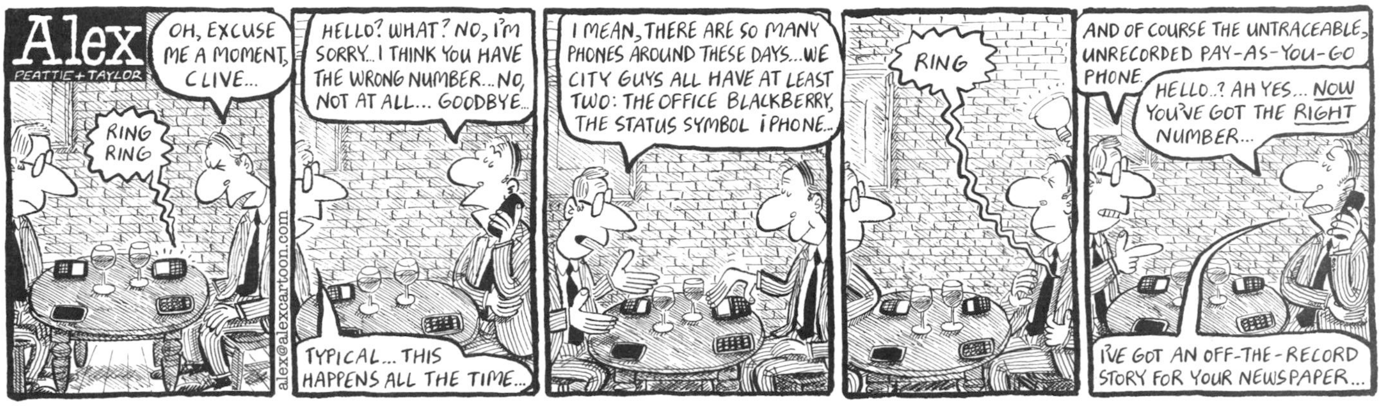
Alex
PEATTIE + TAYLOR
OH, EXCUSE ME A MOMENT, CLIVE...
RING RING
HELLO? WHAT? NO, I'M SORRY... I THINK YOU HAVE THE WRONG NUMBER... NO, NOT AT ALL... GOODBYE...
TYPICAL... THIS HAPPENS ALL THE TIME...
alex@alexcartoon.com
I MEAN, THERE ARE SO MANY PHONES AROUND THESE DAYS... WE CITY GUYS ALL HAVE AT LEAST TWO: THE OFFICE BLACKBERRY, THE STATUS SYMBOL iPHONE...
RING
AND OF COURSE THE UNTRACEABLE, UNRECORDED PAY-AS-YOU-GO PHONE.
HELLO..? AH YES... NOW YOU'VE GOT THE RIGHT NUMBER...
I'VE GOT AN OFF-THE-RECORD STORY FOR YOUR NEWSPAPER...

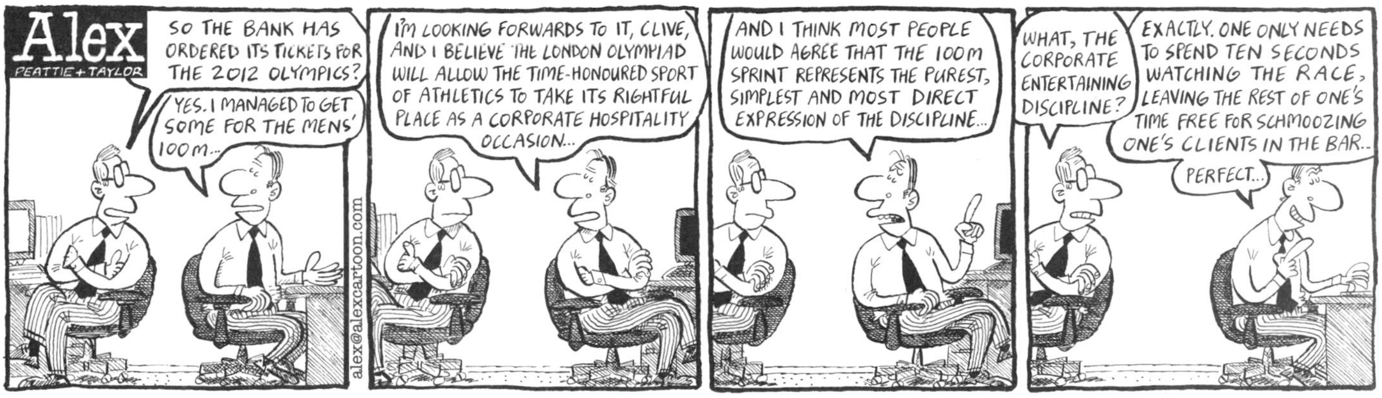
Alex
PEATTIE + TAYLOR
SO THE BANK HAS ORDERED ITS TICKETS FOR THE 2012 OLYMPICS?
YES. I MANAGED TO GET SOME FOR THE MENS' 100M...
alex@alexcartoon.com
I'M LOOKING FORWARDS TO IT, CLIVE, AND I BELIEVE THE LONDON OLYMPIAD WILL ALLOW THE TIME-HONOURED SPORT OF ATHLETICS TO TAKE ITS RIGHTFUL PLACE AS A CORPORATE HOSPITALITY OCCASION...
AND I THINK MOST PEOPLE WOULD AGREE THAT THE 100M SPRINT REPRESENTS THE PUREST, SIMPLEST AND MOST DIRECT EXPRESSION OF THE DISCIPLINE...
WHAT, THE CORPORATE ENTERTAINING DISCIPLINE?
EXACTLY. ONE ONLY NEEDS TO SPEND TEN SECONDS WATCHING THE RACE, LEAVING THE REST OF ONE'S TIME FREE FOR SCHMOOZING ONE'S CLIENTS IN THE BAR...
PERFECT...

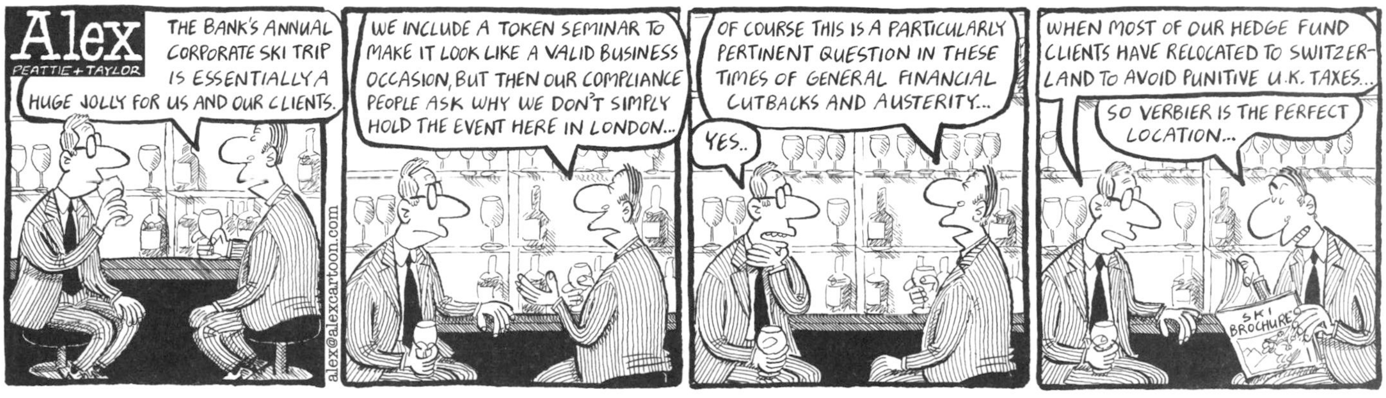
Alex
PEATTIE + TAYLOR
THE BANK'S ANNUAL CORPORATE SKI TRIP IS ESSENTIALLY A HUGE JOLLY FOR US AND OUR CLIENTS.
alex@alexcartoon.com
WE INCLUDE A TOKEN SEMINAR TO MAKE IT LOOK LIKE A VALID BUSINESS OCCASION, BUT THEN OUR COMPLIANCE PEOPLE ASK WHY WE DON'T SIMPLY HOLD THE EVENT HERE IN LONDON...
OF COURSE THIS IS A PARTICULARLY PERTINENT QUESTION IN THESE TIMES OF GENERAL FINANCIAL CUTBACKS AND AUSTERITY...
YES..
WHEN MOST OF OUR HEDGE FUND CLIENTS HAVE RELOCATED TO SWITZERLAND TO AVOID PUNITIVE U.K. TAXES...
SO VERBIER IS THE PERFECT LOCATION...
SKI BROCHURES

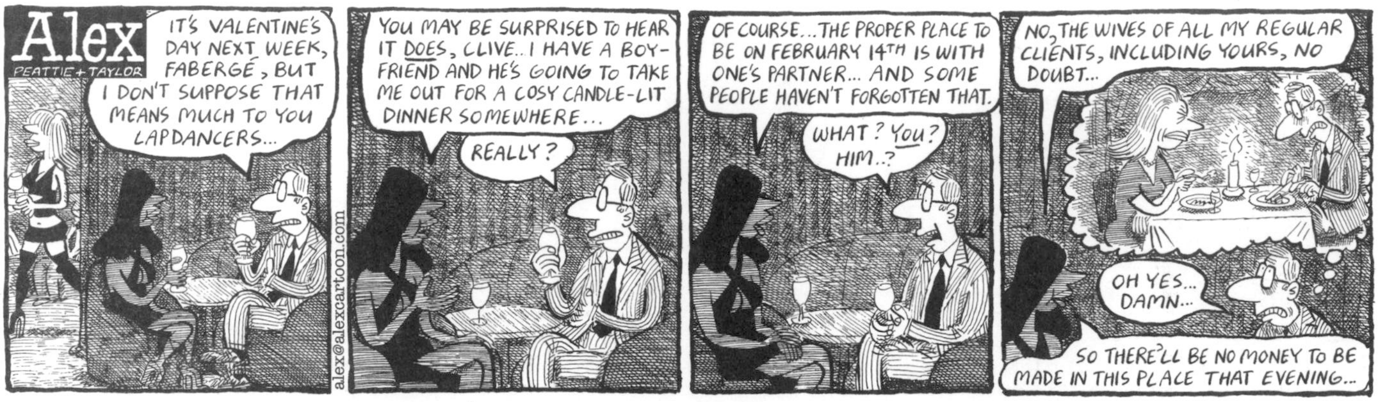
Alex
PEATTIE + TAYLOR
IT'S VALENTINE'S DAY NEXT WEEK, FABERGÉ, BUT I DON'T SUPPOSE THAT MEANS MUCH TO YOU LAPDANCERS...
YOU MAY BE SURPRISED TO HEAR IT DOES, CLIVE.. I HAVE A BOY-FRIEND AND HE'S GOING TO TAKE ME OUT FOR A COSY CANDLE-LIT DINNER SOMEWHERE...
REALLY?
alex@alexcartoon.com
OF COURSE... THE PROPER PLACE TO BE ON FEBRUARY 14TH IS WITH ONE'S PARTNER... AND SOME PEOPLE HAVEN'T FORGOTTEN THAT.
WHAT? YOU? HIM..?
NO, THE WIVES OF ALL MY REGULAR CLIENTS, INCLUDING YOURS, NO DOUBT...
OH YES... DAMN...
SO THERE'LL BE NO MONEY TO BE MADE IN THIS PLACE THAT EVENING...

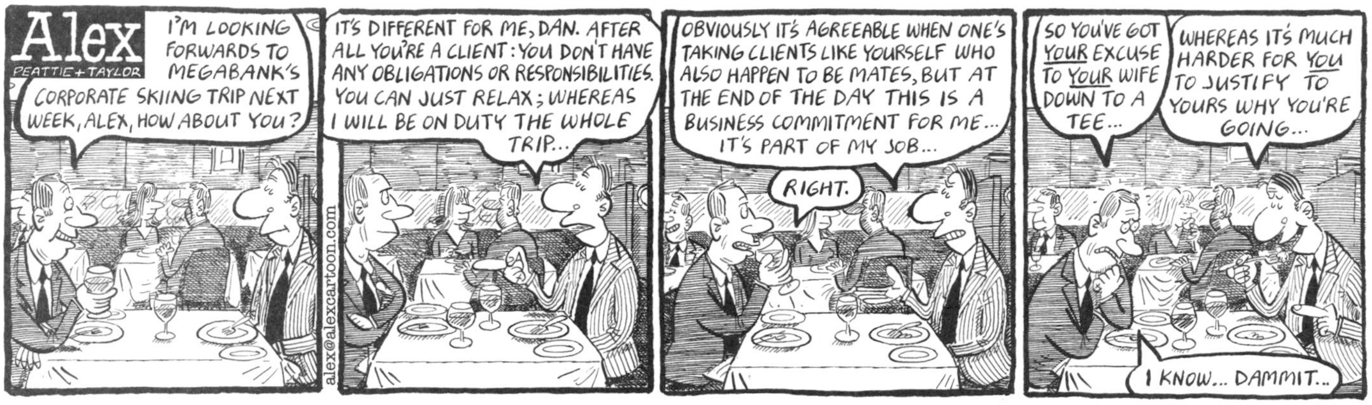
Alex
PEATTIE + TAYLOR
I'M LOOKING FORWARDS TO MEGABANK'S CORPORATE SKIING TRIP NEXT WEEK, ALEX, HOW ABOUT YOU?
IT'S DIFFERENT FOR ME, DAN. AFTER ALL YOU'RE A CLIENT: YOU DON'T HAVE ANY OBLIGATIONS OR RESPONSIBILITIES. YOU CAN JUST RELAX; WHEREAS I WILL BE ON DUTY THE WHOLE TRIP...
alex@alexcartoon.com
OBVIOUSLY IT'S AGREEABLE WHEN ONE'S TAKING CLIENTS LIKE YOURSELF WHO ALSO HAPPEN TO BE MATES, BUT AT THE END OF THE DAY THIS IS A BUSINESS COMMITMENT FOR ME... IT'S PART OF MY JOB...
RIGHT.
SO YOU'VE GOT YOUR EXCUSE TO YOUR WIFE DOWN TO A TEE...
WHEREAS IT'S MUCH HARDER FOR YOU TO JUSTIFY TO YOURS WHY YOU'RE GOING...
I KNOW... DAMMIT...

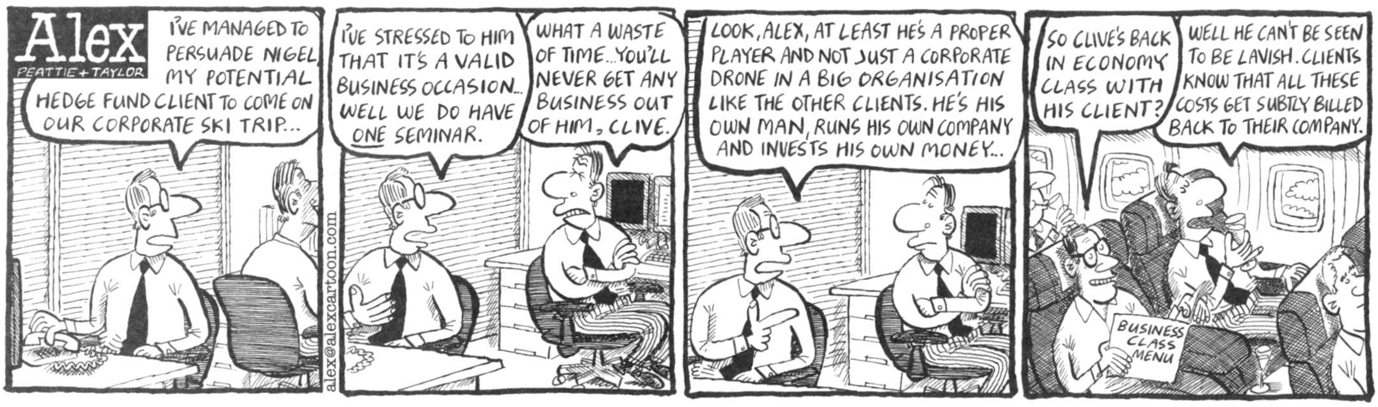
Alex
PEATTIE + TAYLOR
I'VE MANAGED TO PERSUADE NIGEL, MY POTENTIAL HEDGE FUND CLIENT TO COME ON OUR CORPORATE SKI TRIP...
I'VE STRESSED TO HIM THAT IT'S A VALID BUSINESS OCCASION... WELL WE DO HAVE ONE SEMINAR.
WHAT A WASTE OF TIME... YOU'LL NEVER GET ANY BUSINESS OUT OF HIM, CLIVE.
alex@alexcartoon.com
LOOK, ALEX, AT LEAST HE'S A PROPER PLAYER AND NOT JUST A CORPORATE DRONE IN A BIG ORGANISATION LIKE THE OTHER CLIENTS. HE'S HIS OWN MAN, RUNS HIS OWN COMPANY AND INVESTS HIS OWN MONEY...
SO CLIVE'S BACK IN ECONOMY CLASS WITH HIS CLIENT?
WELL HE CAN'T BE SEEN TO BE LAVISH. CLIENTS KNOW THAT ALL THESE COSTS GET SUBTLY BILLED BACK TO THEIR COMPANY.
BUSINESS CLASS MENU

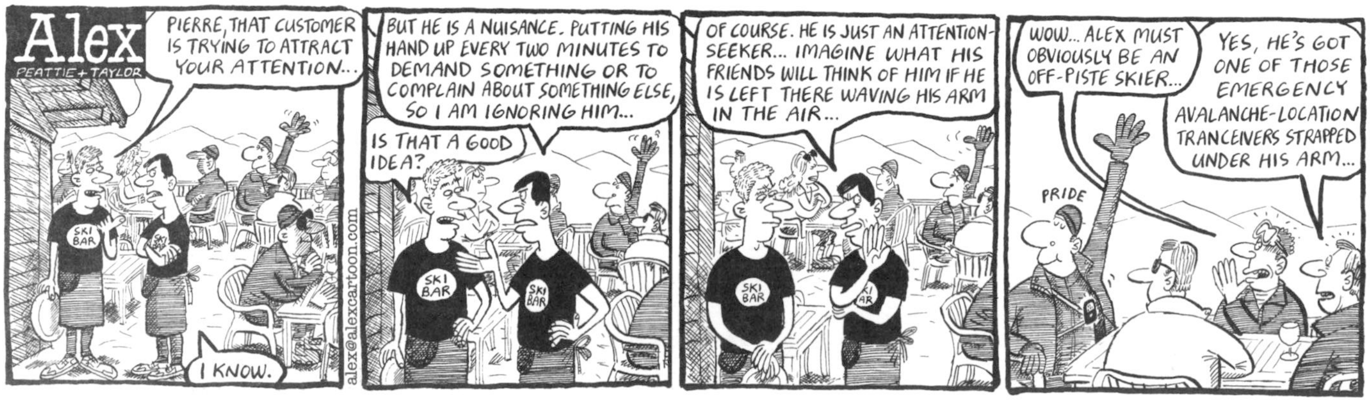
Alex
PEATTIE + TAYLOR
PIERRE, THAT CUSTOMER IS TRYING TO ATTRACT YOUR ATTENTION...
SKI BAR
I KNOW.
alex@alexcartoon.com
BUT HE IS A NUISANCE. PUTTING HIS HAND UP EVERY TWO MINUTES TO DEMAND SOMETHING OR TO COMPLAIN ABOUT SOMETHING ELSE, SO I AM IGNORING HIM...
IS THAT A GOOD IDEA?
OF COURSE. HE IS JUST AN ATTENTION-SEEKER... IMAGINE WHAT HIS FRIENDS WILL THINK OF HIM IF HE IS LEFT THERE WAVING HIS ARM IN THE AIR...
WOW... ALEX MUST OBVIOUSLY BE AN OFF-PISTE SKIER...
YES, HE'S GOT ONE OF THOSE EMERGENCY AVALANCHE-LOCATION TRANCEIVERS STRAPPED UNDER HIS ARM...
PRIDE

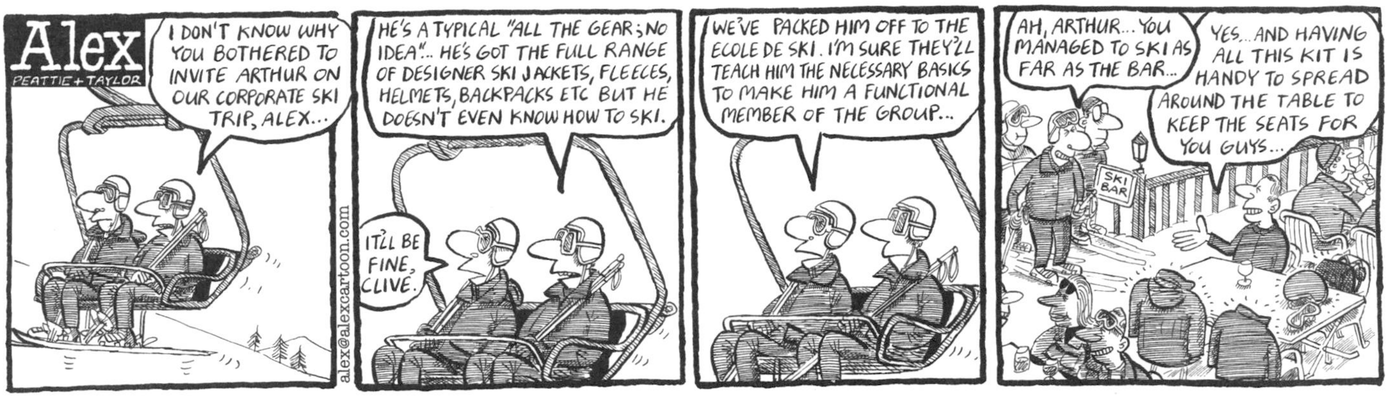
Alex
PEATTIE + TAYLOR
I DON'T KNOW WHY YOU BOTHERED TO INVITE ARTHUR ON OUR CORPORATE SKI TRIP, ALEX...
HE'S A TYPICAL "ALL THE GEAR; NO IDEA"... HE'S GOT THE FULL RANGE OF DESIGNER SKI JACKETS, FLEECES, HELMETS, BACKPACKS ETC BUT HE DOESN'T EVEN KNOW HOW TO SKI.
IT'LL BE FINE, CLIVE.
alex@alexcartoon.com
WE'VE PACKED HIM OFF TO THE ECOLE DE SKI. I'M SURE THEY'LL TEACH HIM THE NECESSARY BASICS TO MAKE HIM A FUNCTIONAL MEMBER OF THE GROUP...
AH, ARTHUR... YOU MANAGED TO SKI AS FAR AS THE BAR...
YES... AND HAVING ALL THIS KIT IS HANDY TO SPREAD AROUND THE TABLE TO KEEP THE SEATS FOR YOU GUYS...
SKI BAR

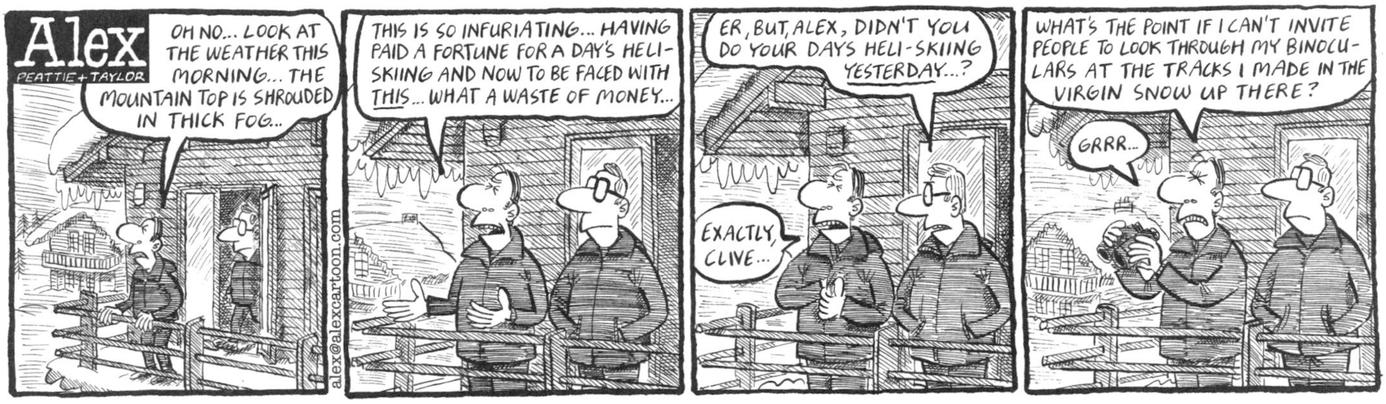
Alex
PEATTIE + TAYLOR
OH NO... LOOK AT THE WEATHER THIS MORNING... THE MOUNTAIN TOP IS SHROUDED IN THICK FOG...
alex@alexcartoon.com
THIS IS SO INFURIATING... HAVING PAID A FORTUNE FOR A DAY'S HELI-SKIING AND NOW TO BE FACED WITH THIS... WHAT A WASTE OF MONEY...
ER, BUT, ALEX, DIDN'T YOU DO YOUR DAY'S HELI-SKIING YESTERDAY...?
EXACTLY, CLIVE...
WHAT'S THE POINT IF I CAN'T INVITE PEOPLE TO LOOK THROUGH MY BINOCULARS AT THE TRACKS I MADE IN THE VIRGIN SNOW UP THERE?
GRRR...

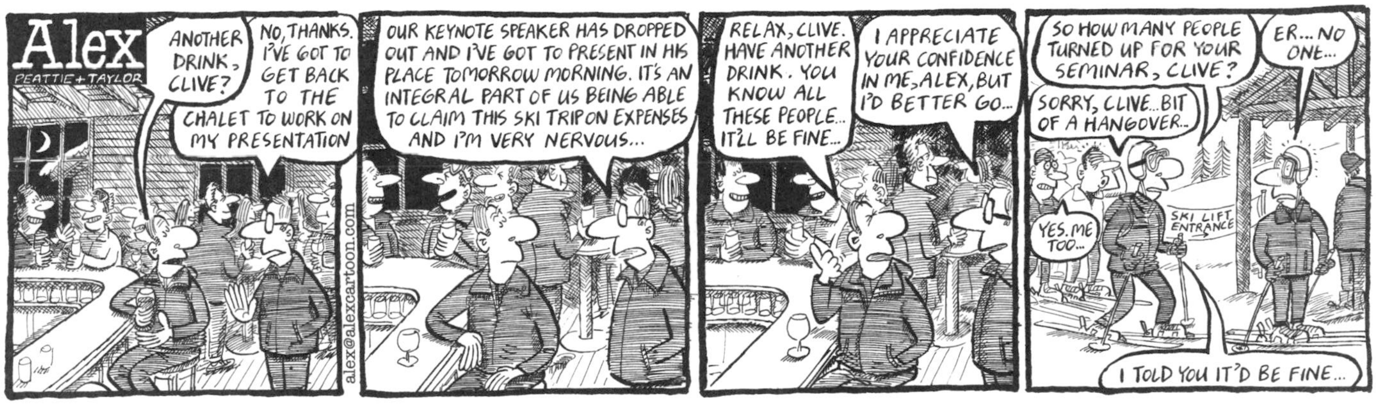
Alex
PEATTIE + TAYLOR
ANOTHER DRINK, CLIVE?
NO, THANKS. I'VE GOT TO GET BACK TO THE CHALET TO WORK ON MY PRESENTATION
alex@alexcartoon.com
OUR KEYNOTE SPEAKER HAS DROPPED OUT AND I'VE GOT TO PRESENT IN HIS PLACE TOMORROW MORNING. IT'S AN INTEGRAL PART OF US BEING ABLE TO CLAIM THIS SKI TRIP ON EXPENSES AND I'M VERY NERVOUS...
RELAX, CLIVE. HAVE ANOTHER DRINK. YOU KNOW ALL THESE PEOPLE... IT'LL BE FINE...
I APPRECIATE YOUR CONFIDENCE IN ME, ALEX, BUT I'D BETTER GO...
SO HOW MANY PEOPLE TURNED UP FOR YOUR SEMINAR, CLIVE?
ER... NO ONE...
SORRY, CLIVE... BIT OF A HANGOVER...
YES. ME TOO...
SKI LIFT ENTRANCE
I TOLD YOU IT'D BE FINE...

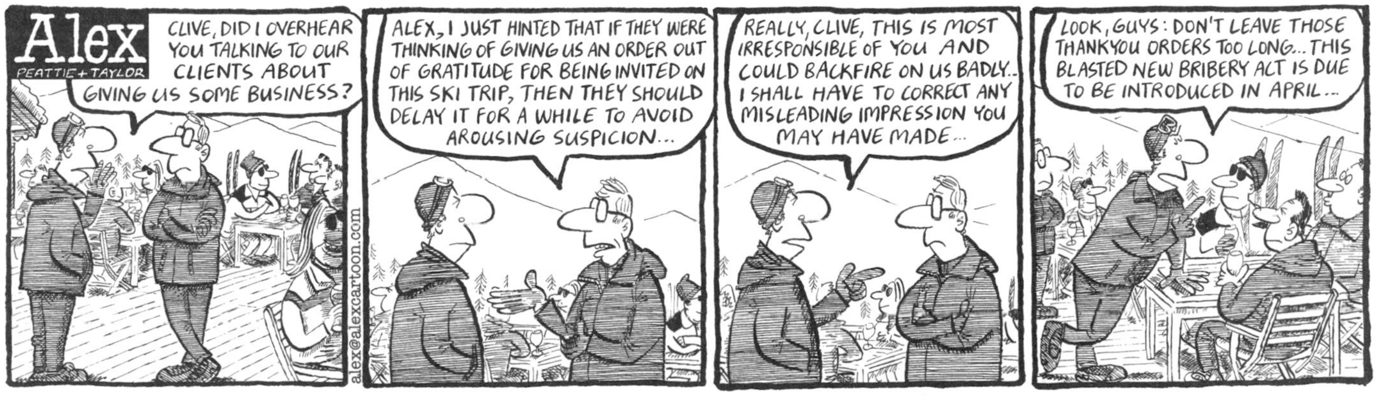
Alex
PEATTIE + TAYLOR
CLIVE, DID I OVERHEAR YOU TALKING TO OUR CLIENTS ABOUT GIVING US SOME BUSINESS?
alex@alexcartoon.com
ALEX, I JUST HINTED THAT IF THEY WERE THINKING OF GIVING US AN ORDER OUT OF GRATITUDE FOR BEING INVITED ON THIS SKI TRIP, THEN THEY SHOULD DELAY IT FOR A WHILE TO AVOID AROUSING SUSPICION...
REALLY, CLIVE, THIS IS MOST IRRESPONSIBLE OF YOU AND COULD BACKFIRE ON US BADLY... I SHALL HAVE TO CORRECT ANY MISLEADING IMPRESSION YOU MAY HAVE MADE...
LOOK, GUYS: DON'T LEAVE THOSE THANKYOU ORDERS TOO LONG... THIS BLASTED NEW BRIBERY ACT IS DUE TO BE INTRODUCED IN APRIL...

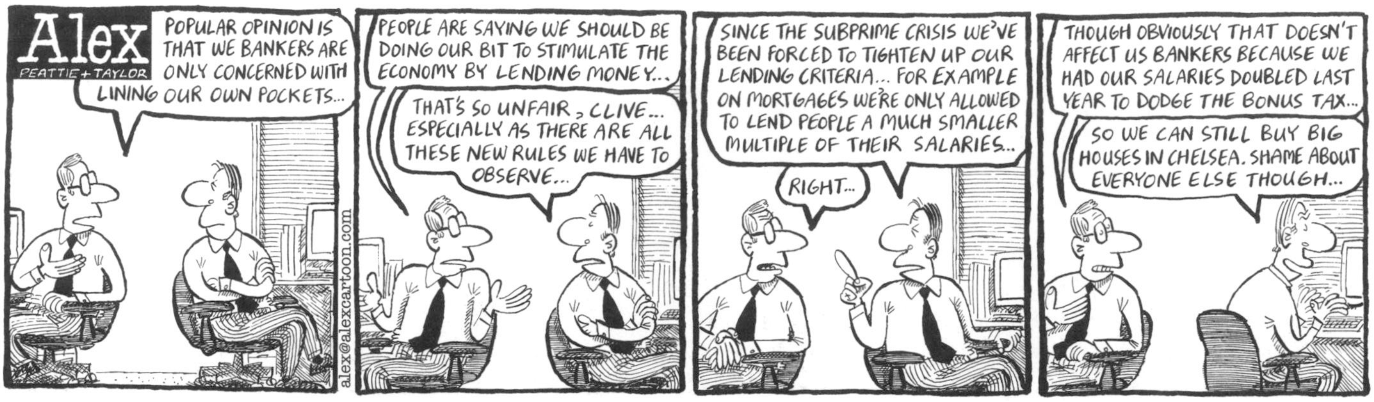
Alex
PEATTIE + TAYLOR
POPULAR OPINION IS THAT WE BANKERS ARE ONLY CONCERNED WITH LINING OUR OWN POCKETS...
PEOPLE ARE SAYING WE SHOULD BE DOING OUR BIT TO STIMULATE THE ECONOMY BY LENDING MONEY...
THAT'S SO UNFAIR, CLIVE... ESPECIALLY AS THERE ARE ALL THESE NEW RULES WE HAVE TO OBSERVE...
SINCE THE SUBPRIME CRISIS WE'VE BEEN FORCED TO TIGHTEN UP OUR LENDING CRITERIA... FOR EXAMPLE ON MORTGAGES WE'RE ONLY ALLOWED TO LEND PEOPLE A MUCH SMALLER MULTIPLE OF THEIR SALARIES...
RIGHT...
THOUGH OBVIOUSLY THAT DOESN'T AFFECT US BANKERS BECAUSE WE HAD OUR SALARIES DOUBLED LAST YEAR TO DODGE THE BONUS TAX...
SO WE CAN STILL BUY BIG HOUSES IN CHELSEA. SHAME ABOUT EVERYONE ELSE THOUGH...
alex@alexcartoon.com

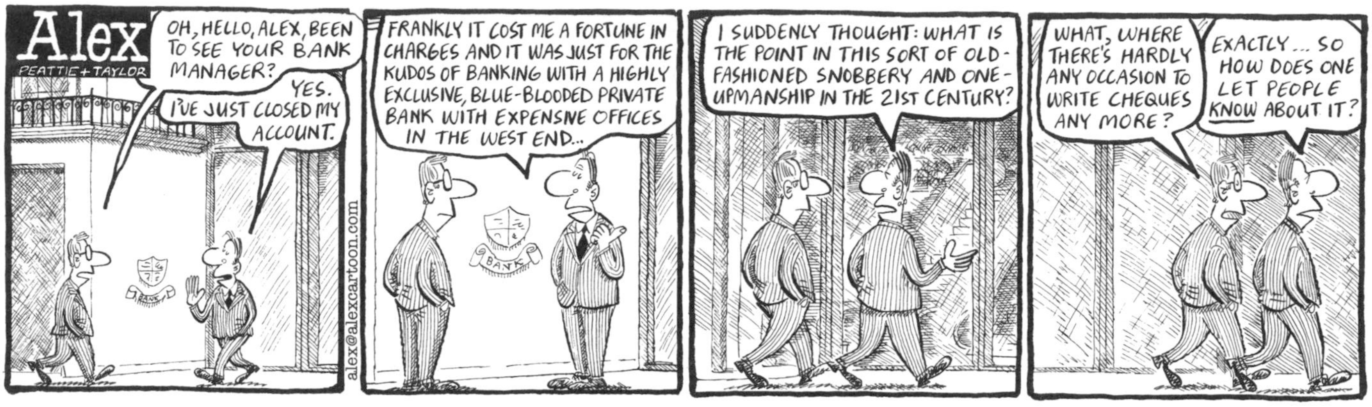
Alex
PEATTIE + TAYLOR
OH, HELLO, ALEX, BEEN TO SEE YOUR BANK MANAGER?
YES. I'VE JUST CLOSED MY ACCOUNT.
FRANKLY IT COST ME A FORTUNE IN CHARGES AND IT WAS JUST FOR THE KUDOS OF BANKING WITH A HIGHLY EXCLUSIVE, BLUE-BLOODED PRIVATE BANK WITH EXPENSIVE OFFICES IN THE WEST END...
BANK
I SUDDENLY THOUGHT: WHAT IS THE POINT IN THIS SORT OF OLD-FASHIONED SNOBBERY AND ONE-UPMANSHIP IN THE 21ST CENTURY?
WHAT, WHERE THERE'S HARDLY ANY OCCASION TO WRITE CHEQUES ANY MORE?
EXACTLY... SO HOW DOES ONE LET PEOPLE KNOW ABOUT IT?
alex@alexcartoon.com

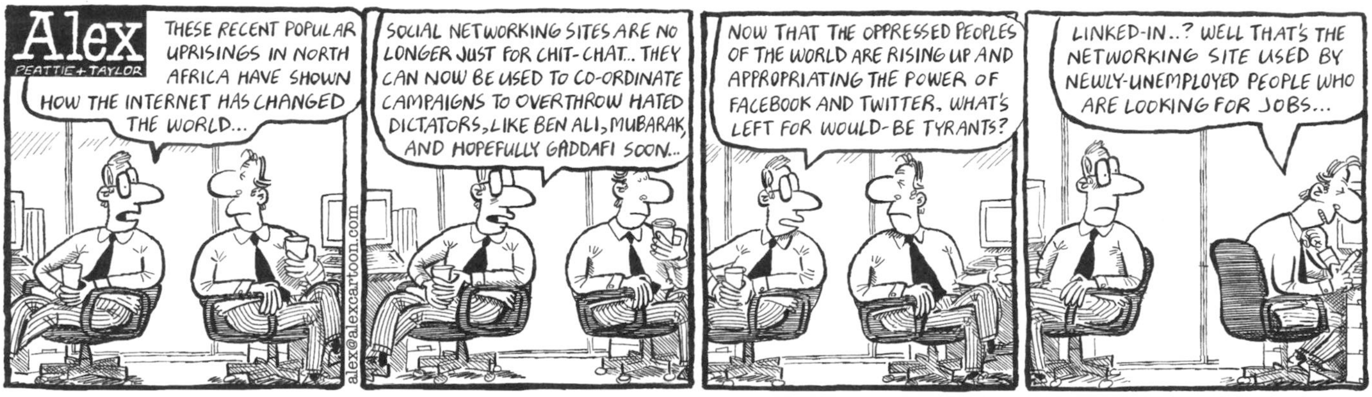
Alex
PEATTIE + TAYLOR
THESE RECENT POPULAR UPRISINGS IN NORTH AFRICA HAVE SHOWN HOW THE INTERNET HAS CHANGED THE WORLD...
SOCIAL NETWORKING SITES ARE NO LONGER JUST FOR CHIT-CHAT... THEY CAN NOW BE USED TO CO-ORDINATE CAMPAIGNS TO OVERTHROW HATED DICTATORS, LIKE BEN ALI, MUBARAK, AND HOPEFULLY GADDAFI SOON...
NOW THAT THE OPPRESSED PEOPLES OF THE WORLD ARE RISING UP AND APPROPRIATING THE POWER OF FACEBOOK AND TWITTER, WHAT'S LEFT FOR WOULD-BE TYRANTS?
LINKED-IN..? WELL THAT'S THE NETWORKING SITE USED BY NEWLY-UNEMPLOYED PEOPLE WHO ARE LOOKING FOR JOBS...
alex@alexcartoon.com

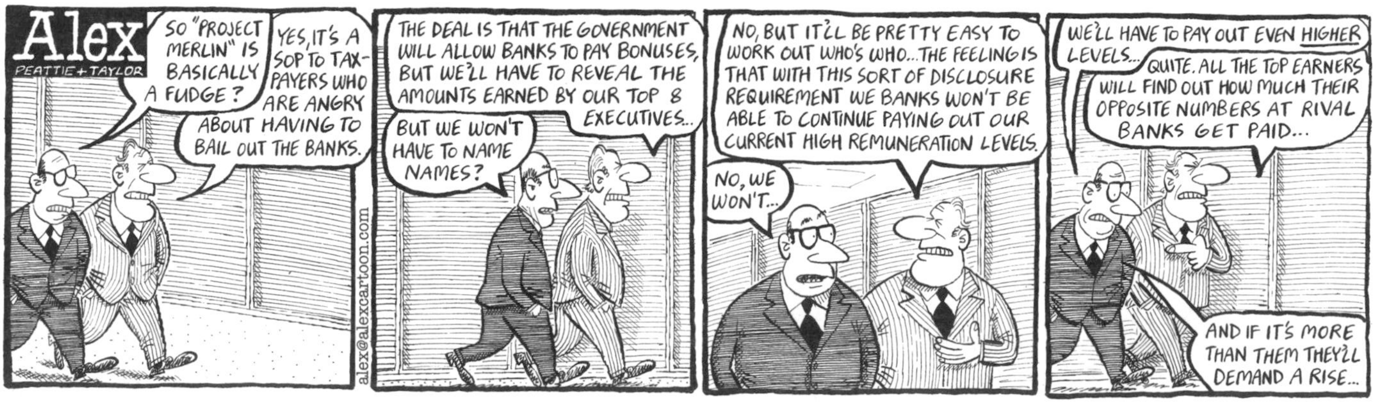
Alex
PEATTIE + TAYLOR
SO "PROJECT MERLIN" IS BASICALLY A FUDGE?
YES, IT'S A SOP TO TAX-PAYERS WHO ARE ANGRY ABOUT HAVING TO BAIL OUT THE BANKS.
THE DEAL IS THAT THE GOVERNMENT WILL ALLOW BANKS TO PAY BONUSES, BUT WE'LL HAVE TO REVEAL THE AMOUNTS EARNED BY OUR TOP 8 EXECUTIVES...
BUT WE WON'T HAVE TO NAME NAMES?
NO, BUT IT'LL BE PRETTY EASY TO WORK OUT WHO'S WHO... THE FEELING IS THAT WITH THIS SORT OF DISCLOSURE REQUIREMENT WE BANKS WON'T BE ABLE TO CONTINUE PAYING OUT OUR CURRENT HIGH REMUNERATION LEVELS.
NO, WE WON'T...
WE'LL HAVE TO PAY OUT EVEN HIGHER LEVELS...
QUITE. ALL THE TOP EARNERS WILL FIND OUT HOW MUCH THEIR OPPOSITE NUMBERS AT RIVAL BANKS GET PAID...
AND IF IT'S MORE THAN THEM THEY'LL DEMAND A RISE...
alex@alexcartoon.com

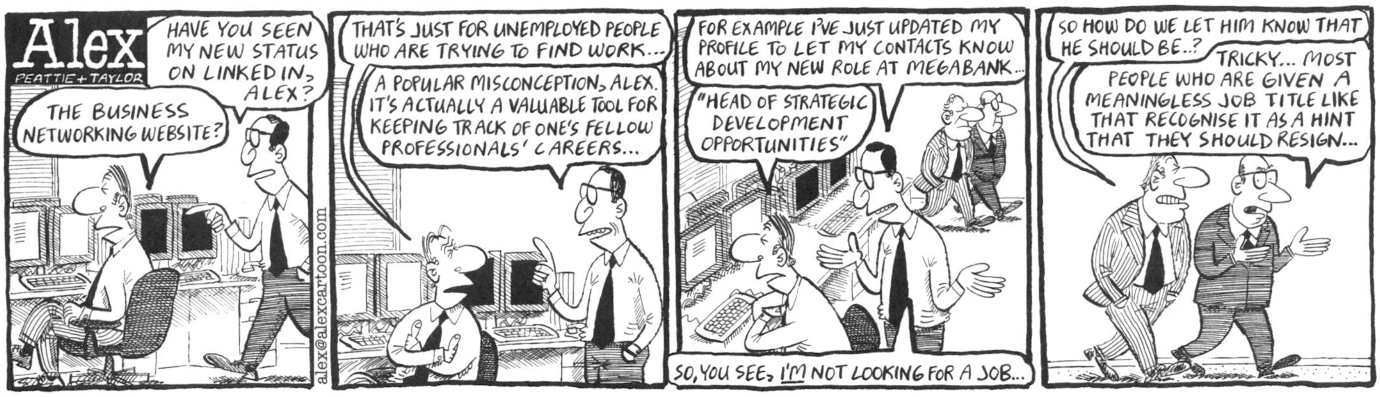
Alex
PEATTIE+TAYLOR
HAVE YOU SEEN MY NEW STATUS ON LINKED IN, ALEX?
THE BUSINESS NETWORKING WEBSITE?
alex@alexcartoon.com
THAT'S JUST FOR UNEMPLOYED PEOPLE WHO ARE TRYING TO FIND WORK...
A POPULAR MISCONCEPTION, ALEX. IT'S ACTUALLY A VALUABLE TOOL FOR KEEPING TRACK OF ONE'S FELLOW PROFESSIONALS' CAREERS...
FOR EXAMPLE I'VE JUST UPDATED MY PROFILE TO LET MY CONTACTS KNOW ABOUT MY NEW ROLE AT MEGABANK...
"HEAD OF STRATEGIC DEVELOPMENT OPPORTUNITIES"
SO, YOU SEE, I'M NOT LOOKING FOR A JOB...
SO HOW DO WE LET HIM KNOW THAT HE SHOULD BE..?
TRICKY... MOST PEOPLE WHO ARE GIVEN A MEANINGLESS JOB TITLE LIKE THAT RECOGNISE IT AS A HINT THAT THEY SHOULD RESIGN...

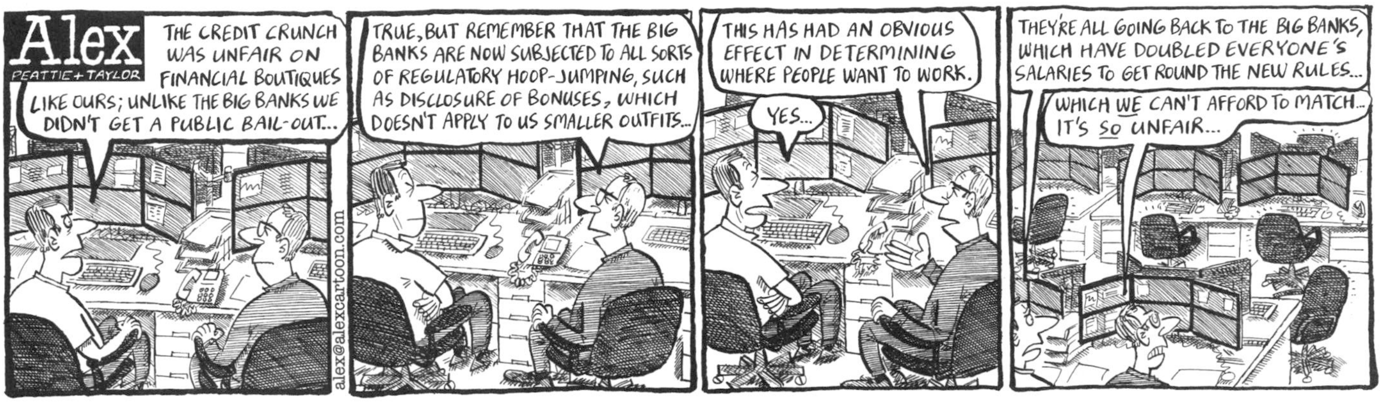
Alex
PEATTIE+TAYLOR
THE CREDIT CRUNCH WAS UNFAIR ON FINANCIAL BOUTIQUES LIKE OURS; UNLIKE THE BIG BANKS WE DIDN'T GET A PUBLIC BAIL-OUT...
alex@alexcartoon.com
TRUE, BUT REMEMBER THAT THE BIG BANKS ARE NOW SUBJECTED TO ALL SORTS OF REGULATORY HOOP-JUMPING, SUCH AS DISCLOSURE OF BONUSES, WHICH DOESN'T APPLY TO US SMALLER OUTFITS...
THIS HAS HAD AN OBVIOUS EFFECT IN DETERMINING WHERE PEOPLE WANT TO WORK.
YES...
THEY'RE ALL GOING BACK TO THE BIG BANKS, WHICH HAVE DOUBLED EVERYONE'S SALARIES TO GET ROUND THE NEW RULES...
WHICH WE CAN'T AFFORD TO MATCH... IT'S SO UNFAIR...

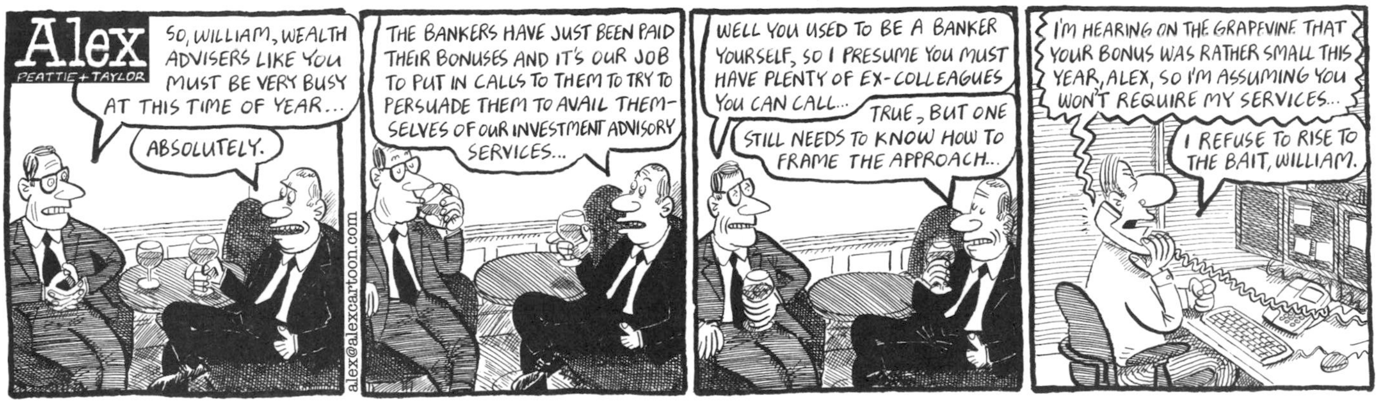
Alex
PEATTIE+TAYLOR
SO, WILLIAM, WEALTH ADVISERS LIKE YOU MUST BE VERY BUSY AT THIS TIME OF YEAR...
ABSOLUTELY.
alex@alexcartoon.com
THE BANKERS HAVE JUST BEEN PAID THEIR BONUSES AND IT'S OUR JOB TO PUT IN CALLS TO THEM TO TRY TO PERSUADE THEM TO AVAIL THEMSELVES OF OUR INVESTMENT ADVISORY SERVICES...
WELL YOU USED TO BE A BANKER YOURSELF, SO I PRESUME YOU MUST HAVE PLENTY OF EX-COLLEAGUES YOU CAN CALL...
TRUE, BUT ONE STILL NEEDS TO KNOW HOW TO FRAME THE APPROACH...
I'M HEARING ON THE GRAPEVINE THAT YOUR BONUS WAS RATHER SMALL THIS YEAR, ALEX, SO I'M ASSUMING YOU WON'T REQUIRE MY SERVICES...
I REFUSE TO RISE TO THE BAIT, WILLIAM.

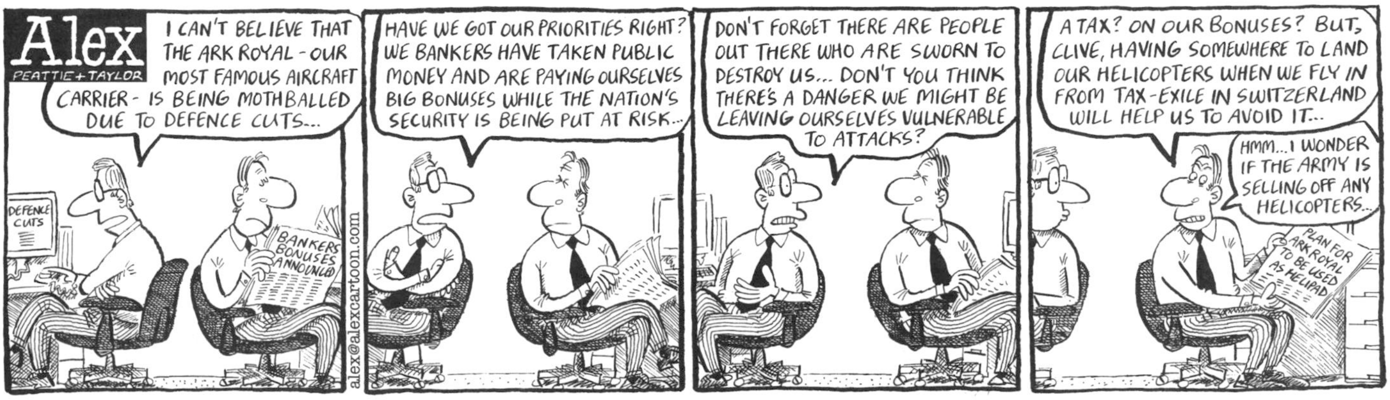
Alex
PEATTIE+TAYLOR
I CAN'T BELIEVE THAT THE ARK ROYAL - OUR MOST FAMOUS AIRCRAFT CARRIER - IS BEING MOTHBALLED DUE TO DEFENCE CUTS...
DEFENCE CUTS
BANKERS BONUSES ANNOUNCED
alex@alexcartoon.com
HAVE WE GOT OUR PRIORITIES RIGHT? WE BANKERS HAVE TAKEN PUBLIC MONEY AND ARE PAYING OURSELVES BIG BONUSES WHILE THE NATION'S SECURITY IS BEING PUT AT RISK...
DON'T FORGET THERE ARE PEOPLE OUT THERE WHO ARE SWORN TO DESTROY US... DON'T YOU THINK THERE'S A DANGER WE MIGHT BE LEAVING OURSELVES VULNERABLE TO ATTACKS?
A TAX? ON OUR BONUSES? BUT, CLIVE, HAVING SOMEWHERE TO LAND OUR HELICOPTERS WHEN WE FLY IN FROM TAX-EXILE IN SWITZERLAND WILL HELP US TO AVOID IT...
HMM... I WONDER IF THE ARMY IS SELLING OFF ANY HELICOPTERS...
PLAN FOR ARK ROYAL TO BE USED AS HELIPAD

45

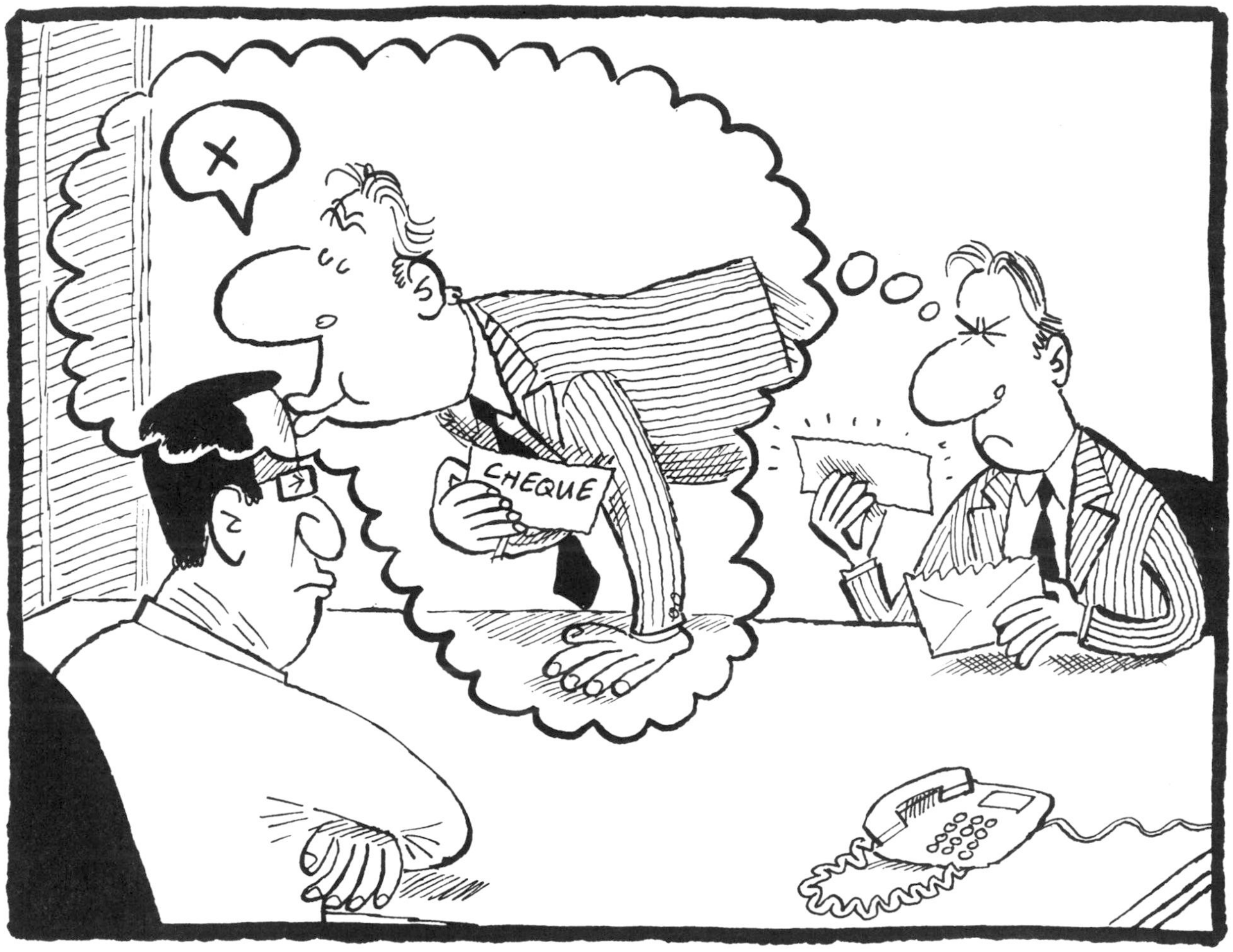
CHEQUE

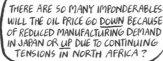

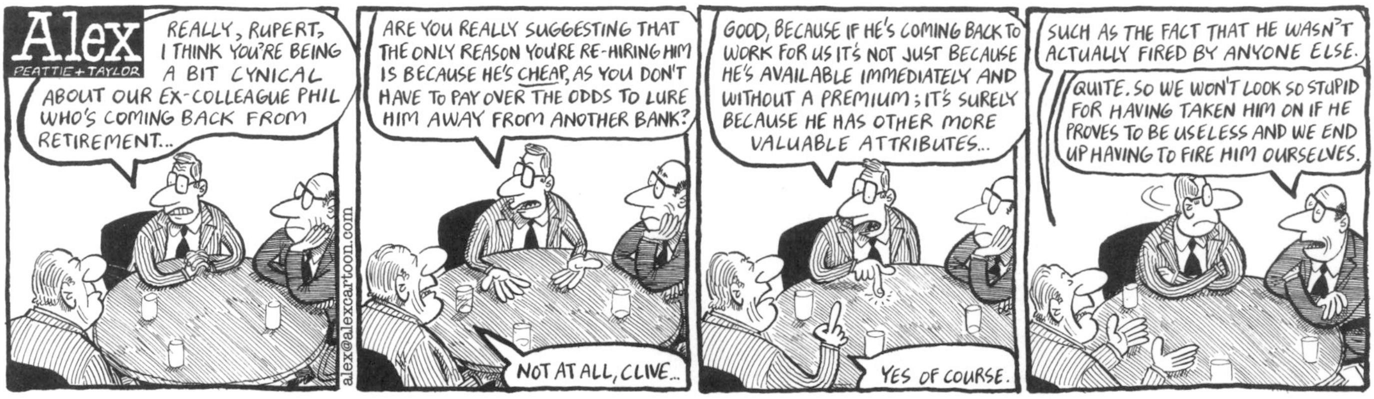
Alex
PEATTIE+TAYLOR
REALLY, RUPERT, I THINK YOU'RE BEING A BIT CYNICAL ABOUT OUR EX-COLLEAGUE PHIL WHO'S COMING BACK FROM RETIREMENT...
ARE YOU REALLY SUGGESTING THAT THE ONLY REASON YOU'RE RE-HIRING HIM IS BECAUSE HE'S CHEAP, AS YOU DON'T HAVE TO PAY OVER THE ODDS TO LURE HIM AWAY FROM ANOTHER BANK?
NOT AT ALL, CLIVE...
alex@alexcartoon.com
GOOD, BECAUSE IF HE'S COMING BACK TO WORK FOR US IT'S NOT JUST BECAUSE HE'S AVAILABLE IMMEDIATELY AND WITHOUT A PREMIUM; IT'S SURELY BECAUSE HE HAS OTHER MORE VALUABLE ATTRIBUTES...
YES OF COURSE.
SUCH AS THE FACT THAT HE WASN'T ACTUALLY FIRED BY ANYONE ELSE.
QUITE. SO WE WON'T LOOK SO STUPID FOR HAVING TAKEN HIM ON IF HE PROVES TO BE USELESS AND WE END UP HAVING TO FIRE HIM OURSELVES.

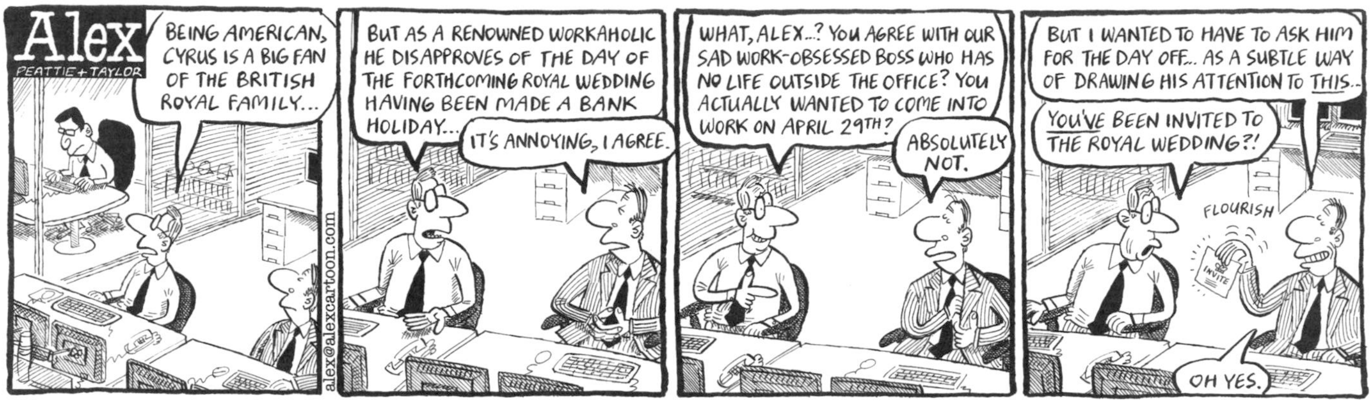
Alex
PEATTIE+TAYLOR
BEING AMERICAN, CYRUS IS A BIG FAN OF THE BRITISH ROYAL FAMILY...
alex@alexcartoon.com
BUT AS A RENOWNED WORKAHOLIC HE DISAPPROVES OF THE DAY OF THE FORTHCOMING ROYAL WEDDING HAVING BEEN MADE A BANK HOLIDAY...
IT'S ANNOYING, I AGREE.
WHAT, ALEX...? YOU AGREE WITH OUR SAD WORK-OBSESSED BOSS WHO HAS NO LIFE OUTSIDE THE OFFICE? YOU ACTUALLY WANTED TO COME INTO WORK ON APRIL 29TH?
ABSOLUTELY NOT.
BUT I WANTED TO HAVE TO ASK HIM FOR THE DAY OFF... AS A SUBTLE WAY OF DRAWING HIS ATTENTION TO THIS...
YOU'VE BEEN INVITED TO THE ROYAL WEDDING?!
FLOURISH
INVITE
OH YES.

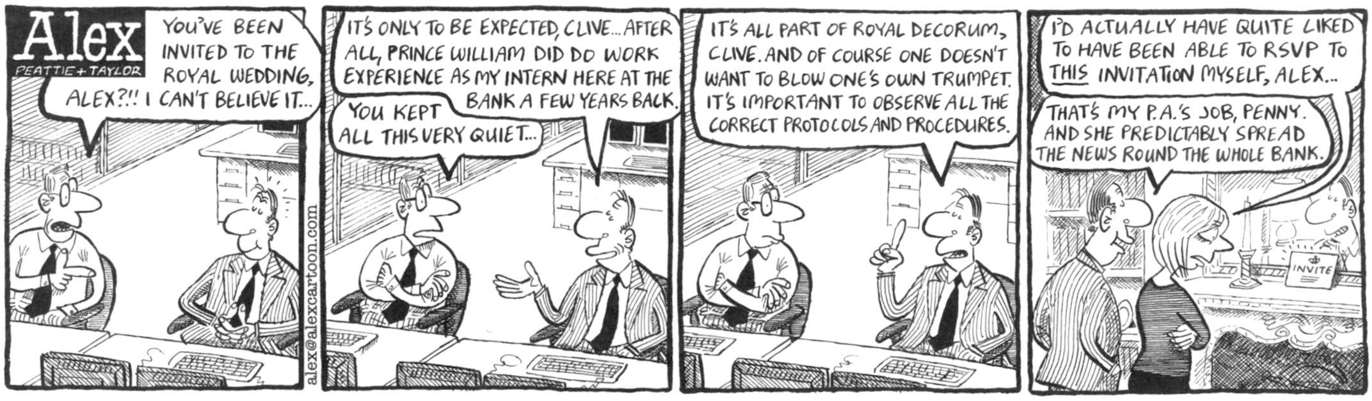
Alex
PEATTIE+TAYLOR
YOU'VE BEEN INVITED TO THE ROYAL WEDDING, ALEX?!! I CAN'T BELIEVE IT...
alex@alexcartoon.com
IT'S ONLY TO BE EXPECTED, CLIVE... AFTER ALL, PRINCE WILLIAM DID DO WORK EXPERIENCE AS MY INTERN HERE AT THE BANK A FEW YEARS BACK.
YOU KEPT ALL THIS VERY QUIET...
IT'S ALL PART OF ROYAL DECORUM, CLIVE. AND OF COURSE ONE DOESN'T WANT TO BLOW ONE'S OWN TRUMPET. IT'S IMPORTANT TO OBSERVE ALL THE CORRECT PROTOCOLS AND PROCEDURES.
I'D ACTUALLY HAVE QUITE LIKED TO HAVE BEEN ABLE TO RSVP TO THIS INVITATION MYSELF, ALEX...
THAT'S MY P.A.'S JOB, PENNY. AND SHE PREDICTABLY SPREAD THE NEWS ROUND THE WHOLE BANK.
INVITE

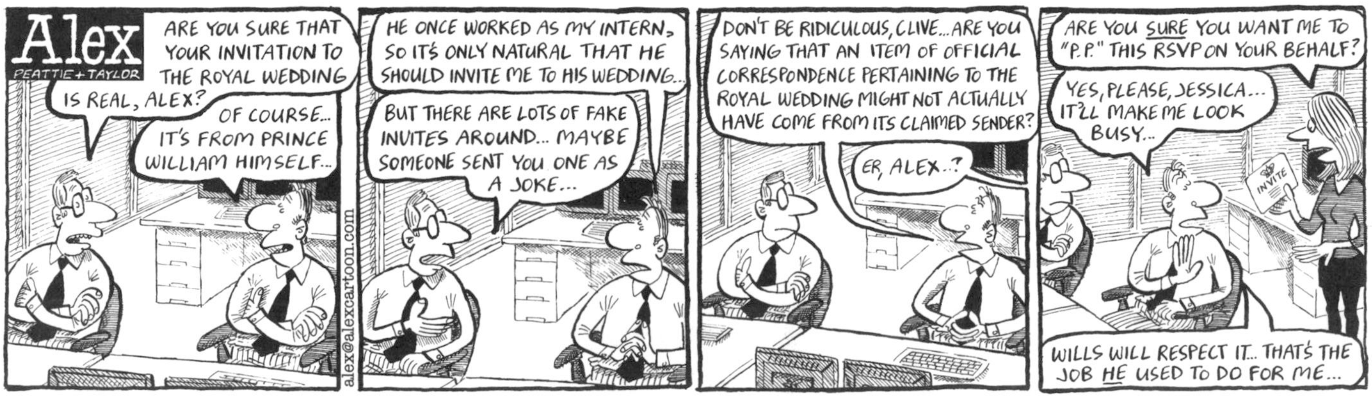
Alex
PEATTIE+TAYLOR
ARE YOU SURE THAT YOUR INVITATION TO THE ROYAL WEDDING IS REAL, ALEX?
OF COURSE... IT'S FROM PRINCE WILLIAM HIMSELF...
alex@alexcartoon.com
HE ONCE WORKED AS MY INTERN, SO IT'S ONLY NATURAL THAT HE SHOULD INVITE ME TO HIS WEDDING...
BUT THERE ARE LOTS OF FAKE INVITES AROUND... MAYBE SOMEONE SENT YOU ONE AS A JOKE...
DON'T BE RIDICULOUS, CLIVE... ARE YOU SAYING THAT AN ITEM OF OFFICIAL CORRESPONDENCE PERTAINING TO THE ROYAL WEDDING MIGHT NOT ACTUALLY HAVE COME FROM ITS CLAIMED SENDER?
ER, ALEX...?
ARE YOU SURE YOU WANT ME TO "P.P." THIS RSVP ON YOUR BEHALF?
YES, PLEASE, JESSICA... IT'LL MAKE ME LOOK BUSY...
INVITE
WILLS WILL RESPECT IT... THAT'S THE JOB HE USED TO DO FOR ME...

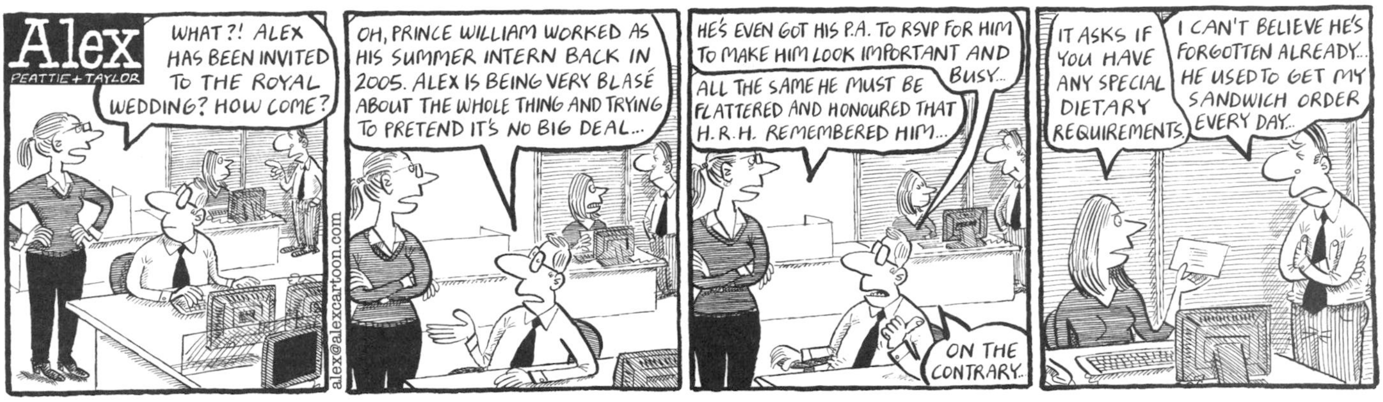
Alex
PEATTIE + TAYLOR
WHAT?! ALEX HAS BEEN INVITED TO THE ROYAL WEDDING? HOW COME?
OH, PRINCE WILLIAM WORKED AS HIS SUMMER INTERN BACK IN 2005. ALEX IS BEING VERY BLASÉ ABOUT THE WHOLE THING AND TRYING TO PRETEND IT'S NO BIG DEAL...
alex@alexcartoon.com
HE'S EVEN GOT HIS P.A. TO RSVP FOR HIM TO MAKE HIM LOOK IMPORTANT AND BUSY...
ALL THE SAME HE MUST BE FLATTERED AND HONOURED THAT H.R.H. REMEMBERED HIM...
ON THE CONTRARY...
IT ASKS IF YOU HAVE ANY SPECIAL DIETARY REQUIREMENTS.
I CAN'T BELIEVE HE'S FORGOTTEN ALREADY... HE USED TO GET MY SANDWICH ORDER EVERY DAY...

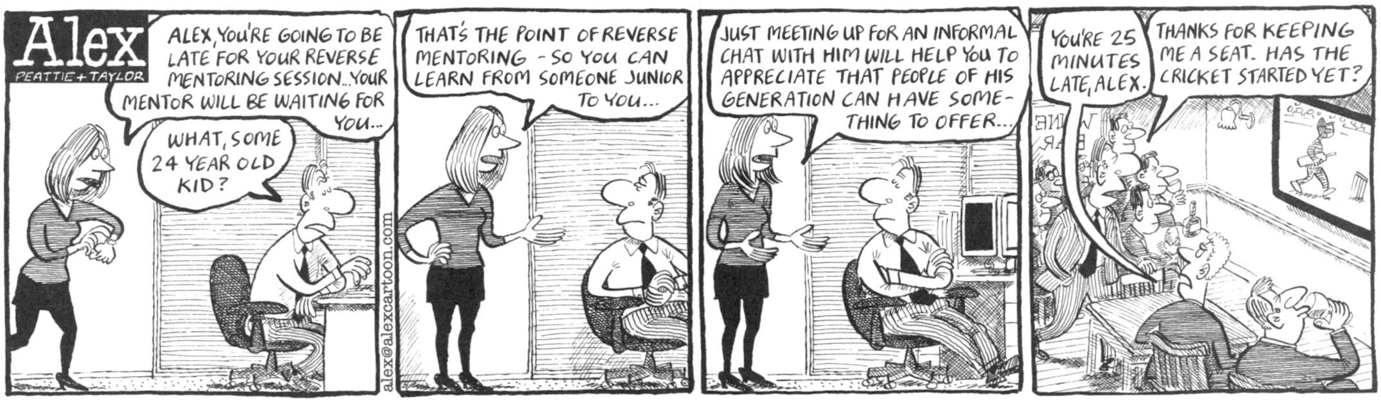
Alex
PEATTIE + TAYLOR
ALEX, YOU'RE GOING TO BE LATE FOR YOUR REVERSE MENTORING SESSION... YOUR MENTOR WILL BE WAITING FOR YOU...
WHAT, SOME 24 YEAR OLD KID?
THAT'S THE POINT OF REVERSE MENTORING - SO YOU CAN LEARN FROM SOMEONE JUNIOR TO YOU...
alex@alexcartoon.com
JUST MEETING UP FOR AN INFORMAL CHAT WITH HIM WILL HELP YOU TO APPRECIATE THAT PEOPLE OF HIS GENERATION CAN HAVE SOMETHING TO OFFER...
YOU'RE 25 MINUTES LATE, ALEX.
THANKS FOR KEEPING ME A SEAT. HAS THE CRICKET STARTED YET?

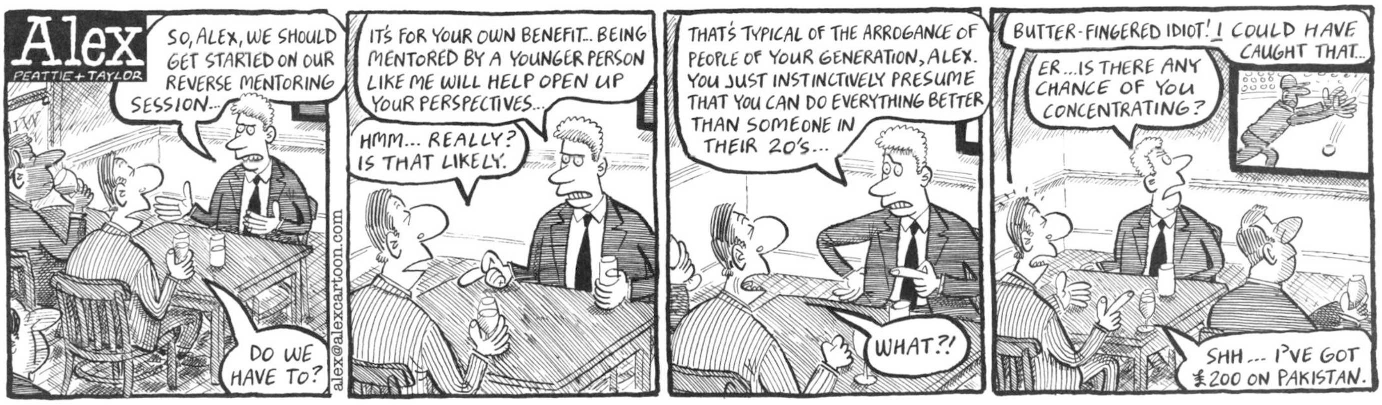
Alex
PEATTIE + TAYLOR
SO, ALEX, WE SHOULD GET STARTED ON OUR REVERSE MENTORING SESSION...
DO WE HAVE TO?
IT'S FOR YOUR OWN BENEFIT... BEING MENTORED BY A YOUNGER PERSON LIKE ME WILL HELP OPEN UP YOUR PERSPECTIVES...
HMM... REALLY? IS THAT LIKELY.
alex@alexcartoon.com
THAT'S TYPICAL OF THE ARROGANCE OF PEOPLE OF YOUR GENERATION, ALEX. YOU JUST INSTINCTIVELY PRESUME THAT YOU CAN DO EVERYTHING BETTER THAN SOMEONE IN THEIR 20'S...
WHAT?!
BUTTER-FINGERED IDIOT! I COULD HAVE CAUGHT THAT...
ER... IS THERE ANY CHANCE OF YOU CONCENTRATING?
SHH... I'VE GOT £200 ON PAKISTAN.

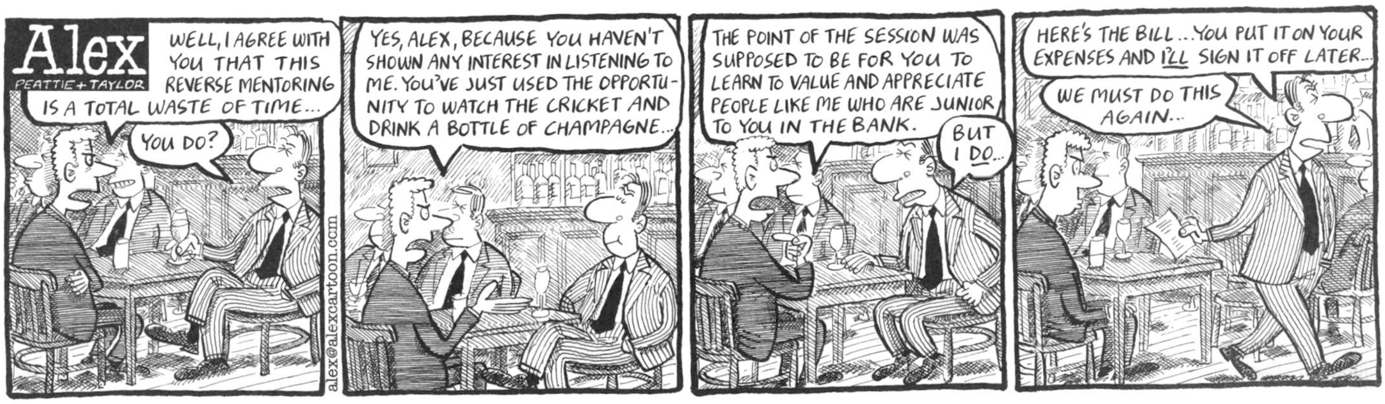
Alex
PEATTIE + TAYLOR
WELL, I AGREE WITH YOU THAT THIS REVERSE MENTORING IS A TOTAL WASTE OF TIME...
YOU DO?
YES, ALEX, BECAUSE YOU HAVEN'T SHOWN ANY INTEREST IN LISTENING TO ME. YOU'VE JUST USED THE OPPORTUNITY TO WATCH THE CRICKET AND DRINK A BOTTLE OF CHAMPAGNE...
alex@alexcartoon.com
THE POINT OF THE SESSION WAS SUPPOSED TO BE FOR YOU TO LEARN TO VALUE AND APPRECIATE PEOPLE LIKE ME WHO ARE JUNIOR TO YOU IN THE BANK.
BUT I DO...
HERE'S THE BILL... YOU PUT IT ON YOUR EXPENSES AND I'LL SIGN IT OFF LATER...
WE MUST DO THIS AGAIN...

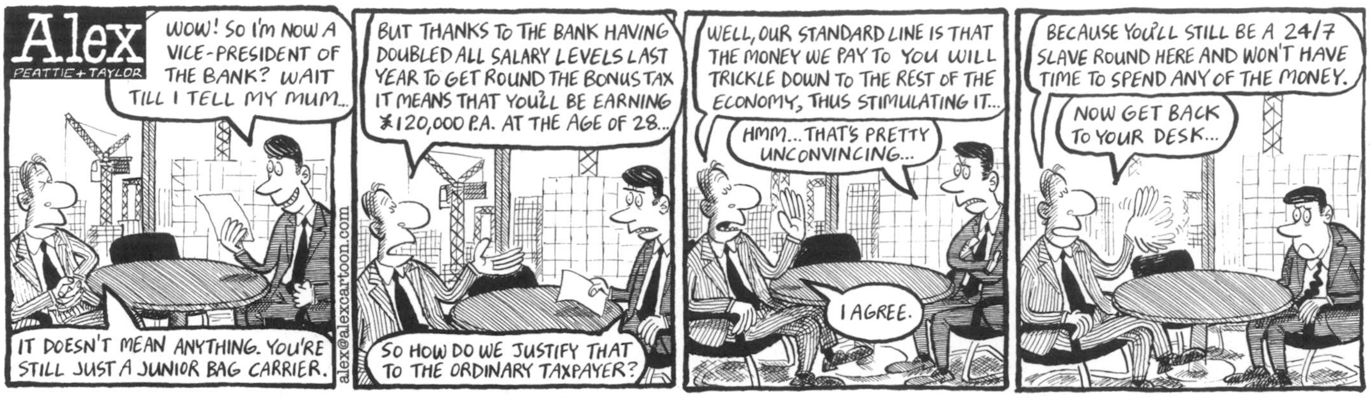
Alex
PEATTIE + TAYLOR
WOW! SO I'M NOW A VICE-PRESIDENT OF THE BANK? WAIT TILL I TELL MY MUM...
IT DOESN'T MEAN ANYTHING. YOU'RE STILL JUST A JUNIOR BAG CARRIER.
alex@alexcartoon.com
BUT THANKS TO THE BANK HAVING DOUBLED ALL SALARY LEVELS LAST YEAR TO GET ROUND THE BONUS TAX IT MEANS THAT YOU'LL BE EARNING ¥120,000 P.A. AT THE AGE OF 28...
SO HOW DO WE JUSTIFY THAT TO THE ORDINARY TAXPAYER?
WELL, OUR STANDARD LINE IS THAT THE MONEY WE PAY TO YOU WILL TRICKLE DOWN TO THE REST OF THE ECONOMY, THUS STIMULATING IT...
HMM... THAT'S PRETTY UNCONVINCING...
I AGREE.
BECAUSE YOU'LL STILL BE A 24/7 SLAVE ROUND HERE AND WON'T HAVE TIME TO SPEND ANY OF THE MONEY.
NOW GET BACK TO YOUR DESK...

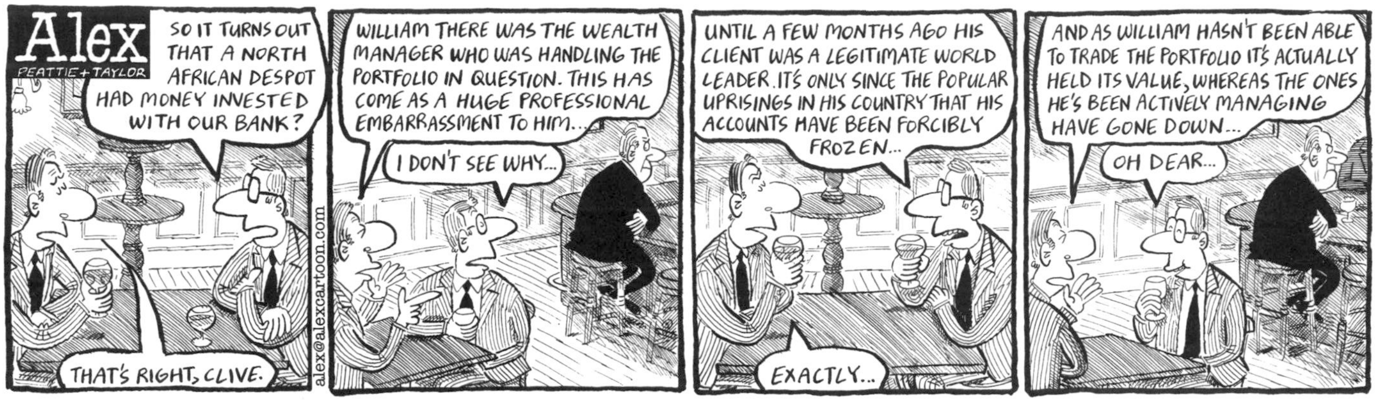
Alex
PEATTIE + TAYLOR
SO IT TURNS OUT THAT A NORTH AFRICAN DESPOT HAD MONEY INVESTED WITH OUR BANK?
THAT'S RIGHT, CLIVE.
alex@alexcartoon.com
WILLIAM THERE WAS THE WEALTH MANAGER WHO WAS HANDLING THE PORTFOLIO IN QUESTION. THIS HAS COME AS A HUGE PROFESSIONAL EMBARRASSMENT TO HIM...
I DON'T SEE WHY...
UNTIL A FEW MONTHS AGO HIS CLIENT WAS A LEGITIMATE WORLD LEADER. IT'S ONLY SINCE THE POPULAR UPRISINGS IN HIS COUNTRY THAT HIS ACCOUNTS HAVE BEEN FORCIBLY FROZEN...
EXACTLY...
AND AS WILLIAM HASN'T BEEN ABLE TO TRADE THE PORTFOLIO IT'S ACTUALLY HELD ITS VALUE, WHEREAS THE ONES HE'S BEEN ACTIVELY MANAGING HAVE GONE DOWN...
OH DEAR...

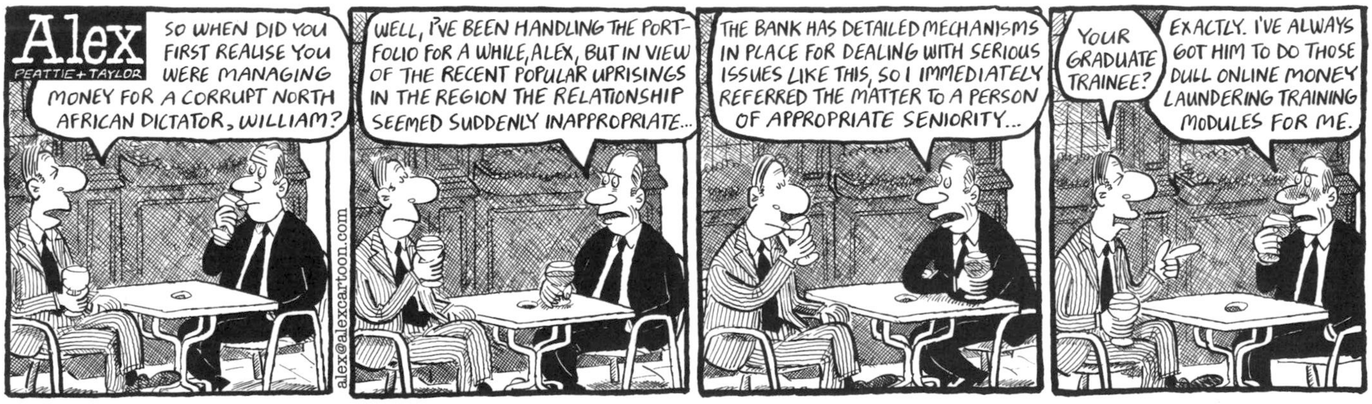
Alex
PEATTIE + TAYLOR
SO WHEN DID YOU FIRST REALISE YOU WERE MANAGING MONEY FOR A CORRUPT NORTH AFRICAN DICTATOR, WILLIAM?
alex@alexcartoon.com
WELL, I'VE BEEN HANDLING THE PORTFOLIO FOR A WHILE, ALEX, BUT IN VIEW OF THE RECENT POPULAR UPRISINGS IN THE REGION THE RELATIONSHIP SEEMED SUDDENLY INAPPROPRIATE...
THE BANK HAS DETAILED MECHANISMS IN PLACE FOR DEALING WITH SERIOUS ISSUES LIKE THIS, SO I IMMEDIATELY REFERRED THE MATTER TO A PERSON OF APPROPRIATE SENIORITY...
YOUR GRADUATE TRAINEE?
EXACTLY. I'VE ALWAYS GOT HIM TO DO THOSE DULL ONLINE MONEY LAUNDERING TRAINING MODULES FOR ME.

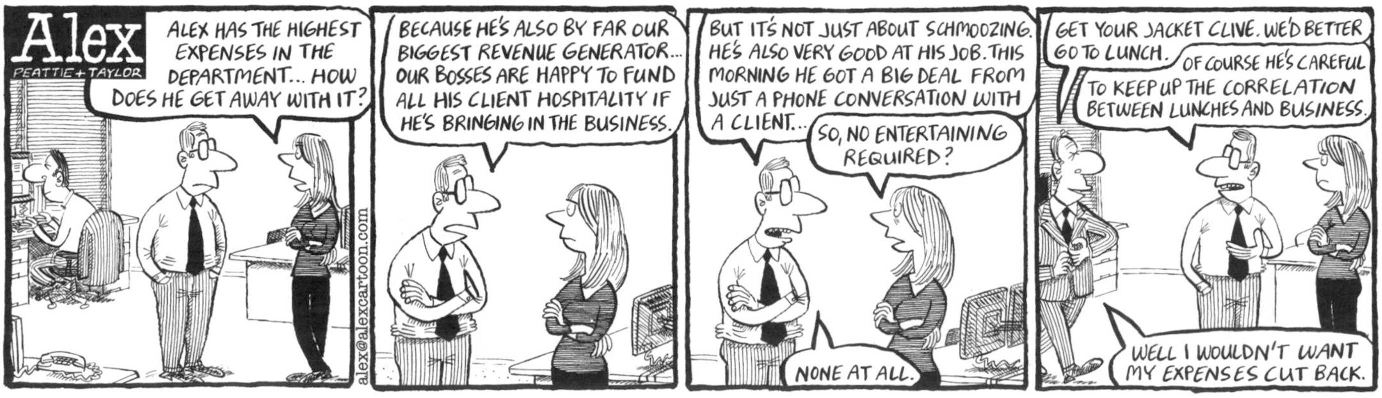
Alex
PEATTIE + TAYLOR
ALEX HAS THE HIGHEST EXPENSES IN THE DEPARTMENT... HOW DOES HE GET AWAY WITH IT?
alex@alexcartoon.com
BECAUSE HE'S ALSO BY FAR OUR BIGGEST REVENUE GENERATOR... OUR BOSSES ARE HAPPY TO FUND ALL HIS CLIENT HOSPITALITY IF HE'S BRINGING IN THE BUSINESS.
BUT IT'S NOT JUST ABOUT SCHMOOZING. HE'S ALSO VERY GOOD AT HIS JOB. THIS MORNING HE GOT A BIG DEAL FROM JUST A PHONE CONVERSATION WITH A CLIENT...
SO, NO ENTERTAINING REQUIRED?
NONE AT ALL.
GET YOUR JACKET CLIVE. WE'D BETTER GO TO LUNCH.
OF COURSE HE'S CAREFUL TO KEEP UP THE CORRELATION BETWEEN LUNCHES AND BUSINESS.
WELL I WOULDN'T WANT MY EXPENSES CUT BACK.

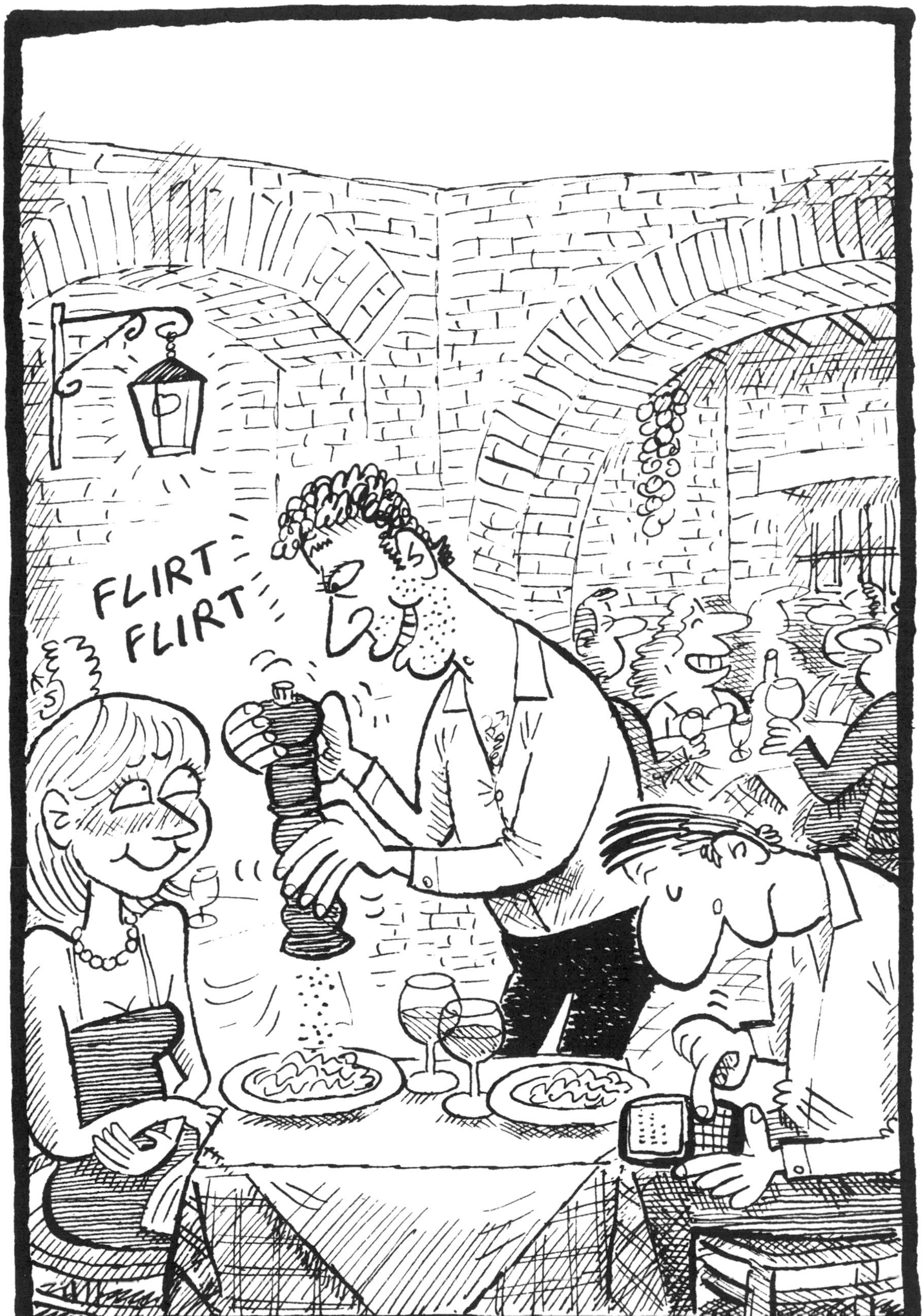
FLIRT
FLIRT

ALEX WENT ON HOLIDAY TO ITALY...

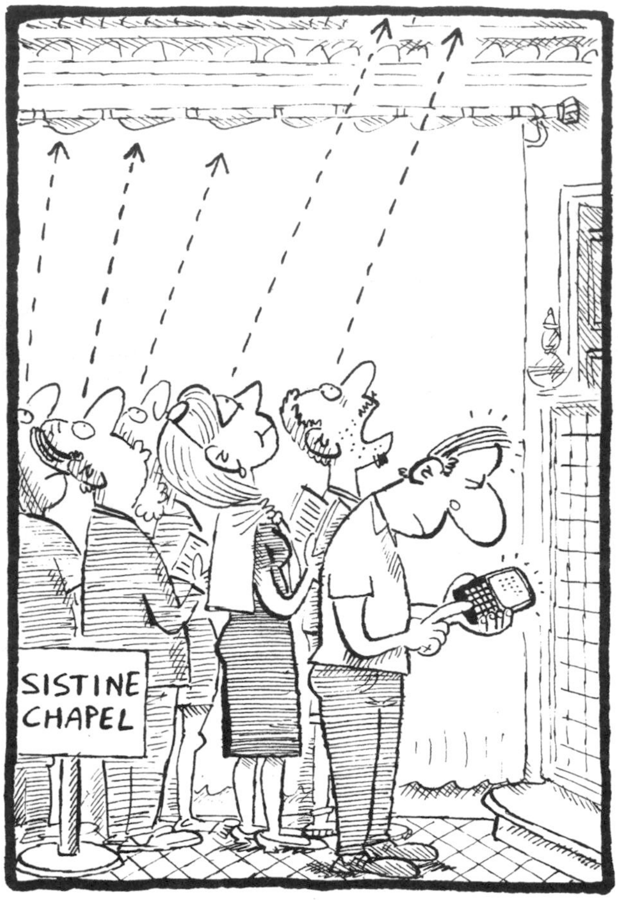
SISTINE
CHAPEL

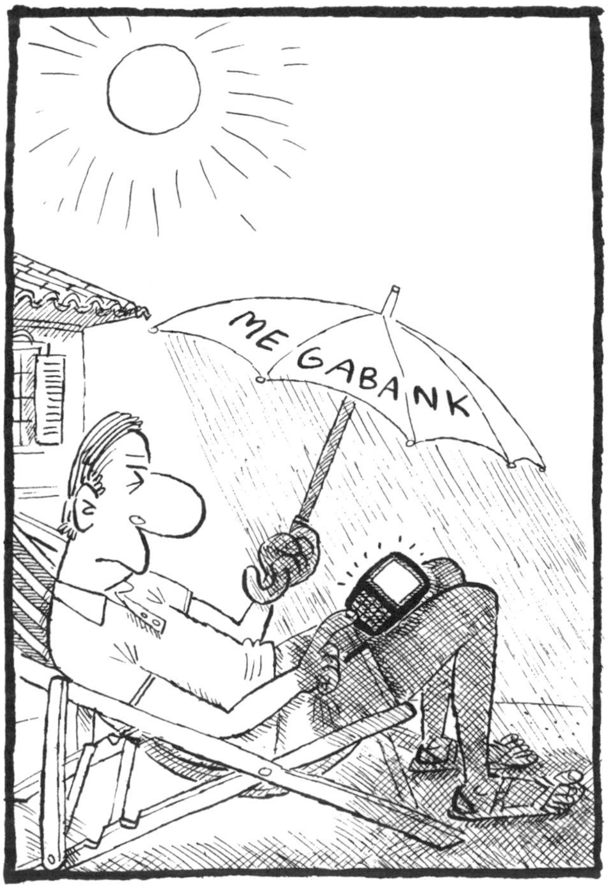
MEGABANK

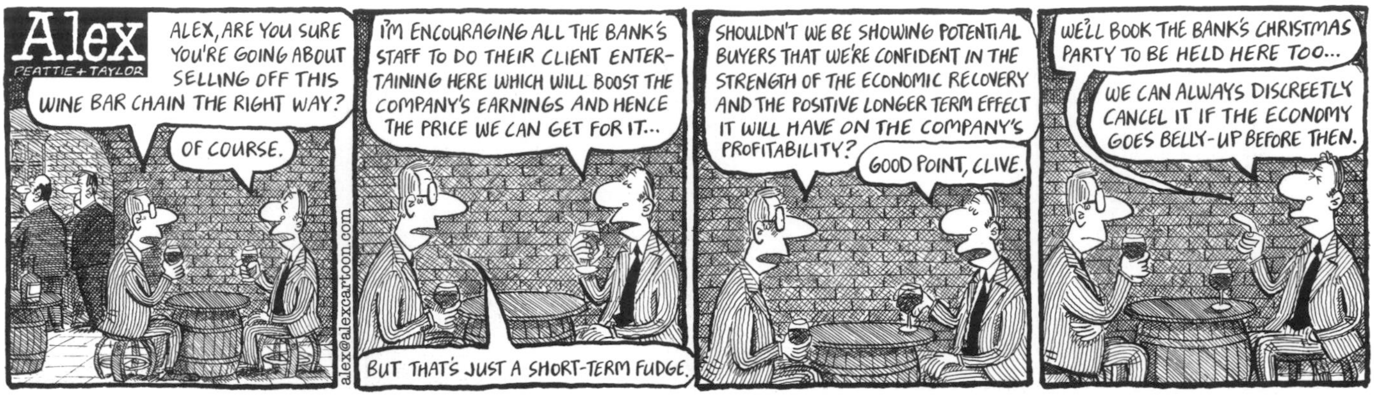
Alex
PEATTIE + TAYLOR
ALEX, ARE YOU SURE YOU'RE GOING ABOUT SELLING OFF THIS WINE BAR CHAIN THE RIGHT WAY?
OF COURSE.
I'M ENCOURAGING ALL THE BANK'S STAFF TO DO THEIR CLIENT ENTERTAINING HERE WHICH WILL BOOST THE COMPANY'S EARNINGS AND HENCE THE PRICE WE CAN GET FOR IT...
BUT THAT'S JUST A SHORT-TERM FUDGE.
alex@alexcartoon.com
SHOULDN'T WE BE SHOWING POTENTIAL BUYERS THAT WE'RE CONFIDENT IN THE STRENGTH OF THE ECONOMIC RECOVERY AND THE POSITIVE LONGER TERM EFFECT IT WILL HAVE ON THE COMPANY'S PROFITABILITY?
GOOD POINT, CLIVE.
WE'LL BOOK THE BANK'S CHRISTMAS PARTY TO BE HELD HERE TOO...
WE CAN ALWAYS DISCREETLY CANCEL IT IF THE ECONOMY GOES BELLY-UP BEFORE THEN.

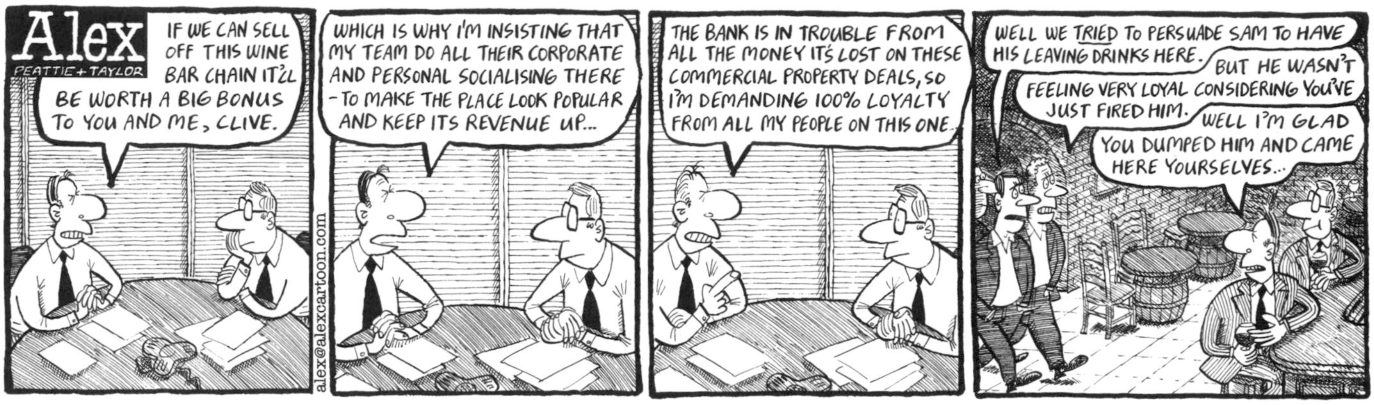
Alex
PEATTIE + TAYLOR
IF WE CAN SELL OFF THIS WINE BAR CHAIN IT'LL BE WORTH A BIG BONUS TO YOU AND ME, CLIVE.
alex@alexcartoon.com
WHICH IS WHY I'M INSISTING THAT MY TEAM DO ALL THEIR CORPORATE AND PERSONAL SOCIALISING THERE - TO MAKE THE PLACE LOOK POPULAR AND KEEP ITS REVENUE UP...
THE BANK IS IN TROUBLE FROM ALL THE MONEY IT'S LOST ON THESE COMMERCIAL PROPERTY DEALS, SO I'M DEMANDING 100% LOYALTY FROM ALL MY PEOPLE ON THIS ONE.
WELL WE TRIED TO PERSUADE SAM TO HAVE HIS LEAVING DRINKS HERE.
BUT HE WASN'T FEELING VERY LOYAL CONSIDERING YOU'VE JUST FIRED HIM.
WELL I'M GLAD YOU DUMPED HIM AND CAME HERE YOURSELVES...

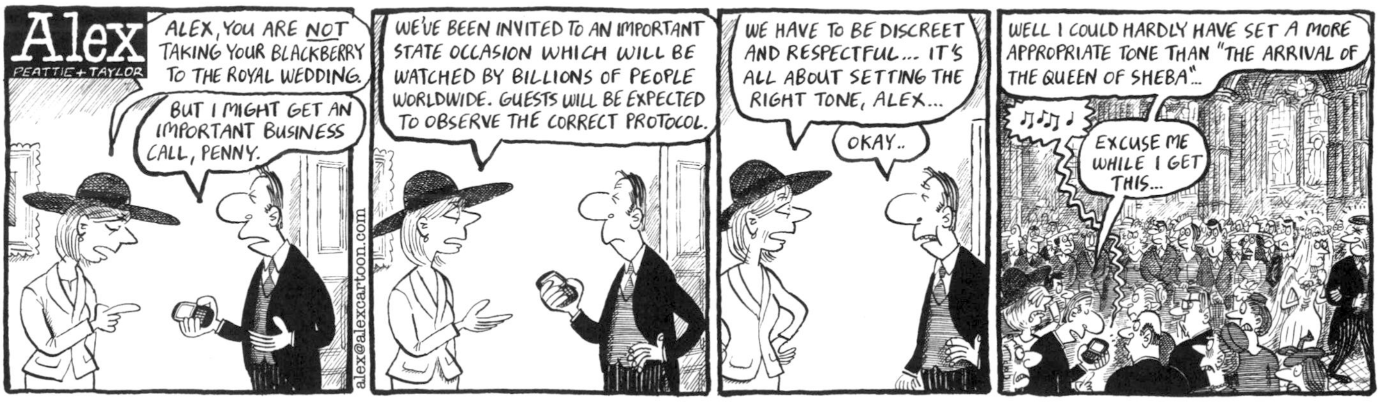
Alex
PEATTIE + TAYLOR
ALEX, YOU ARE NOT TAKING YOUR BLACKBERRY TO THE ROYAL WEDDING.
BUT I MIGHT GET AN IMPORTANT BUSINESS CALL, PENNY.
alex@alexcartoon.com
WE'VE BEEN INVITED TO AN IMPORTANT STATE OCCASION WHICH WILL BE WATCHED BY BILLIONS OF PEOPLE WORLDWIDE. GUESTS WILL BE EXPECTED TO OBSERVE THE CORRECT PROTOCOL.
WE HAVE TO BE DISCREET AND RESPECTFUL... IT'S ALL ABOUT SETTING THE RIGHT TONE, ALEX...
OKAY..
WELL I COULD HARDLY HAVE SET A MORE APPROPRIATE TONE THAN "THE ARRIVAL OF THE QUEEN OF SHEBA"...
EXCUSE ME WHILE I GET THIS...

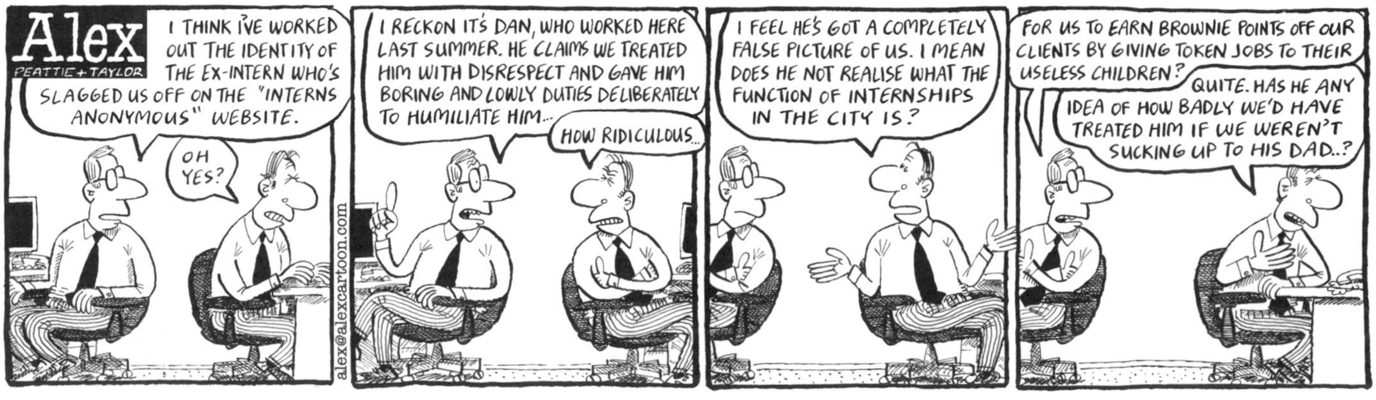
Alex
PEATTIE + TAYLOR
I THINK I'VE WORKED OUT THE IDENTITY OF THE EX-INTERN WHO'S SLAGGED US OFF ON THE "INTERNS ANONYMOUS" WEBSITE.
OH YES?
alex@alexcartoon.com
I RECKON IT'S DAN, WHO WORKED HERE LAST SUMMER. HE CLAIMS WE TREATED HIM WITH DISRESPECT AND GAVE HIM BORING AND LOWLY DUTIES DELIBERATELY TO HUMILIATE HIM...
HOW RIDICULOUS...
I FEEL HE'S GOT A COMPLETELY FALSE PICTURE OF US. I MEAN DOES HE NOT REALISE WHAT THE FUNCTION OF INTERNSHIPS IN THE CITY IS?
FOR US TO EARN BROWNIE POINTS OFF OUR CLIENTS BY GIVING TOKEN JOBS TO THEIR USELESS CHILDREN?
QUITE. HAS HE ANY IDEA OF HOW BADLY WE'D HAVE TREATED HIM IF WE WEREN'T SUCKING UP TO HIS DAD..?

55

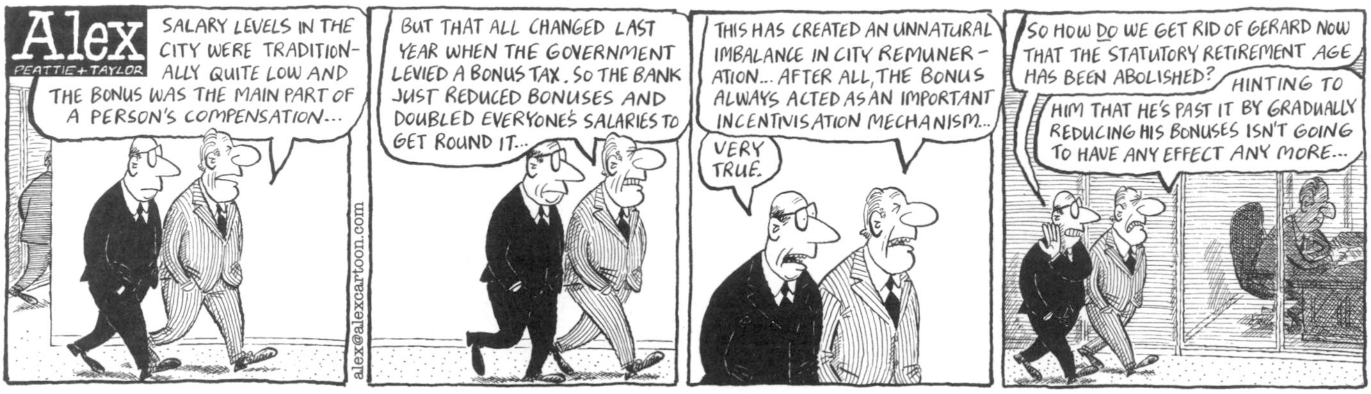
Alex
PEATTIE + TAYLOR
SALARY LEVELS IN THE CITY WERE TRADITIONALLY QUITE LOW AND THE BONUS WAS THE MAIN PART OF A PERSON'S COMPENSATION...
alex@alexcartoon.com
BUT THAT ALL CHANGED LAST YEAR WHEN THE GOVERNMENT LEVIED A BONUS TAX. SO THE BANK JUST REDUCED BONUSES AND DOUBLED EVERYONE'S SALARIES TO GET ROUND IT...
THIS HAS CREATED AN UNNATURAL IMBALANCE IN CITY REMUNERATION... AFTER ALL, THE BONUS ALWAYS ACTED AS AN IMPORTANT INCENTIVISATION MECHANISM...
VERY TRUE.
SO HOW DO WE GET RID OF GERARD NOW THAT THE STATUTORY RETIREMENT AGE HAS BEEN ABOLISHED?
HINTING TO HIM THAT HE'S PAST IT BY GRADUALLY REDUCING HIS BONUSES ISN'T GOING TO HAVE ANY EFFECT ANY MORE...

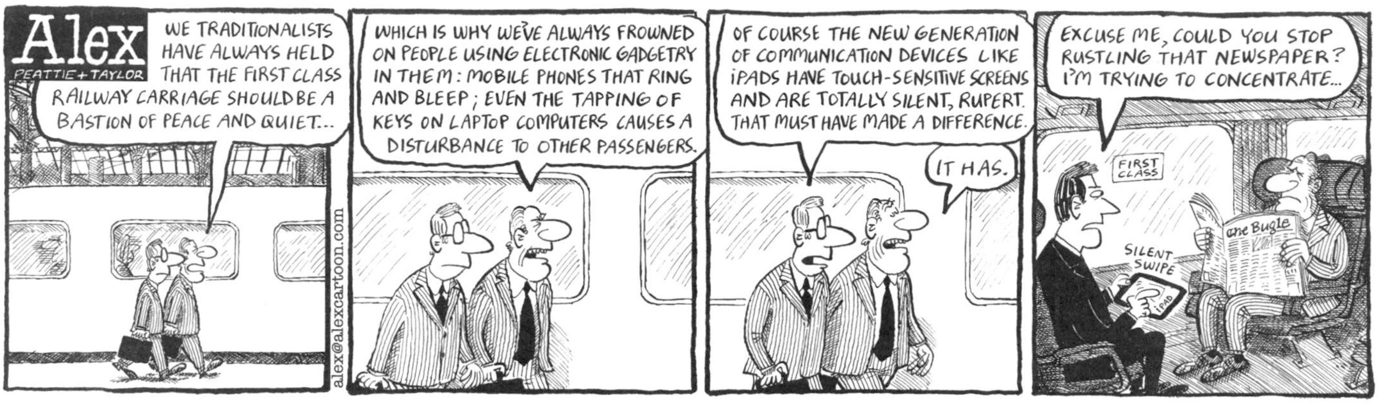
Alex
PEATTIE + TAYLOR
WE TRADITIONALISTS HAVE ALWAYS HELD THAT THE FIRST CLASS RAILWAY CARRIAGE SHOULD BE A BASTION OF PEACE AND QUIET...
alex@alexcartoon.com
WHICH IS WHY WE'VE ALWAYS FROWNED ON PEOPLE USING ELECTRONIC GADGETRY IN THEM: MOBILE PHONES THAT RING AND BLEEP; EVEN THE TAPPING OF KEYS ON LAPTOP COMPUTERS CAUSES A DISTURBANCE TO OTHER PASSENGERS.
OF COURSE THE NEW GENERATION OF COMMUNICATION DEVICES LIKE iPADS HAVE TOUCH-SENSITIVE SCREENS AND ARE TOTALLY SILENT, RUPERT. THAT MUST HAVE MADE A DIFFERENCE.
IT HAS.
EXCUSE ME, COULD YOU STOP RUSTLING THAT NEWSPAPER? I'M TRYING TO CONCENTRATE...
FIRST CLASS
SILENT SWIPE
iPAD
the Bugle

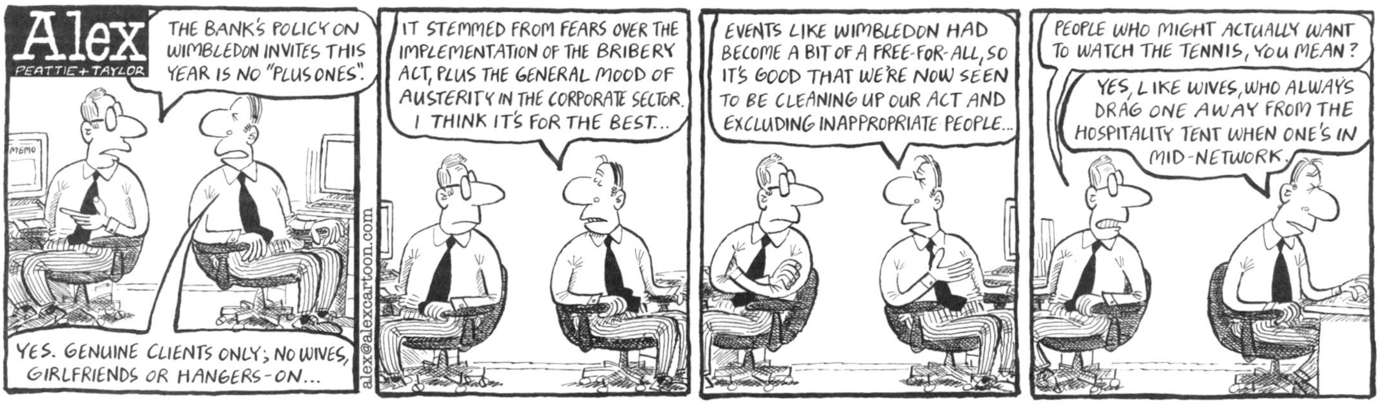
Alex
PEATTIE + TAYLOR
THE BANK'S POLICY ON WIMBLEDON INVITES THIS YEAR IS NO "PLUS ONES".
MEMO
YES. GENUINE CLIENTS ONLY; NO WIVES, GIRLFRIENDS OR HANGERS-ON...
alex@alexcartoon.com
IT STEMMED FROM FEARS OVER THE IMPLEMENTATION OF THE BRIBERY ACT, PLUS THE GENERAL MOOD OF AUSTERITY IN THE CORPORATE SECTOR. I THINK IT'S FOR THE BEST...
EVENTS LIKE WIMBLEDON HAD BECOME A BIT OF A FREE-FOR-ALL, SO IT'S GOOD THAT WE'RE NOW SEEN TO BE CLEANING UP OUR ACT AND EXCLUDING INAPPROPRIATE PEOPLE...
PEOPLE WHO MIGHT ACTUALLY WANT TO WATCH THE TENNIS, YOU MEAN?
YES, LIKE WIVES, WHO ALWAYS DRAG ONE AWAY FROM THE HOSPITALITY TENT WHEN ONE'S IN MID-NETWORK.

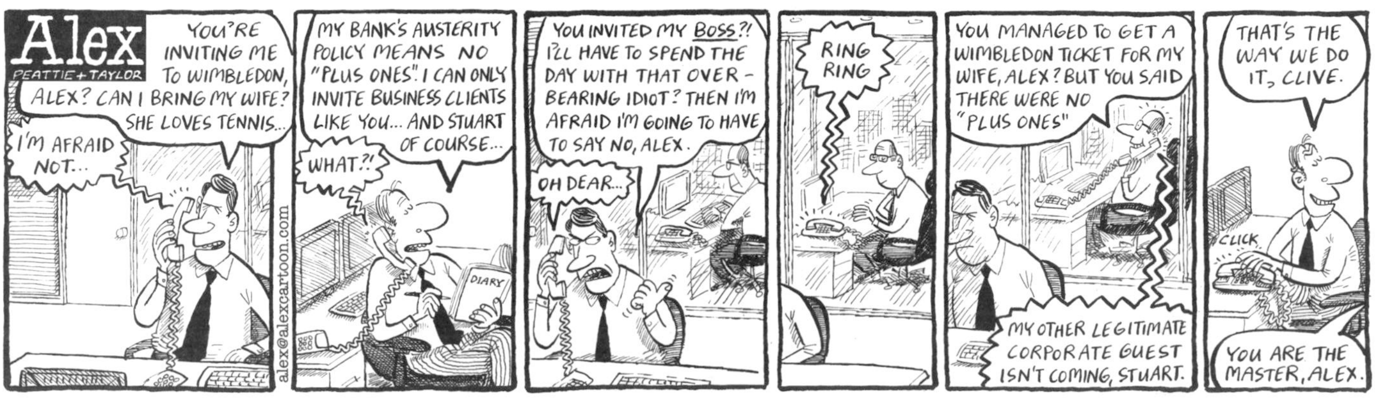
Alex
PEATTIE + TAYLOR
YOU'RE INVITING ME TO WIMBLEDON, ALEX? CAN I BRING MY WIFE? SHE LOVES TENNIS...
I'M AFRAID NOT...
alex@alexcartoon.com
MY BANK'S AUSTERITY POLICY MEANS NO "PLUS ONES". I CAN ONLY INVITE BUSINESS CLIENTS LIKE YOU... AND STUART OF COURSE...
WHAT?!
DIARY
YOU INVITED MY BOSS?! I'LL HAVE TO SPEND THE DAY WITH THAT OVER-BEARING IDIOT? THEN I'M AFRAID I'M GOING TO HAVE TO SAY NO, ALEX.
OH DEAR...
RING RING
YOU MANAGED TO GET A WIMBLEDON TICKET FOR MY WIFE, ALEX? BUT YOU SAID THERE WERE NO "PLUS ONES"
MY OTHER LEGITIMATE CORPORATE GUEST ISN'T COMING, STUART.
THAT'S THE WAY WE DO IT, CLIVE.
CLICK
YOU ARE THE MASTER, ALEX.

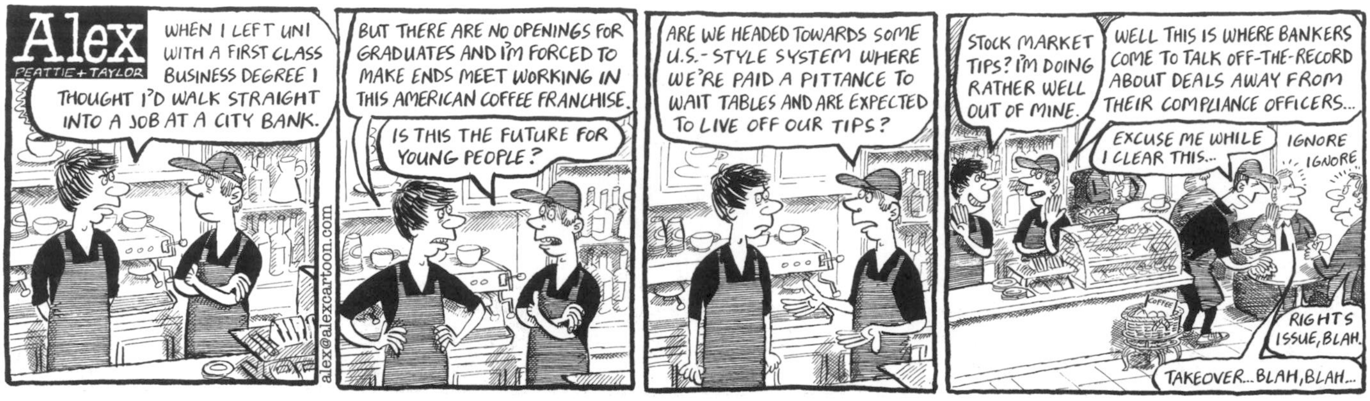
Alex
PEATTIE + TAYLOR
WHEN I LEFT UNI WITH A FIRST CLASS BUSINESS DEGREE I THOUGHT I'D WALK STRAIGHT INTO A JOB AT A CITY BANK.
BUT THERE ARE NO OPENINGS FOR GRADUATES AND I'M FORCED TO MAKE ENDS MEET WORKING IN THIS AMERICAN COFFEE FRANCHISE.
IS THIS THE FUTURE FOR YOUNG PEOPLE?
alex@alexcartoon.com
ARE WE HEADED TOWARDS SOME U.S.-STYLE SYSTEM WHERE WE'RE PAID A PITTANCE TO WAIT TABLES AND ARE EXPECTED TO LIVE OFF OUR TIPS?
STOCK MARKET TIPS? I'M DOING RATHER WELL OUT OF MINE.
WELL THIS IS WHERE BANKERS COME TO TALK OFF-THE-RECORD ABOUT DEALS AWAY FROM THEIR COMPLIANCE OFFICERS...
EXCUSE ME WHILE I CLEAR THIS...
IGNORE IGNORE
RIGHTS ISSUE, BLAH.
TAKEOVER... BLAH, BLAH...

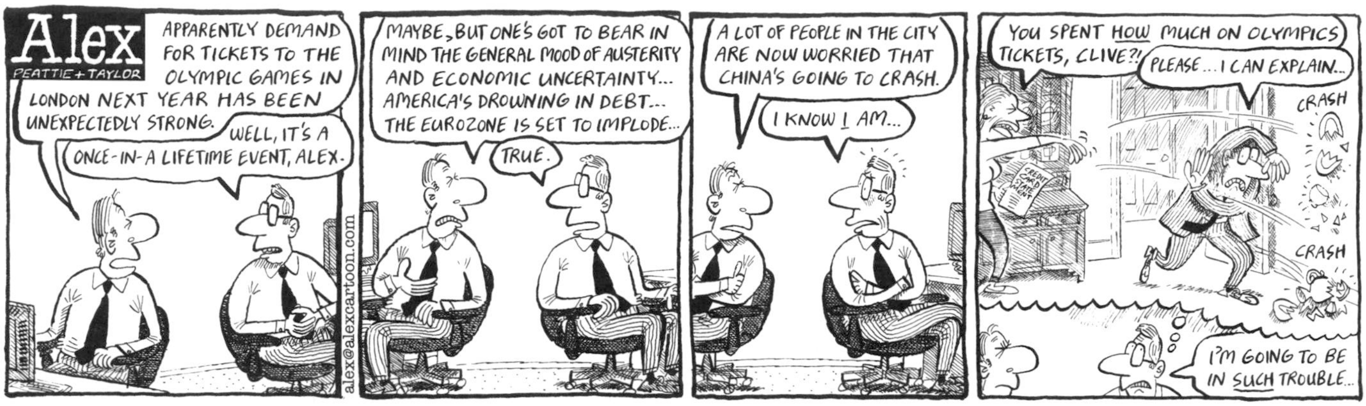
Alex
PEATTIE + TAYLOR
APPARENTLY DEMAND FOR TICKETS TO THE OLYMPIC GAMES IN LONDON NEXT YEAR HAS BEEN UNEXPECTEDLY STRONG.
WELL, IT'S A ONCE-IN-A LIFETIME EVENT, ALEX.
alex@alexcartoon.com
MAYBE, BUT ONE'S GOT TO BEAR IN MIND THE GENERAL MOOD OF AUSTERITY AND ECONOMIC UNCERTAINTY... AMERICA'S DROWNING IN DEBT... THE EUROZONE IS SET TO IMPLODE...
TRUE.
A LOT OF PEOPLE IN THE CITY ARE NOW WORRIED THAT CHINA'S GOING TO CRASH.
I KNOW I AM...
YOU SPENT HOW MUCH ON OLYMPICS TICKETS, CLIVE?!
PLEASE... I CAN EXPLAIN...
CRASH
CRASH
I'M GOING TO BE IN SUCH TROUBLE...

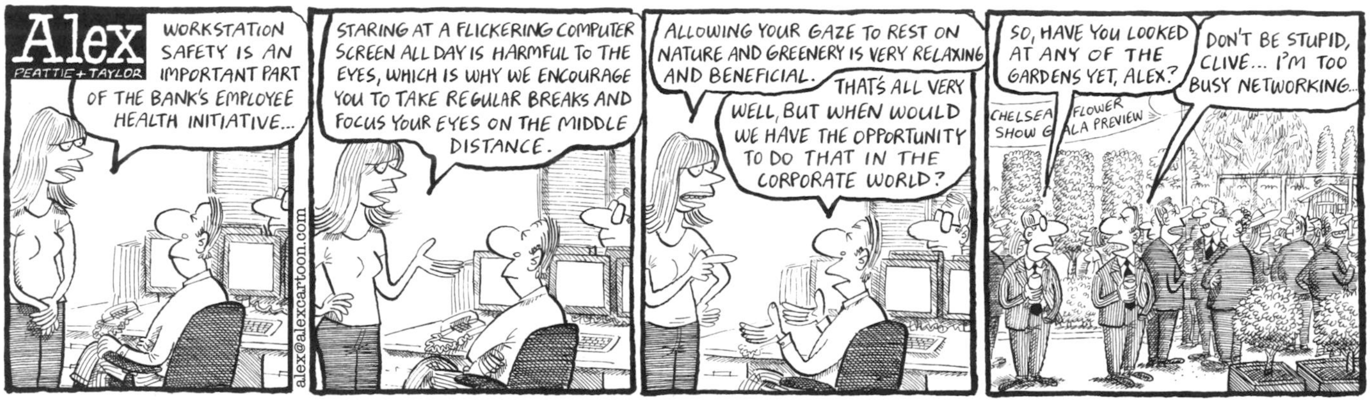
Alex
PEATTIE + TAYLOR
WORKSTATION SAFETY IS AN IMPORTANT PART OF THE BANK'S EMPLOYEE HEALTH INITIATIVE...
alex@alexcartoon.com
STARING AT A FLICKERING COMPUTER SCREEN ALL DAY IS HARMFUL TO THE EYES, WHICH IS WHY WE ENCOURAGE YOU TO TAKE REGULAR BREAKS AND FOCUS YOUR EYES ON THE MIDDLE DISTANCE.
ALLOWING YOUR GAZE TO REST ON NATURE AND GREENERY IS VERY RELAXING AND BENEFICIAL.
THAT'S ALL VERY WELL, BUT WHEN WOULD WE HAVE THE OPPORTUNITY TO DO THAT IN THE CORPORATE WORLD?
SO, HAVE YOU LOOKED AT ANY OF THE GARDENS YET, ALEX?
DON'T BE STUPID, CLIVE... I'M TOO BUSY NETWORKING...
CHELSEA FLOWER SHOW GALA PREVIEW

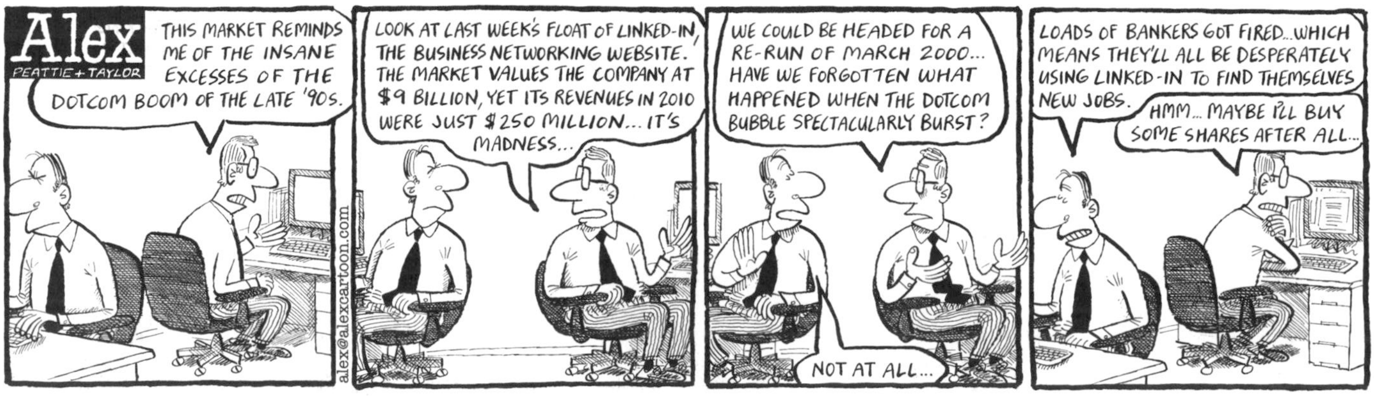
Alex
PEATTIE + TAYLOR
THIS MARKET REMINDS ME OF THE INSANE EXCESSES OF THE DOTCOM BOOM OF THE LATE '90s.
alex@alexcartoon.com
LOOK AT LAST WEEK'S FLOAT OF LINKED-IN, THE BUSINESS NETWORKING WEBSITE. THE MARKET VALUES THE COMPANY AT $9 BILLION, YET ITS REVENUES IN 2010 WERE JUST $250 MILLION... IT'S MADNESS...
WE COULD BE HEADED FOR A RE-RUN OF MARCH 2000... HAVE WE FORGOTTEN WHAT HAPPENED WHEN THE DOTCOM BUBBLE SPECTACULARLY BURST?
NOT AT ALL...
LOADS OF BANKERS GOT FIRED... WHICH MEANS THEY'LL ALL BE DESPERATELY USING LINKED-IN TO FIND THEMSELVES NEW JOBS.
HMM... MAYBE I'LL BUY SOME SHARES AFTER ALL...

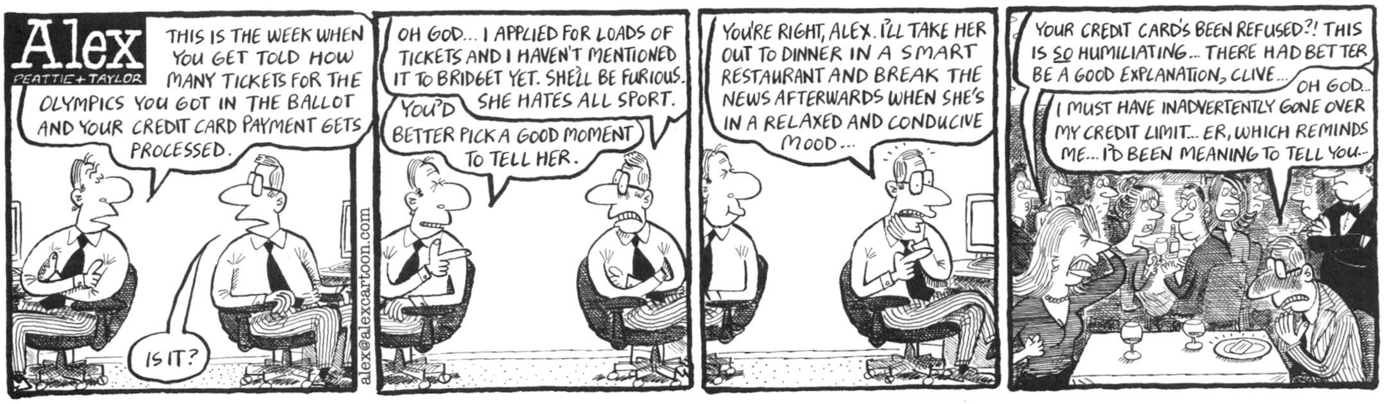
Alex
PEATTIE + TAYLOR
THIS IS THE WEEK WHEN YOU GET TOLD HOW MANY TICKETS FOR THE OLYMPICS YOU GOT IN THE BALLOT AND YOUR CREDIT CARD PAYMENT GETS PROCESSED.
IS IT?
alex@alexcartoon.com
OH GOD... I APPLIED FOR LOADS OF TICKETS AND I HAVEN'T MENTIONED IT TO BRIDGET YET. SHE'LL BE FURIOUS. SHE HATES ALL SPORT.
YOU'D BETTER PICK A GOOD MOMENT TO TELL HER.
YOU'RE RIGHT, ALEX. I'LL TAKE HER OUT TO DINNER IN A SMART RESTAURANT AND BREAK THE NEWS AFTERWARDS WHEN SHE'S IN A RELAXED AND CONDUCIVE MOOD...
YOUR CREDIT CARD'S BEEN REFUSED?! THIS IS SO HUMILIATING... THERE HAD BETTER BE A GOOD EXPLANATION, CLIVE...
OH GOD... I MUST HAVE INADVERTENTLY GONE OVER MY CREDIT LIMIT... ER, WHICH REMINDS ME... I'D BEEN MEANING TO TELL YOU...

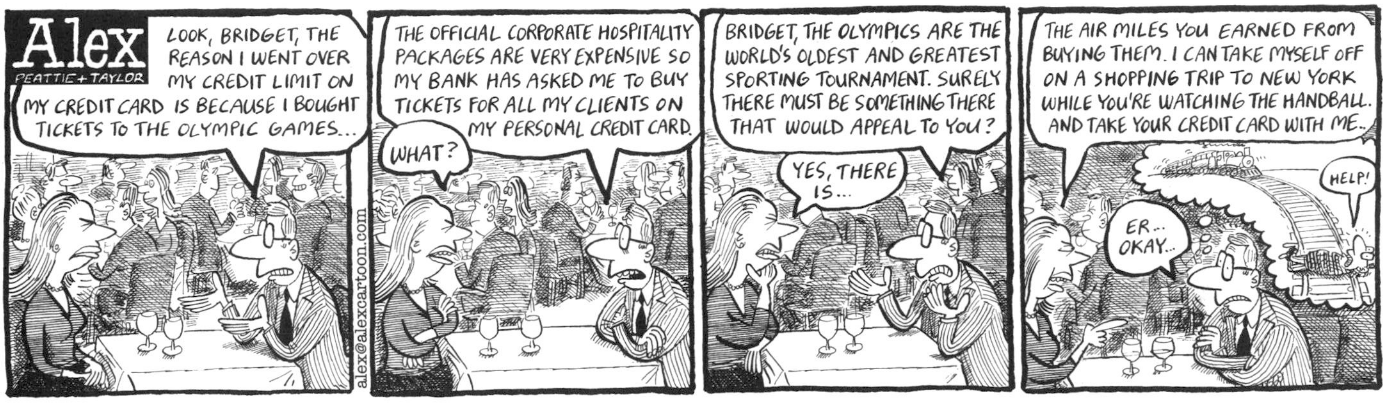
Alex
PEATTIE + TAYLOR
LOOK, BRIDGET, THE REASON I WENT OVER MY CREDIT LIMIT ON MY CREDIT CARD IS BECAUSE I BOUGHT TICKETS TO THE OLYMPIC GAMES...
alex@alexcartoon.com
THE OFFICIAL CORPORATE HOSPITALITY PACKAGES ARE VERY EXPENSIVE SO MY BANK HAS ASKED ME TO BUY TICKETS FOR ALL MY CLIENTS ON MY PERSONAL CREDIT CARD.
WHAT?
BRIDGET, THE OLYMPICS ARE THE WORLD'S OLDEST AND GREATEST SPORTING TOURNAMENT. SURELY THERE MUST BE SOMETHING THERE THAT WOULD APPEAL TO YOU?
YES, THERE IS...
THE AIR MILES YOU EARNED FROM BUYING THEM. I CAN TAKE MYSELF OFF ON A SHOPPING TRIP TO NEW YORK WHILE YOU'RE WATCHING THE HANDBALL. AND TAKE YOUR CREDIT CARD WITH ME...
ER... OKAY...
HELP!

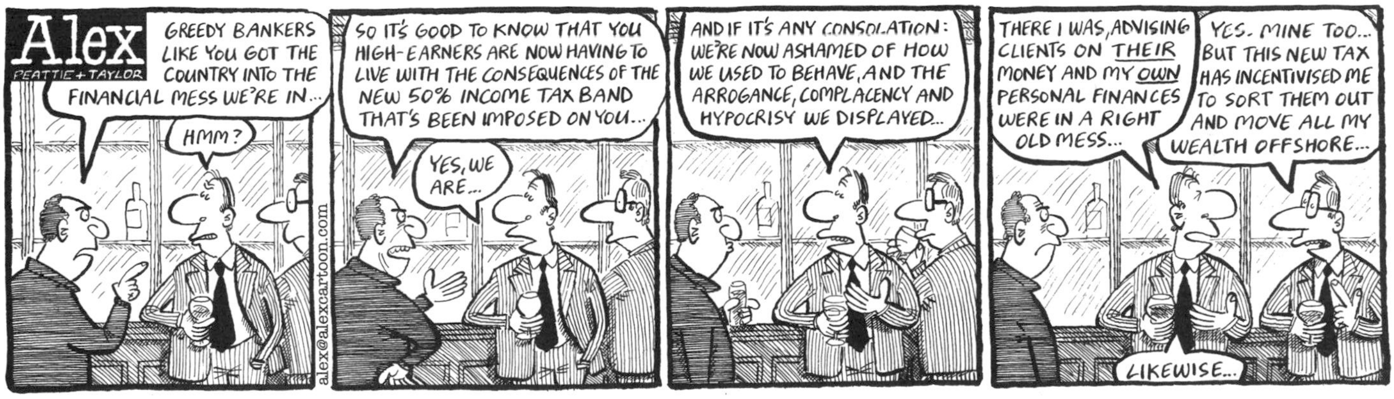
Alex
PEATTIE + TAYLOR
GREEDY BANKERS LIKE YOU GOT THE COUNTRY INTO THE FINANCIAL MESS WE'RE IN...
HMM?
alex@alexcartoon.com
SO IT'S GOOD TO KNOW THAT YOU HIGH-EARNERS ARE NOW HAVING TO LIVE WITH THE CONSEQUENCES OF THE NEW 50% INCOME TAX BAND THAT'S BEEN IMPOSED ON YOU...
YES, WE ARE...
AND IF IT'S ANY CONSOLATION: WE'RE NOW ASHAMED OF HOW WE USED TO BEHAVE, AND THE ARROGANCE, COMPLACENCY AND HYPOCRISY WE DISPLAYED...
THERE I WAS, ADVISING CLIENTS ON THEIR MONEY AND MY OWN PERSONAL FINANCES WERE IN A RIGHT OLD MESS...
YES. MINE TOO... BUT THIS NEW TAX HAS INCENTIVISED ME TO SORT THEM OUT AND MOVE ALL MY WEALTH OFFSHORE...
LIKEWISE...

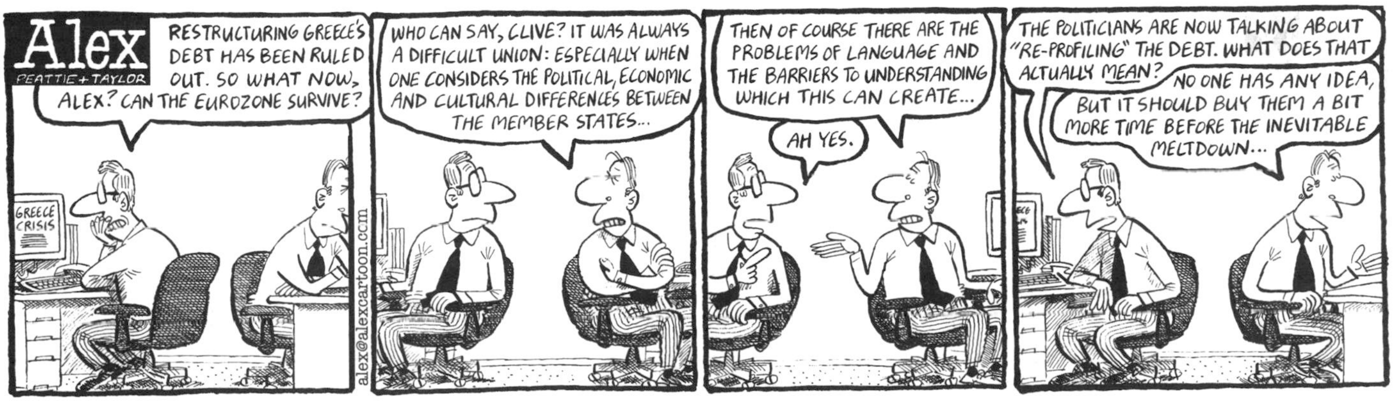
Alex
PEATTIE + TAYLOR
RESTRUCTURING GREECE'S DEBT HAS BEEN RULED OUT. SO WHAT NOW, ALEX? CAN THE EUROZONE SURVIVE?
GREECE CRISIS
alex@alexcartoon.com
WHO CAN SAY, CLIVE? IT WAS ALWAYS A DIFFICULT UNION: ESPECIALLY WHEN ONE CONSIDERS THE POLITICAL, ECONOMIC AND CULTURAL DIFFERENCES BETWEEN THE MEMBER STATES...
THEN OF COURSE THERE ARE THE PROBLEMS OF LANGUAGE AND THE BARRIERS TO UNDERSTANDING WHICH THIS CAN CREATE...
AH YES.
THE POLITICIANS ARE NOW TALKING ABOUT "RE-PROFILING" THE DEBT. WHAT DOES THAT ACTUALLY MEAN?
NO ONE HAS ANY IDEA, BUT IT SHOULD BUY THEM A BIT MORE TIME BEFORE THE INEVITABLE MELTDOWN...

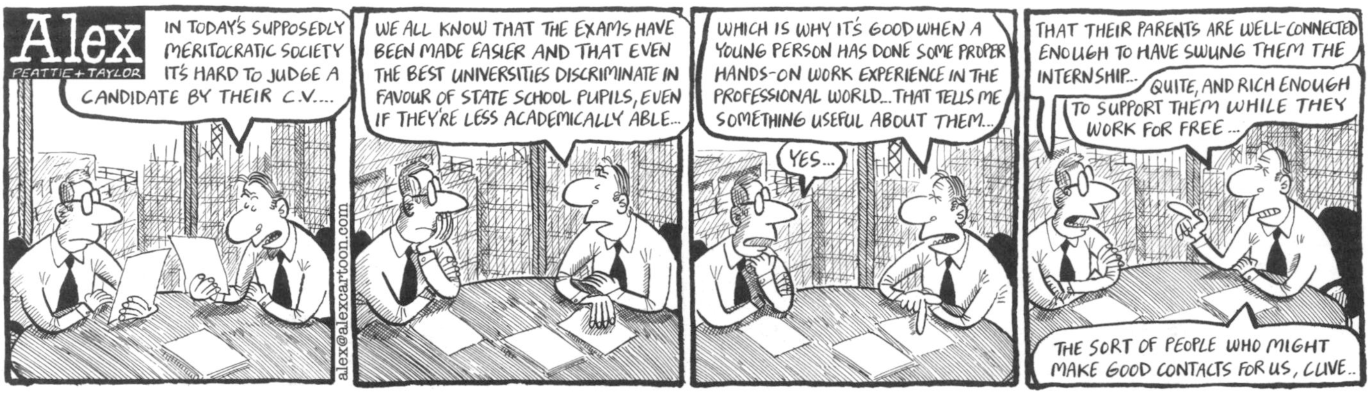
Alex
PEATTIE + TAYLOR
IN TODAY'S SUPPOSEDLY MERITOCRATIC SOCIETY IT'S HARD TO JUDGE A CANDIDATE BY THEIR C.V....
WE ALL KNOW THAT THE EXAMS HAVE BEEN MADE EASIER AND THAT EVEN THE BEST UNIVERSITIES DISCRIMINATE IN FAVOUR OF STATE SCHOOL PUPILS, EVEN IF THEY'RE LESS ACADEMICALLY ABLE...
WHICH IS WHY IT'S GOOD WHEN A YOUNG PERSON HAS DONE SOME PROPER HANDS-ON WORK EXPERIENCE IN THE PROFESSIONAL WORLD... THAT TELLS ME SOMETHING USEFUL ABOUT THEM...
YES...
THAT THEIR PARENTS ARE WELL-CONNECTED ENOUGH TO HAVE SWUNG THEM THE INTERNSHIP...
QUITE, AND RICH ENOUGH TO SUPPORT THEM WHILE THEY WORK FOR FREE...
THE SORT OF PEOPLE WHO MIGHT MAKE GOOD CONTACTS FOR US, CLIVE...
alex@alexcartoon.com

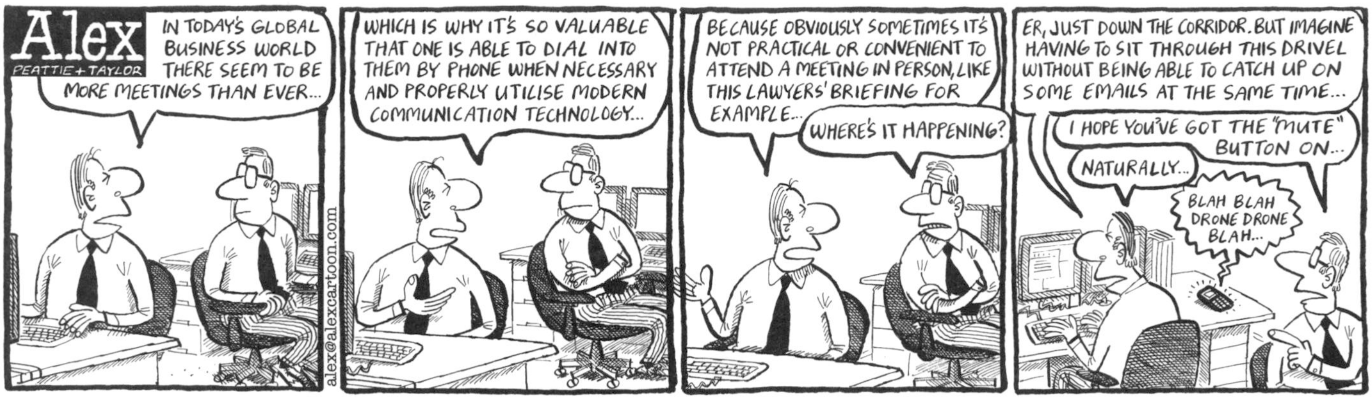
Alex
PEATTIE + TAYLOR
IN TODAY'S GLOBAL BUSINESS WORLD THERE SEEM TO BE MORE MEETINGS THAN EVER...
WHICH IS WHY IT'S SO VALUABLE THAT ONE IS ABLE TO DIAL INTO THEM BY PHONE WHEN NECESSARY AND PROPERLY UTILISE MODERN COMMUNICATION TECHNOLOGY...
BECAUSE OBVIOUSLY SOMETIMES IT'S NOT PRACTICAL OR CONVENIENT TO ATTEND A MEETING IN PERSON, LIKE THIS LAWYERS' BRIEFING FOR EXAMPLE...
WHERE'S IT HAPPENING?
ER, JUST DOWN THE CORRIDOR. BUT IMAGINE HAVING TO SIT THROUGH THIS DRIVEL WITHOUT BEING ABLE TO CATCH UP ON SOME EMAILS AT THE SAME TIME...
I HOPE YOU'VE GOT THE "MUTE" BUTTON ON...
NATURALLY...
BLAH BLAH DRONE DRONE BLAH...
alex@alexcartoon.com

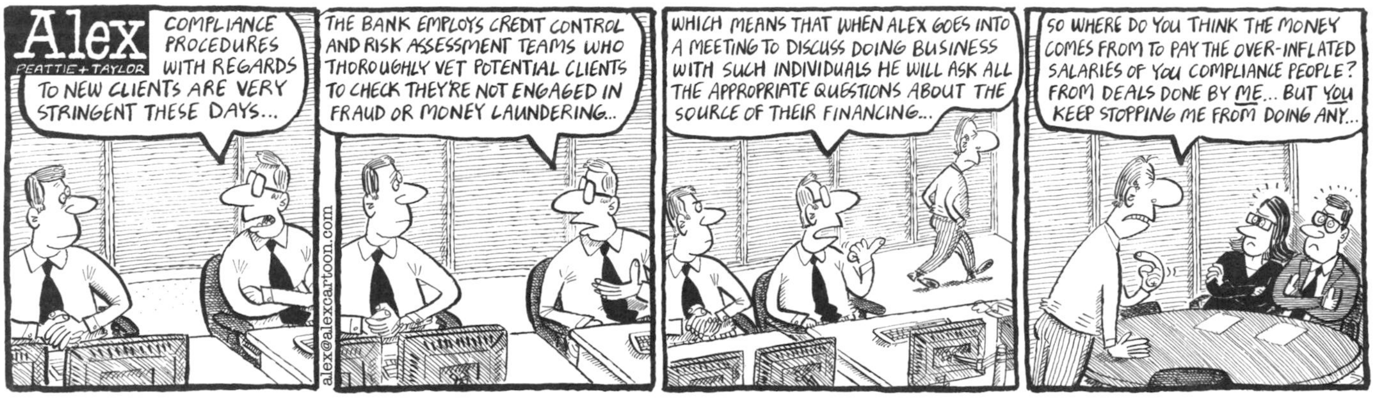
Alex
PEATTIE + TAYLOR
COMPLIANCE PROCEDURES WITH REGARDS TO NEW CLIENTS ARE VERY STRINGENT THESE DAYS...
THE BANK EMPLOYS CREDIT CONTROL AND RISK ASSESSMENT TEAMS WHO THOROUGHLY VET POTENTIAL CLIENTS TO CHECK THEY'RE NOT ENGAGED IN FRAUD OR MONEY LAUNDERING...
WHICH MEANS THAT WHEN ALEX GOES INTO A MEETING TO DISCUSS DOING BUSINESS WITH SUCH INDIVIDUALS HE WILL ASK ALL THE APPROPRIATE QUESTIONS ABOUT THE SOURCE OF THEIR FINANCING...
SO WHERE DO YOU THINK THE MONEY COMES FROM TO PAY THE OVER-INFLATED SALARIES OF YOU COMPLIANCE PEOPLE? FROM DEALS DONE BY ME... BUT YOU KEEP STOPPING ME FROM DOING ANY...
alex@alexcartoon.com

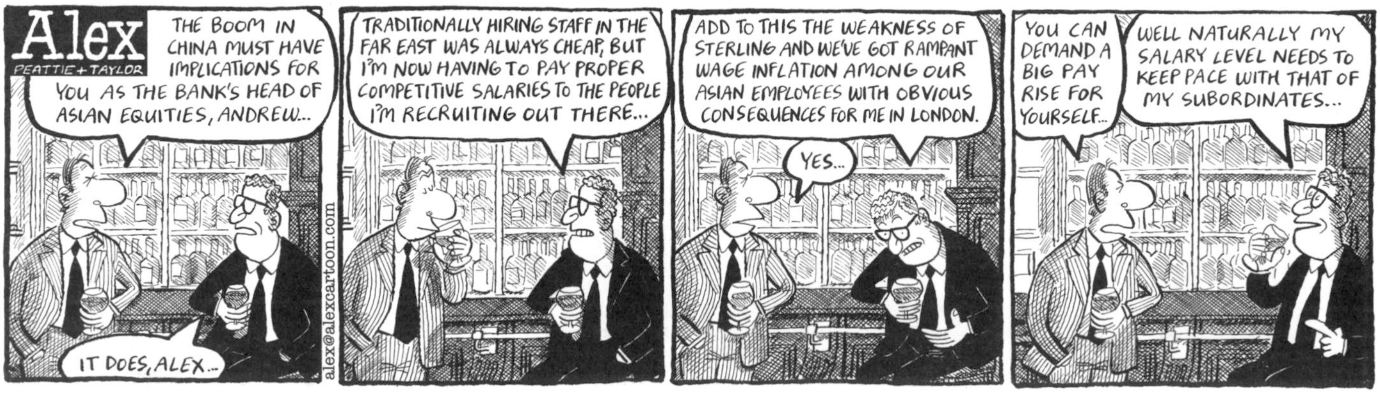
Alex
PEATTIE + TAYLOR
THE BOOM IN CHINA MUST HAVE IMPLICATIONS FOR YOU AS THE BANK'S HEAD OF ASIAN EQUITIES, ANDREW...
IT DOES, ALEX...
TRADITIONALLY HIRING STAFF IN THE FAR EAST WAS ALWAYS CHEAP, BUT I'M NOW HAVING TO PAY PROPER COMPETITIVE SALARIES TO THE PEOPLE I'M RECRUITING OUT THERE...
ADD TO THIS THE WEAKNESS OF STERLING AND WE'VE GOT RAMPANT WAGE INFLATION AMONG OUR ASIAN EMPLOYEES WITH OBVIOUS CONSEQUENCES FOR ME IN LONDON.
YES...
YOU CAN DEMAND A BIG PAY RISE FOR YOURSELF...
WELL NATURALLY MY SALARY LEVEL NEEDS TO KEEP PACE WITH THAT OF MY SUBORDINATES...
alex@alexcartoon.com

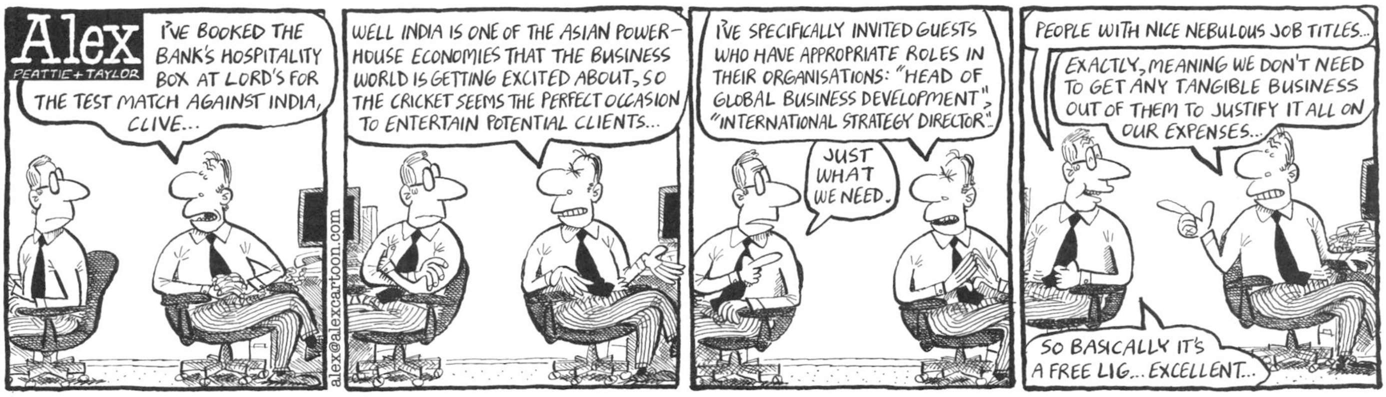
Alex
PEATTIE + TAYLOR
I'VE BOOKED THE BANK'S HOSPITALITY BOX AT LORD'S FOR THE TEST MATCH AGAINST INDIA, CLIVE...
alex@alexcartoon.com
WELL INDIA IS ONE OF THE ASIAN POWER-HOUSE ECONOMIES THAT THE BUSINESS WORLD IS GETTING EXCITED ABOUT, SO THE CRICKET SEEMS THE PERFECT OCCASION TO ENTERTAIN POTENTIAL CLIENTS...
I'VE SPECIFICALLY INVITED GUESTS WHO HAVE APPROPRIATE ROLES IN THEIR ORGANISATIONS: "HEAD OF GLOBAL BUSINESS DEVELOPMENT", "INTERNATIONAL STRATEGY DIRECTOR"...
JUST WHAT WE NEED.
PEOPLE WITH NICE NEBULOUS JOB TITLES...
EXACTLY, MEANING WE DON'T NEED TO GET ANY TANGIBLE BUSINESS OUT OF THEM TO JUSTIFY IT ALL ON OUR EXPENSES...
SO BASICALLY IT'S A FREE LIG... EXCELLENT...

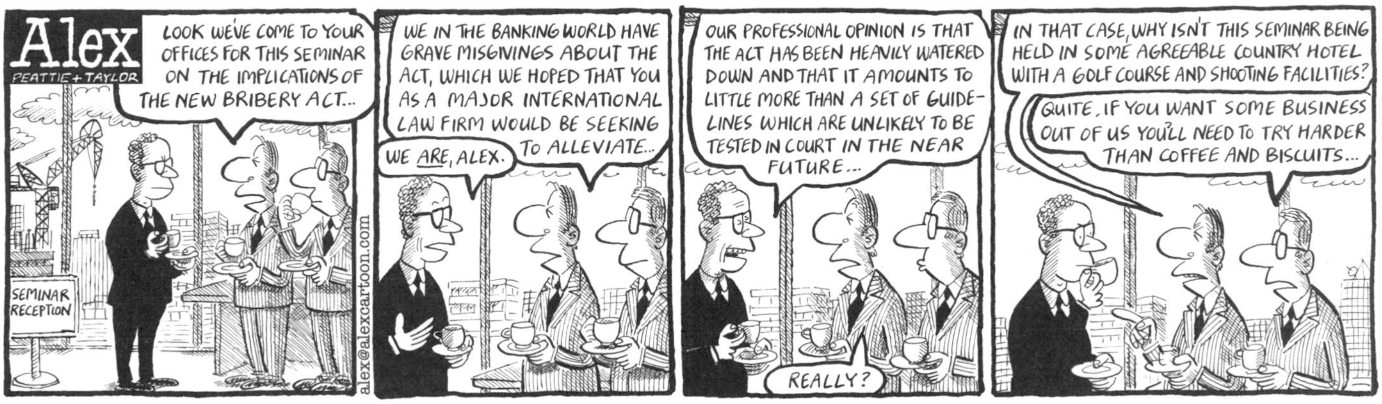
Alex
PEATTIE + TAYLOR
LOOK WE'VE COME TO YOUR OFFICES FOR THIS SEMINAR ON THE IMPLICATIONS OF THE NEW BRIBERY ACT...
SEMINAR RECEPTION
alex@alexcartoon.com
WE IN THE BANKING WORLD HAVE GRAVE MISGIVINGS ABOUT THE ACT, WHICH WE HOPED THAT YOU AS A MAJOR INTERNATIONAL LAW FIRM WOULD BE SEEKING TO ALLEVIATE...
WE ARE, ALEX.
OUR PROFESSIONAL OPINION IS THAT THE ACT HAS BEEN HEAVILY WATERED DOWN AND THAT IT AMOUNTS TO LITTLE MORE THAN A SET OF GUIDE-LINES WHICH ARE UNLIKELY TO BE TESTED IN COURT IN THE NEAR FUTURE...
REALLY?
IN THAT CASE, WHY ISN'T THIS SEMINAR BEING HELD IN SOME AGREEABLE COUNTRY HOTEL WITH A GOLF COURSE AND SHOOTING FACILITIES?
QUITE. IF YOU WANT SOME BUSINESS OUT OF US YOU'LL NEED TO TRY HARDER THAN COFFEE AND BISCUITS...

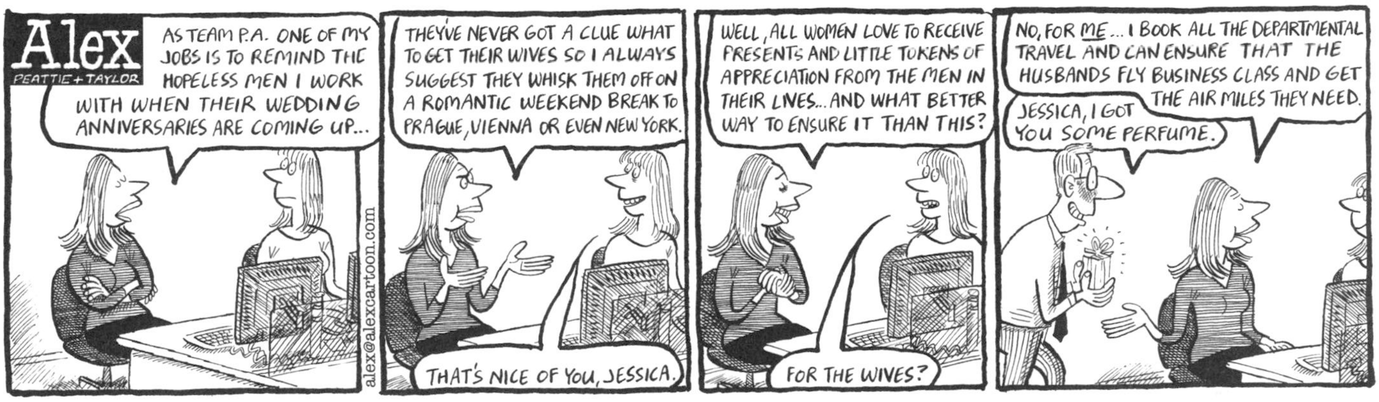
Alex
PEATTIE + TAYLOR
AS TEAM P.A. ONE OF MY JOBS IS TO REMIND THE HOPELESS MEN I WORK WITH WHEN THEIR WEDDING ANNIVERSARIES ARE COMING UP...
alex@alexcartoon.com
THEY'VE NEVER GOT A CLUE WHAT TO GET THEIR WIVES SO I ALWAYS SUGGEST THEY WHISK THEM OFF ON A ROMANTIC WEEKEND BREAK TO PRAGUE, VIENNA OR EVEN NEW YORK.
THAT'S NICE OF YOU, JESSICA.
WELL, ALL WOMEN LOVE TO RECEIVE PRESENTS AND LITTLE TOKENS OF APPRECIATION FROM THE MEN IN THEIR LIVES... AND WHAT BETTER WAY TO ENSURE IT THAN THIS?
FOR THE WIVES?
NO, FOR ME... I BOOK ALL THE DEPARTMENTAL TRAVEL AND CAN ENSURE THAT THE HUSBANDS FLY BUSINESS CLASS AND GET THE AIR MILES THEY NEED.
JESSICA, I GOT YOU SOME PERFUME.

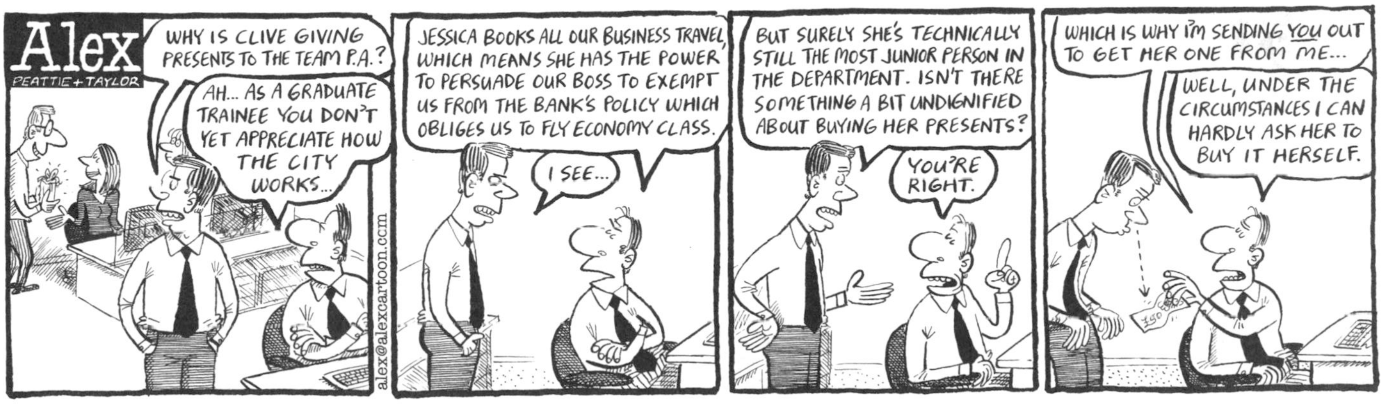
Alex
PEATTIE + TAYLOR
WHY IS CLIVE GIVING PRESENTS TO THE TEAM P.A.?
AH... AS A GRADUATE TRAINEE YOU DON'T YET APPRECIATE HOW THE CITY WORKS...
alex@alexcartoon.com
JESSICA BOOKS ALL OUR BUSINESS TRAVEL, WHICH MEANS SHE HAS THE POWER TO PERSUADE OUR BOSS TO EXEMPT US FROM THE BANK'S POLICY WHICH OBLIGES US TO FLY ECONOMY CLASS.
I SEE...
BUT SURELY SHE'S TECHNICALLY STILL THE MOST JUNIOR PERSON IN THE DEPARTMENT. ISN'T THERE SOMETHING A BIT UNDIGNIFIED ABOUT BUYING HER PRESENTS?
YOU'RE RIGHT.
WHICH IS WHY I'M SENDING YOU OUT TO GET HER ONE FROM ME...
WELL, UNDER THE CIRCUMSTANCES I CAN HARDLY ASK HER TO BUY IT HERSELF.

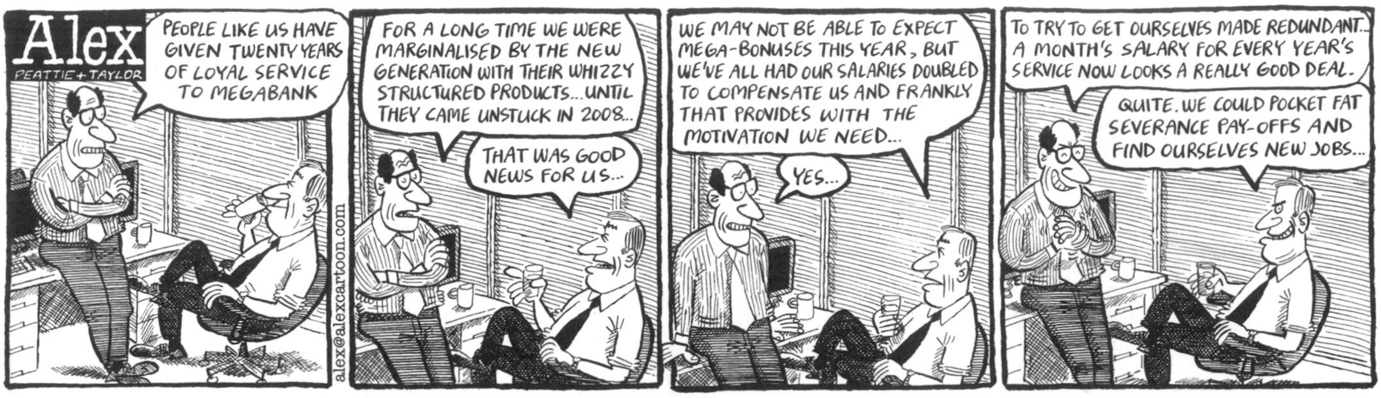
Alex
PEATTIE+TAYLOR
PEOPLE LIKE US HAVE GIVEN TWENTY YEARS OF LOYAL SERVICE TO MEGABANK
FOR A LONG TIME WE WERE MARGINALISED BY THE NEW GENERATION WITH THEIR WHIZZY STRUCTURED PRODUCTS... UNTIL THEY CAME UNSTUCK IN 2008...
THAT WAS GOOD NEWS FOR US...
alex@alexcartoon.com
WE MAY NOT BE ABLE TO EXPECT MEGA-BONUSES THIS YEAR, BUT WE'VE ALL HAD OUR SALARIES DOUBLED TO COMPENSATE US AND FRANKLY THAT PROVIDES US WITH THE MOTIVATION WE NEED...
YES...
TO TRY TO GET OURSELVES MADE REDUNDANT... A MONTH'S SALARY FOR EVERY YEAR'S SERVICE NOW LOOKS A REALLY GOOD DEAL.
QUITE. WE COULD POCKET FAT SEVERANCE PAY-OFFS AND FIND OURSELVES NEW JOBS...

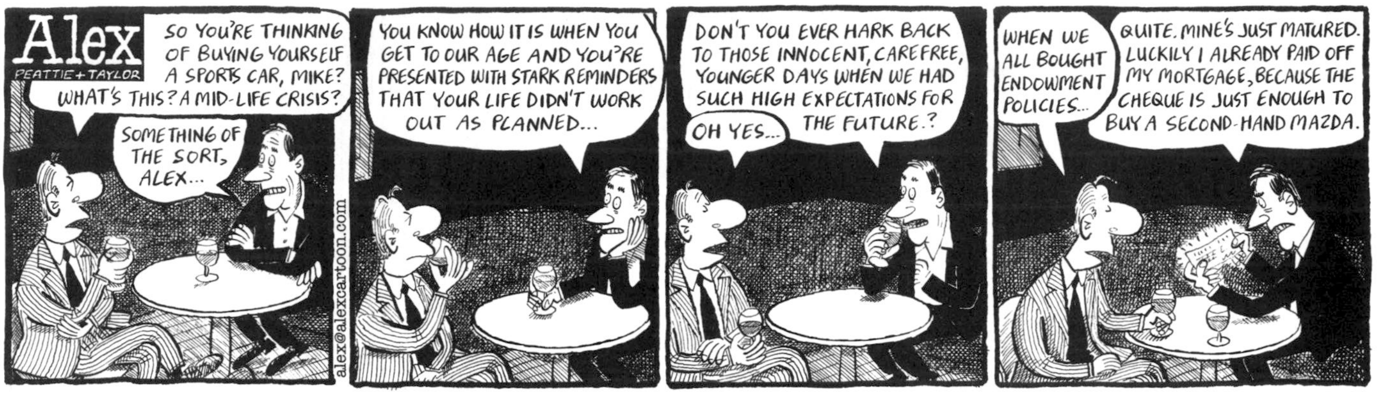
Alex
PEATTIE+TAYLOR
SO YOU'RE THINKING OF BUYING YOURSELF A SPORTS CAR, MIKE? WHAT'S THIS? A MID-LIFE CRISIS?
SOMETHING OF THE SORT, ALEX...
YOU KNOW HOW IT IS WHEN YOU GET TO OUR AGE AND YOU'RE PRESENTED WITH STARK REMINDERS THAT YOUR LIFE DIDN'T WORK OUT AS PLANNED...
alex@alexcartoon.com
DON'T YOU EVER HARK BACK TO THOSE INNOCENT, CAREFREE, YOUNGER DAYS WHEN WE HAD SUCH HIGH EXPECTATIONS FOR THE FUTURE.?
OH YES...
WHEN WE ALL BOUGHT ENDOWMENT POLICIES...
QUITE. MINE'S JUST MATURED. LUCKILY I ALREADY PAID OFF MY MORTGAGE, BECAUSE THE CHEQUE IS JUST ENOUGH TO BUY A SECOND-HAND MAZDA.

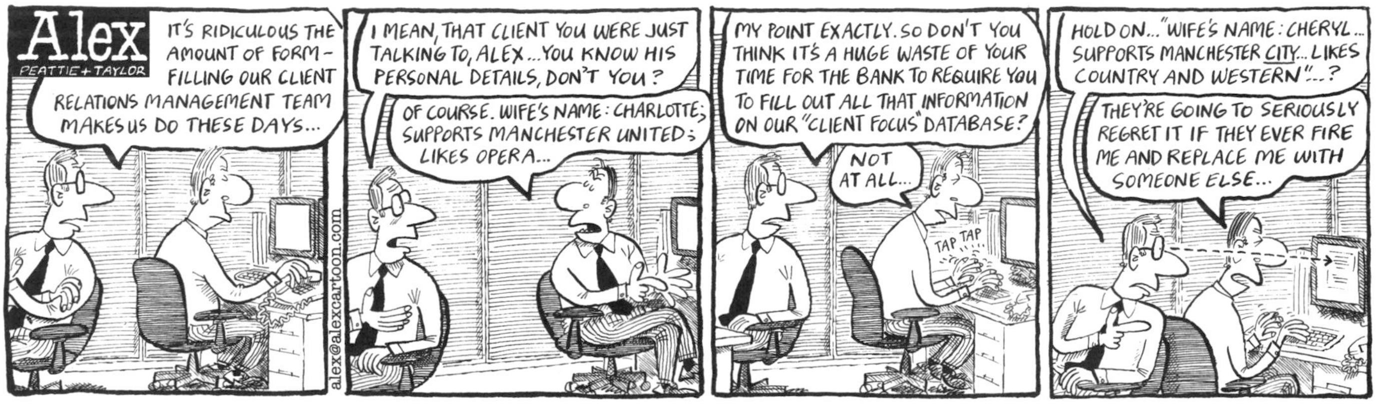
Alex
PEATTIE+TAYLOR
IT'S RIDICULOUS THE AMOUNT OF FORM-FILLING OUR CLIENT RELATIONS MANAGEMENT TEAM MAKES US DO THESE DAYS...
I MEAN, THAT CLIENT YOU WERE JUST TALKING TO, ALEX... YOU KNOW HIS PERSONAL DETAILS, DON'T YOU?
OF COURSE. WIFE'S NAME: CHARLOTTE; SUPPORTS MANCHESTER UNITED; LIKES OPERA...
alex@alexcartoon.com
MY POINT EXACTLY. SO DON'T YOU THINK IT'S A HUGE WASTE OF YOUR TIME FOR THE BANK TO REQUIRE YOU TO FILL OUT ALL THAT INFORMATION ON OUR "CLIENT FOCUS" DATABASE?
NOT AT ALL...
TAP TAP
HOLD ON... "WIFE'S NAME: CHERYL... SUPPORTS MANCHESTER CITY... LIKES COUNTRY AND WESTERN"...?
THEY'RE GOING TO SERIOUSLY REGRET IT IF THEY EVER FIRE ME AND REPLACE ME WITH SOMEONE ELSE...

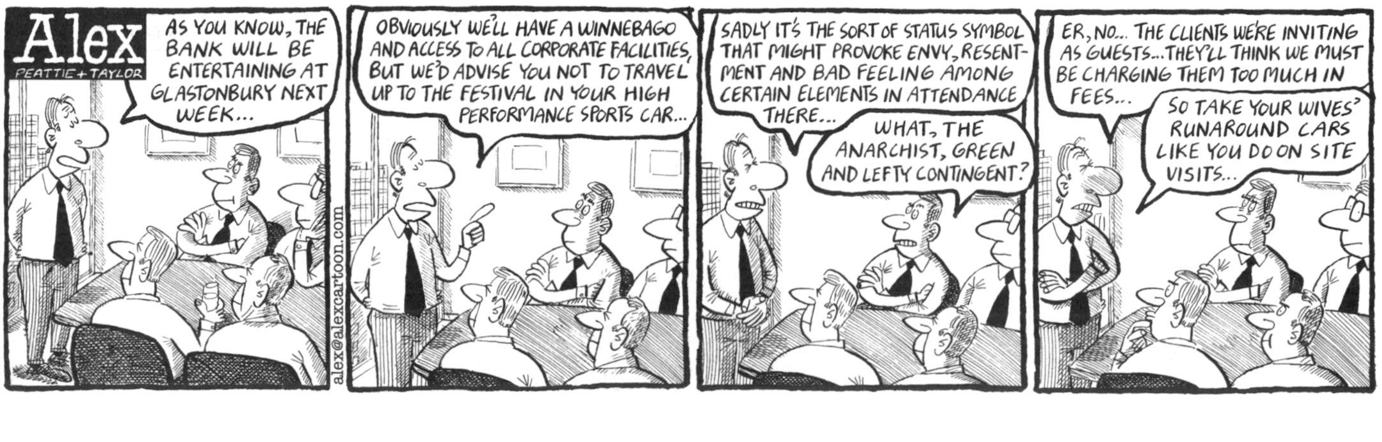
Alex
PEATTIE+TAYLOR
AS YOU KNOW, THE BANK WILL BE ENTERTAINING AT GLASTONBURY NEXT WEEK...
OBVIOUSLY WE'LL HAVE A WINNEBAGO AND ACCESS TO ALL CORPORATE FACILITIES, BUT WE'D ADVISE YOU NOT TO TRAVEL UP TO THE FESTIVAL IN YOUR HIGH PERFORMANCE SPORTS CAR...
alex@alexcartoon.com
SADLY IT'S THE SORT OF STATUS SYMBOL THAT MIGHT PROVOKE ENVY, RESENTMENT AND BAD FEELING AMONG CERTAIN ELEMENTS IN ATTENDANCE THERE...
WHAT, THE ANARCHIST, GREEN AND LEFTY CONTINGENT?
ER, NO... THE CLIENTS WE'RE INVITING AS GUESTS... THEY'LL THINK WE MUST BE CHARGING THEM TOO MUCH IN FEES...
SO TAKE YOUR WIVES' RUNAROUND CARS LIKE YOU DO ON SITE VISITS...

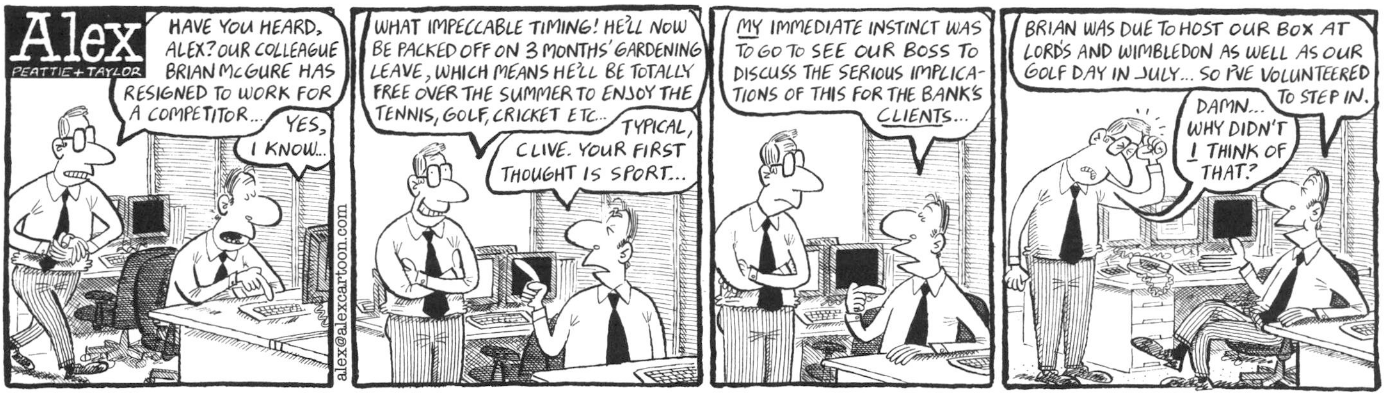
Alex
PEATTIE + TAYLOR
HAVE YOU HEARD, ALEX? OUR COLLEAGUE BRIAN McGURE HAS RESIGNED TO WORK FOR A COMPETITOR...
YES, I KNOW...
WHAT IMPECCABLE TIMING! HE'LL NOW BE PACKED OFF ON 3 MONTHS' GARDENING LEAVE, WHICH MEANS HE'LL BE TOTALLY FREE OVER THE SUMMER TO ENJOY THE TENNIS, GOLF, CRICKET ETC...
TYPICAL, CLIVE. YOUR FIRST THOUGHT IS SPORT...
alex@alexcartoon.com
MY IMMEDIATE INSTINCT WAS TO GO TO SEE OUR BOSS TO DISCUSS THE SERIOUS IMPLICATIONS OF THIS FOR THE BANK'S CLIENTS...
BRIAN WAS DUE TO HOST OUR BOX AT LORDS AND WIMBLEDON AS WELL AS OUR GOLF DAY IN JULY... SO I'VE VOLUNTEERED TO STEP IN.
DAMN... WHY DIDN'T I THINK OF THAT?

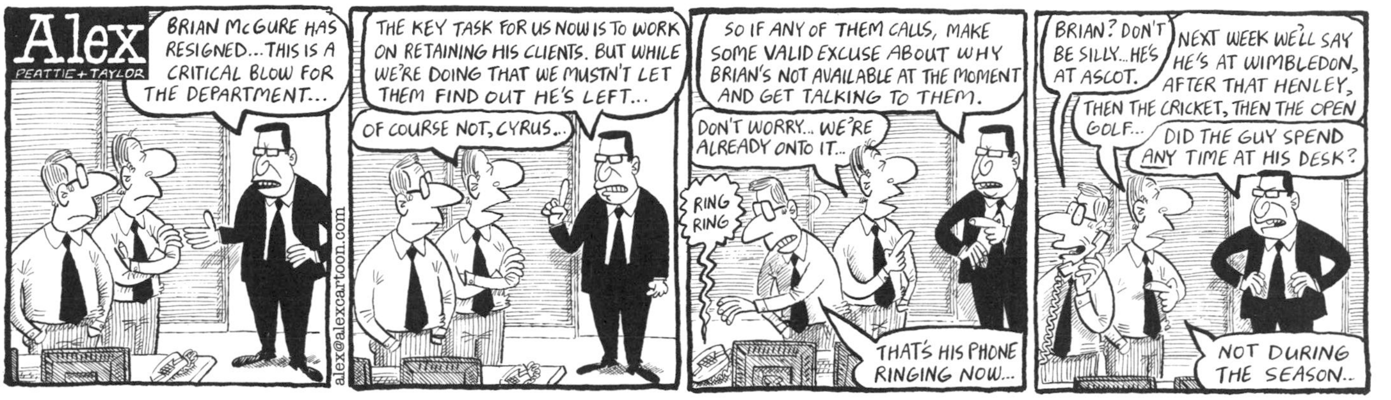
Alex
PEATTIE + TAYLOR
BRIAN McGURE HAS RESIGNED... THIS IS A CRITICAL BLOW FOR THE DEPARTMENT...
THE KEY TASK FOR US NOW IS TO WORK ON RETAINING HIS CLIENTS. BUT WHILE WE'RE DOING THAT WE MUSTN'T LET THEM FIND OUT HE'S LEFT...
OF COURSE NOT, CYRUS...
alex@alexcartoon.com
SO IF ANY OF THEM CALLS, MAKE SOME VALID EXCUSE ABOUT WHY BRIAN'S NOT AVAILABLE AT THE MOMENT AND GET TALKING TO THEM.
DON'T WORRY... WE'RE ALREADY ONTO IT...
RING RING
THAT'S HIS PHONE RINGING NOW...
BRIAN? DON'T BE SILLY... HE'S AT ASCOT.
NEXT WEEK WE'LL SAY HE'S AT WIMBLEDON, AFTER THAT HENLEY, THEN THE CRICKET, THEN THE OPEN GOLF...
DID THE GUY SPEND ANY TIME AT HIS DESK?
NOT DURING THE SEASON...

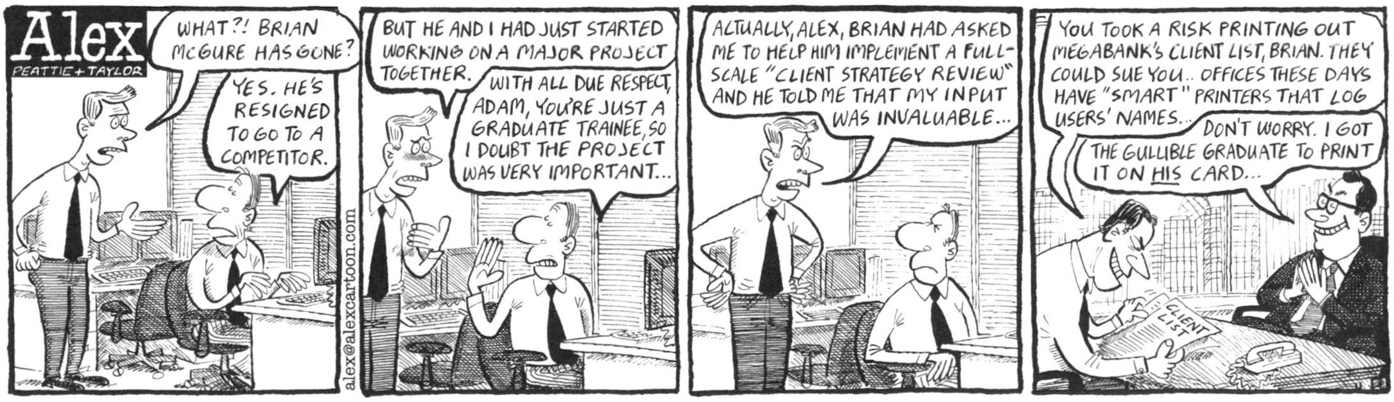
Alex
PEATTIE + TAYLOR
WHAT?! BRIAN McGURE HAS GONE?
YES. HE'S RESIGNED TO GO TO A COMPETITOR.
alex@alexcartoon.com
BUT HE AND I HAD JUST STARTED WORKING ON A MAJOR PROJECT TOGETHER.
WITH ALL DUE RESPECT, ADAM, YOU'RE JUST A GRADUATE TRAINEE, SO I DOUBT THE PROJECT WAS VERY IMPORTANT...
ACTUALLY, ALEX, BRIAN HAD ASKED ME TO HELP HIM IMPLEMENT A FULL-SCALE "CLIENT STRATEGY REVIEW" AND HE TOLD ME THAT MY INPUT WAS INVALUABLE...
YOU TOOK A RISK PRINTING OUT MEGABANK'S CLIENT LIST, BRIAN. THEY COULD SUE YOU.. OFFICES THESE DAYS HAVE "SMART" PRINTERS THAT LOG USERS' NAMES...
DON'T WORRY. I GOT THE GULLIBLE GRADUATE TO PRINT IT ON HIS CARD...
CLIENT LIST

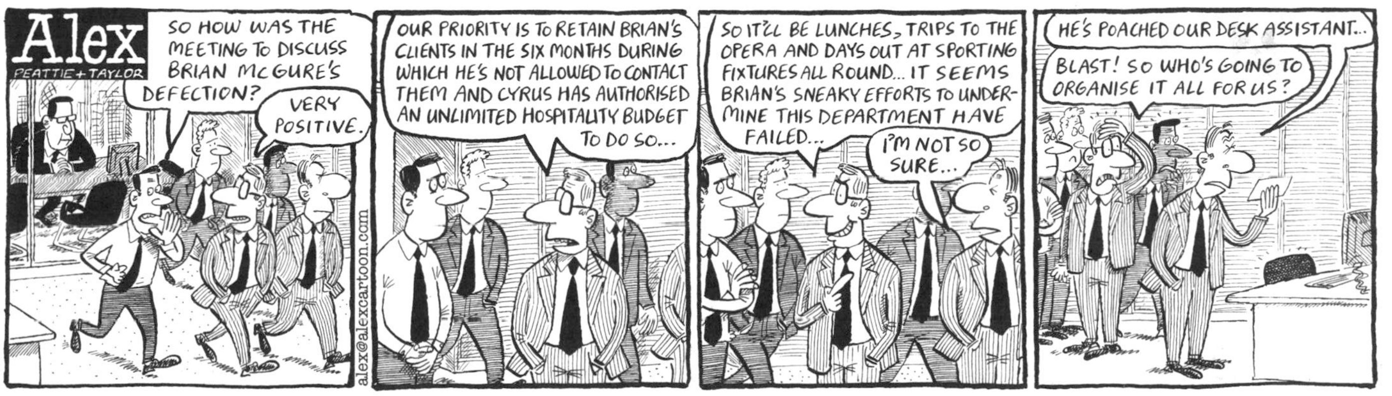
Alex
PEATTIE + TAYLOR
SO HOW WAS THE MEETING TO DISCUSS BRIAN McGURE'S DEFECTION?
VERY POSITIVE.
alex@alexcartoon.com
OUR PRIORITY IS TO RETAIN BRIAN'S CLIENTS IN THE SIX MONTHS DURING WHICH HE'S NOT ALLOWED TO CONTACT THEM AND CYRUS HAS AUTHORISED AN UNLIMITED HOSPITALITY BUDGET TO DO SO...
SO IT'LL BE LUNCHES, TRIPS TO THE OPERA AND DAYS OUT AT SPORTING FIXTURES ALL ROUND... IT SEEMS BRIAN'S SNEAKY EFFORTS TO UNDERMINE THIS DEPARTMENT HAVE FAILED...
I'M NOT SO SURE...
HE'S POACHED OUR DESK ASSISTANT...
BLAST! SO WHO'S GOING TO ORGANISE IT ALL FOR US?

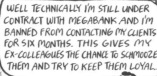

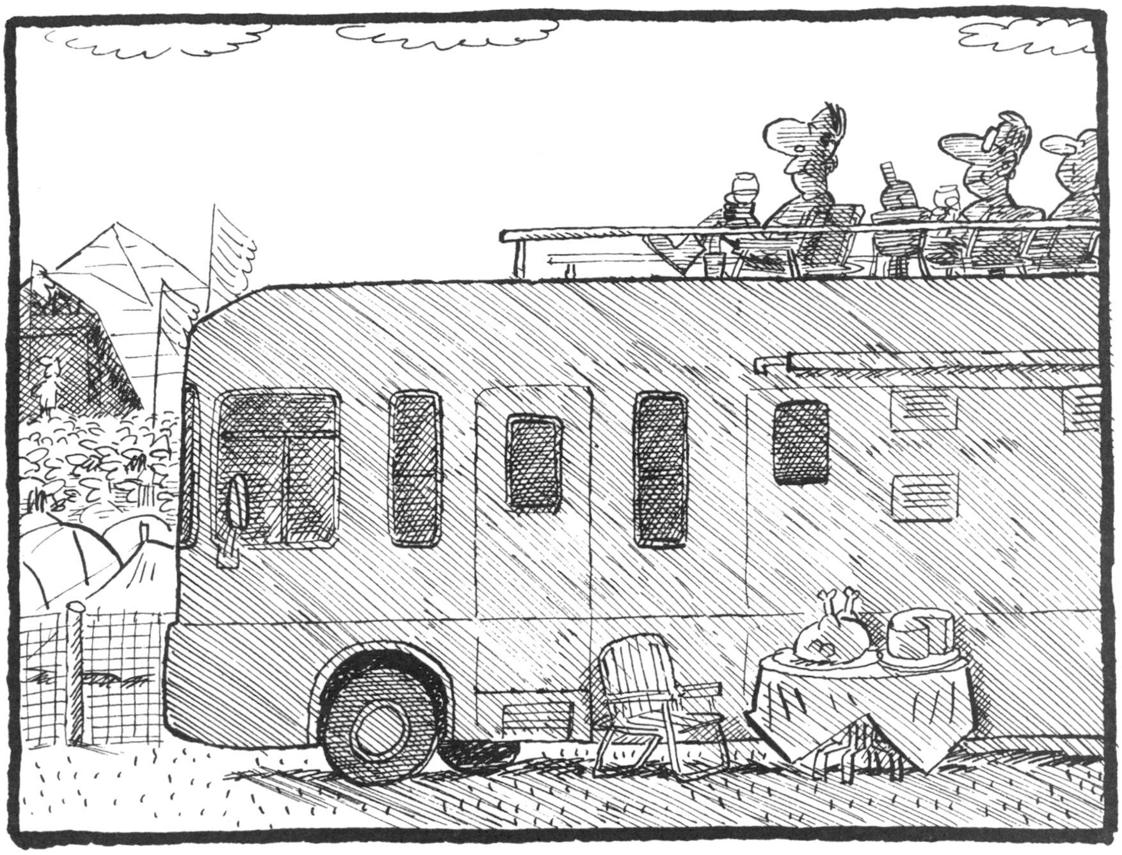

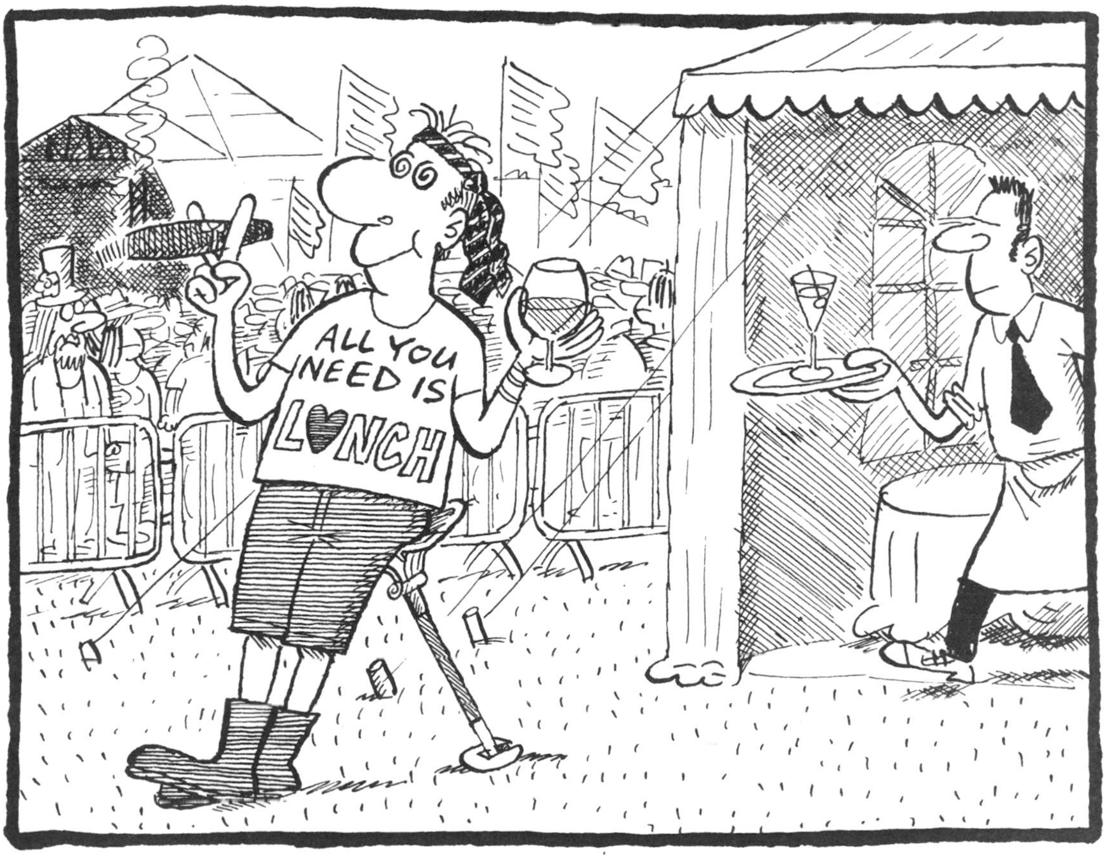
ALL YOU NEED IS L♥NCH

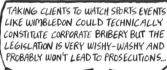

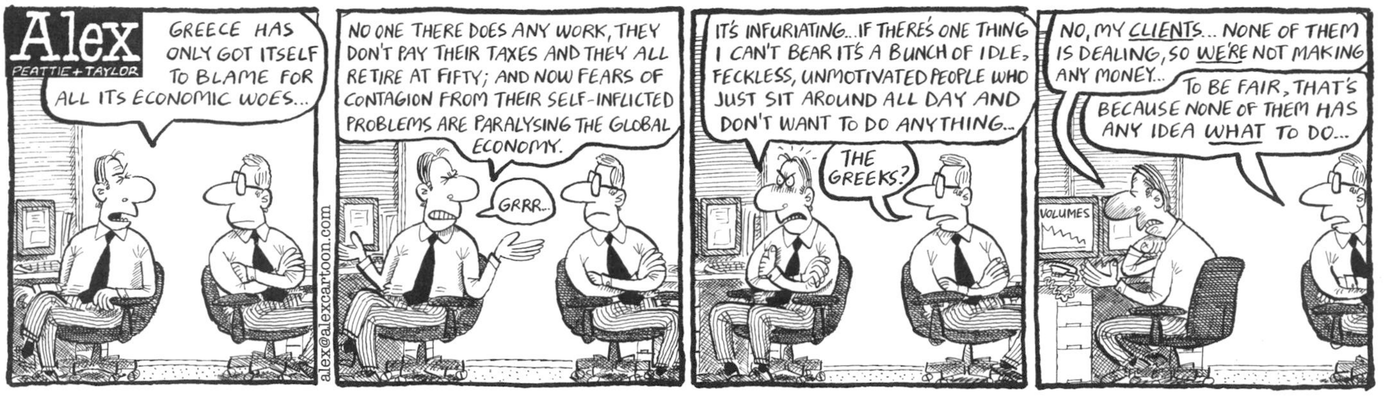
Alex
PEATTIE + TAYLOR
GREECE HAS ONLY GOT ITSELF TO BLAME FOR ALL ITS ECONOMIC WOES...
NO ONE THERE DOES ANY WORK, THEY DON'T PAY THEIR TAXES AND THEY ALL RETIRE AT FIFTY; AND NOW FEARS OF CONTAGION FROM THEIR SELF-INFLICTED PROBLEMS ARE PARALYSING THE GLOBAL ECONOMY.
GRRR...
alex@alexcartoon.com
IT'S INFURIATING... IF THERE'S ONE THING I CAN'T BEAR IT'S A BUNCH OF IDLE, FECKLESS, UNMOTIVATED PEOPLE WHO JUST SIT AROUND ALL DAY AND DON'T WANT TO DO ANYTHING...
THE GREEKS?
NO, MY CLIENTS... NONE OF THEM IS DEALING, SO WE'RE NOT MAKING ANY MONEY...
TO BE FAIR, THAT'S BECAUSE NONE OF THEM HAS ANY IDEA WHAT TO DO...
VOLUMES

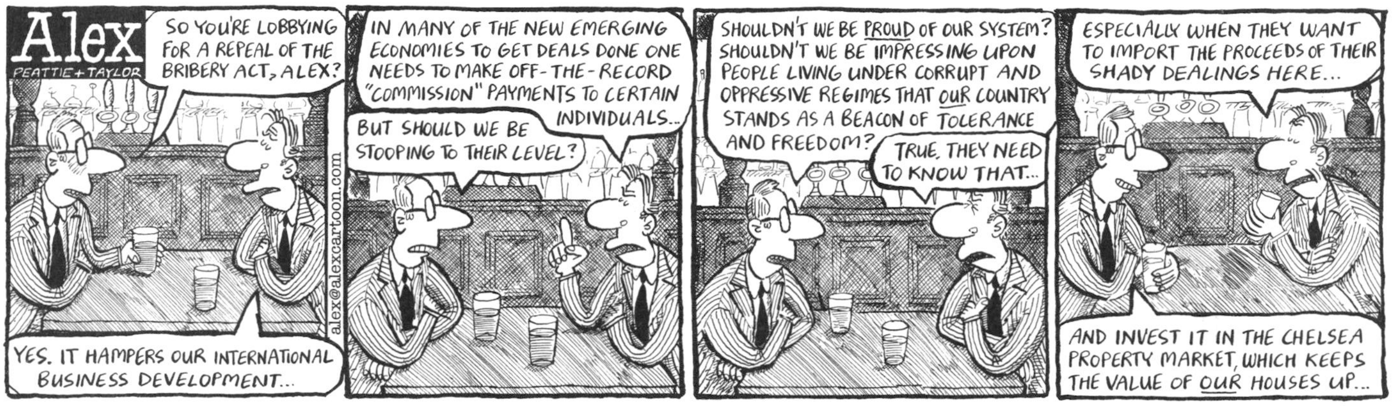
Alex
PEATTIE + TAYLOR
SO YOU'RE LOBBYING FOR A REPEAL OF THE BRIBERY ACT, ALEX?
YES. IT HAMPERS OUR INTERNATIONAL BUSINESS DEVELOPMENT...
alex@alexcartoon.com
IN MANY OF THE NEW EMERGING ECONOMIES TO GET DEALS DONE ONE NEEDS TO MAKE OFF-THE-RECORD "COMMISSION" PAYMENTS TO CERTAIN INDIVIDUALS...
BUT SHOULD WE BE STOOPING TO THEIR LEVEL?
SHOULDN'T WE BE PROUD OF OUR SYSTEM? SHOULDN'T WE BE IMPRESSING UPON PEOPLE LIVING UNDER CORRUPT AND OPPRESSIVE REGIMES THAT OUR COUNTRY STANDS AS A BEACON OF TOLERANCE AND FREEDOM?
TRUE. THEY NEED TO KNOW THAT...
ESPECIALLY WHEN THEY WANT TO IMPORT THE PROCEEDS OF THEIR SHADY DEALINGS HERE...
AND INVEST IT IN THE CHELSEA PROPERTY MARKET, WHICH KEEPS THE VALUE OF OUR HOUSES UP...

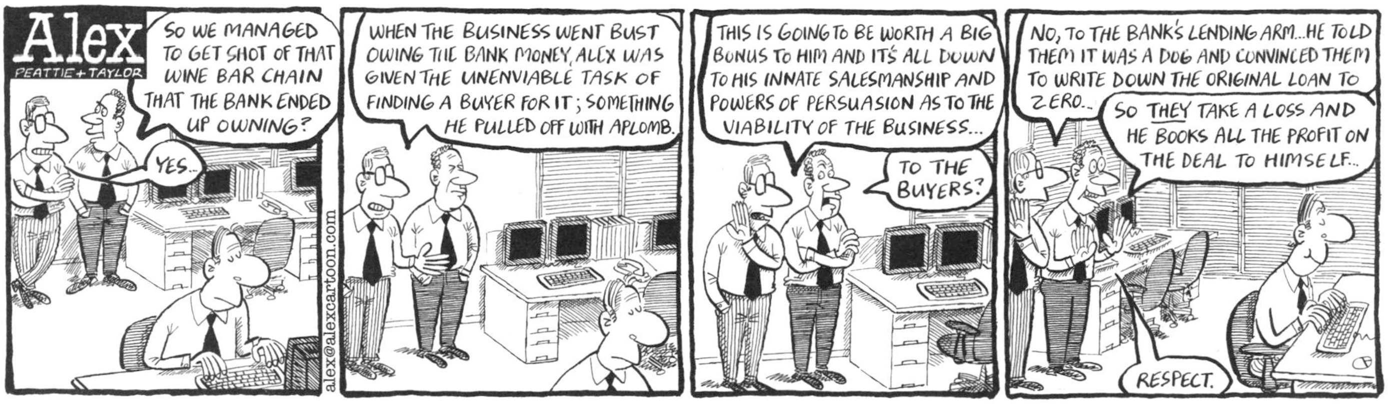
Alex
PEATTIE + TAYLOR
SO WE MANAGED TO GET SHOT OF THAT WINE BAR CHAIN THAT THE BANK ENDED UP OWNING?
YES...
alex@alexcartoon.com
WHEN THE BUSINESS WENT BUST OWING THE BANK MONEY, ALEX WAS GIVEN THE UNENVIABLE TASK OF FINDING A BUYER FOR IT; SOMETHING HE PULLED OFF WITH APLOMB.
THIS IS GOING TO BE WORTH A BIG BONUS TO HIM AND IT'S ALL DOWN TO HIS INNATE SALESMANSHIP AND POWERS OF PERSUASION AS TO THE VIABILITY OF THE BUSINESS...
TO THE BUYERS?
NO, TO THE BANK'S LENDING ARM... HE TOLD THEM IT WAS A DOG AND CONVINCED THEM TO WRITE DOWN THE ORIGINAL LOAN TO ZERO...
SO THEY TAKE A LOSS AND HE BOOKS ALL THE PROFIT ON THE DEAL TO HIMSELF...
RESPECT.

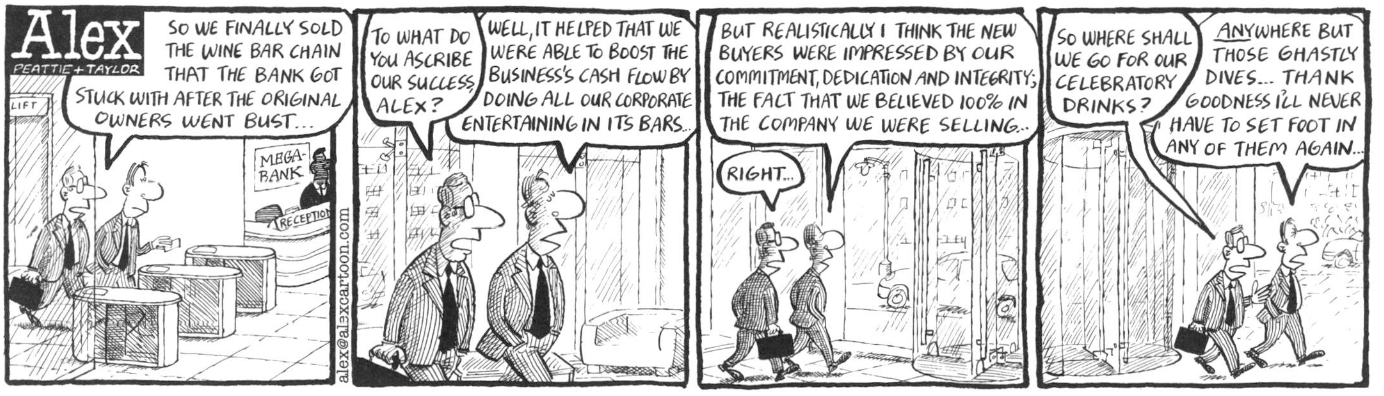
Alex
PEATTIE + TAYLOR
SO WE FINALLY SOLD THE WINE BAR CHAIN THAT THE BANK GOT STUCK WITH AFTER THE ORIGINAL OWNERS WENT BUST...
LIFT
MEGA-BANK
RECEPTION
alex@alexcartoon.com
TO WHAT DO YOU ASCRIBE OUR SUCCESS, ALEX?
WELL, IT HELPED THAT WE WERE ABLE TO BOOST THE BUSINESS'S CASH FLOW BY DOING ALL OUR CORPORATE ENTERTAINING IN ITS BARS...
BUT REALISTICALLY I THINK THE NEW BUYERS WERE IMPRESSED BY OUR COMMITMENT, DEDICATION AND INTEGRITY; THE FACT THAT WE BELIEVED 100% IN THE COMPANY WE WERE SELLING...
RIGHT...
SO WHERE SHALL WE GO FOR OUR CELEBRATORY DRINKS?
ANYWHERE BUT THOSE GHASTLY DIVES... THANK GOODNESS I'LL NEVER HAVE TO SET FOOT IN ANY OF THEM AGAIN...

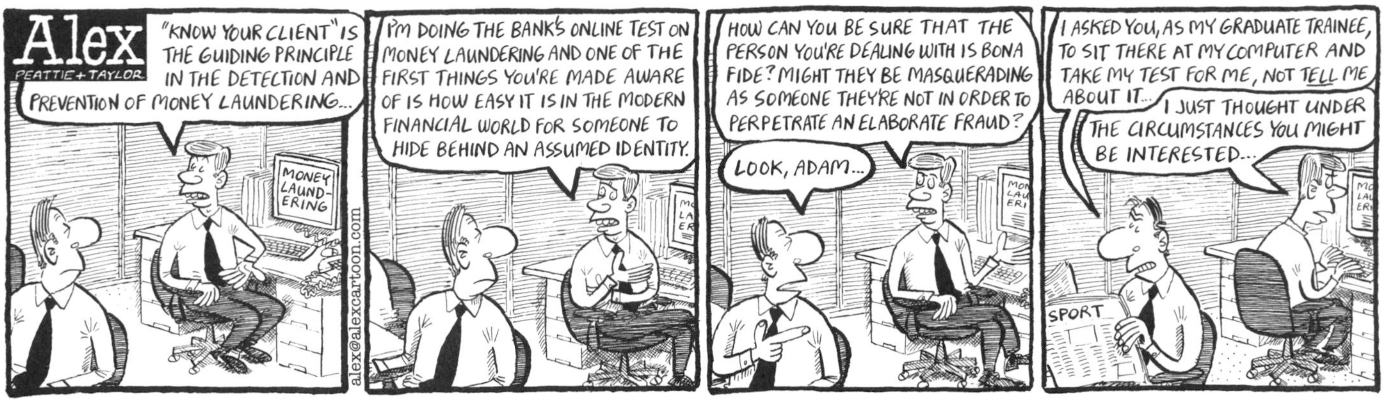
Alex
PEATTIE+TAYLOR
"KNOW YOUR CLIENT" IS THE GUIDING PRINCIPLE IN THE DETECTION AND PREVENTION OF MONEY LAUNDERING...
MONEY LAUNDERING
alex@alexcartoon.com
I'M DOING THE BANK'S ONLINE TEST ON MONEY LAUNDERING AND ONE OF THE FIRST THINGS YOU'RE MADE AWARE OF IS HOW EASY IT IS IN THE MODERN FINANCIAL WORLD FOR SOMEONE TO HIDE BEHIND AN ASSUMED IDENTITY.
HOW CAN YOU BE SURE THAT THE PERSON YOU'RE DEALING WITH IS BONA FIDE? MIGHT THEY BE MASQUERADING AS SOMEONE THEY'RE NOT IN ORDER TO PERPETRATE AN ELABORATE FRAUD?
LOOK, ADAM...
I ASKED YOU, AS MY GRADUATE TRAINEE, TO SIT THERE AT MY COMPUTER AND TAKE MY TEST FOR ME, NOT TELL ME ABOUT IT...
I JUST THOUGHT UNDER THE CIRCUMSTANCES YOU MIGHT BE INTERESTED...
SPORT

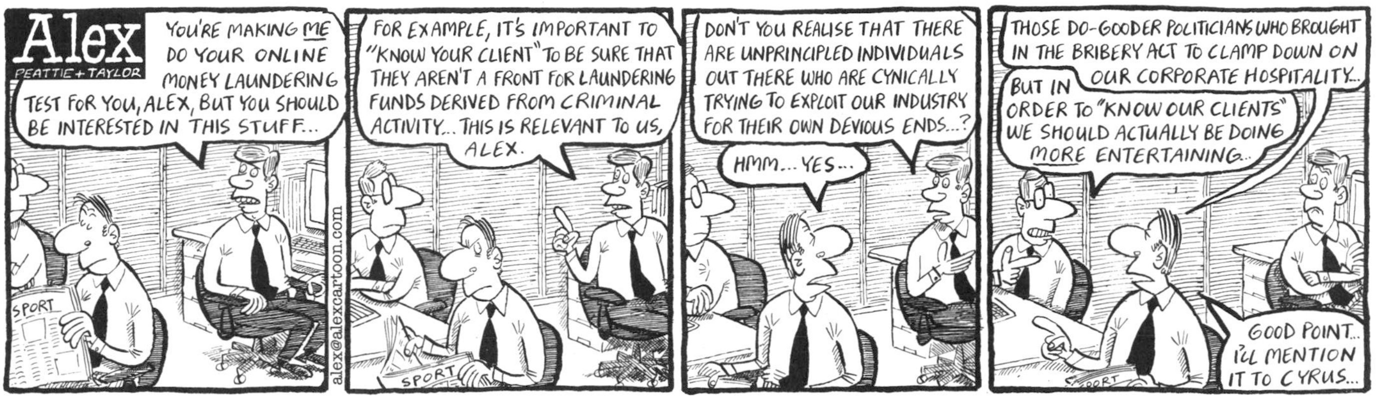
Alex
PEATTIE+TAYLOR
YOU'RE MAKING ME DO YOUR ONLINE MONEY LAUNDERING TEST FOR YOU, ALEX, BUT YOU SHOULD BE INTERESTED IN THIS STUFF...
SPORT
alex@alexcartoon.com
FOR EXAMPLE, IT'S IMPORTANT TO "KNOW YOUR CLIENT" TO BE SURE THAT THEY AREN'T A FRONT FOR LAUNDERING FUNDS DERIVED FROM CRIMINAL ACTIVITY... THIS IS RELEVANT TO US, ALEX.
SPORT
DON'T YOU REALISE THAT THERE ARE UNPRINCIPLED INDIVIDUALS OUT THERE WHO ARE CYNICALLY TRYING TO EXPLOIT OUR INDUSTRY FOR THEIR OWN DEVIOUS ENDS...?
HMM... YES...
THOSE DO-GOODER POLITICIANS WHO BROUGHT IN THE BRIBERY ACT TO CLAMP DOWN ON OUR CORPORATE HOSPITALITY...
BUT IN ORDER TO "KNOW OUR CLIENTS" WE SHOULD ACTUALLY BE DOING MORE ENTERTAINING...
GOOD POINT... I'LL MENTION IT TO CYRUS...

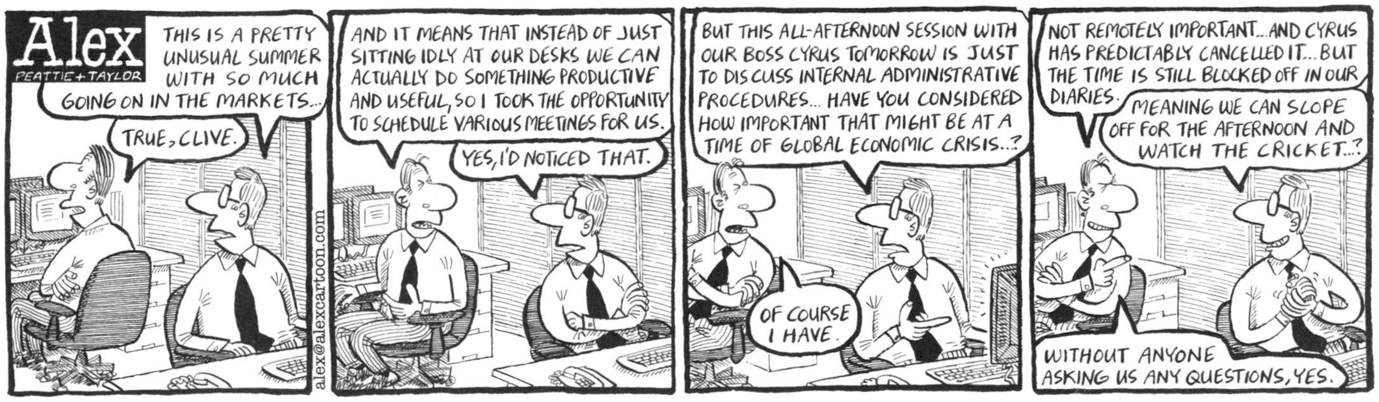
Alex
PEATTIE+TAYLOR
THIS IS A PRETTY UNUSUAL SUMMER WITH SO MUCH GOING ON IN THE MARKETS...
TRUE, CLIVE.
alex@alexcartoon.com
AND IT MEANS THAT INSTEAD OF JUST SITTING IDLY AT OUR DESKS WE CAN ACTUALLY DO SOMETHING PRODUCTIVE AND USEFUL, SO I TOOK THE OPPORTUNITY TO SCHEDULE VARIOUS MEETINGS FOR US.
YES, I'D NOTICED THAT.
BUT THIS ALL-AFTERNOON SESSION WITH OUR BOSS CYRUS TOMORROW IS JUST TO DISCUSS INTERNAL ADMINISTRATIVE PROCEDURES... HAVE YOU CONSIDERED HOW IMPORTANT THAT MIGHT BE AT A TIME OF GLOBAL ECONOMIC CRISIS...?
OF COURSE I HAVE.
NOT REMOTELY IMPORTANT... AND CYRUS HAS PREDICTABLY CANCELLED IT... BUT THE TIME IS STILL BLOCKED OFF IN OUR DIARIES.
MEANING WE CAN SLOPE OFF FOR THE AFTERNOON AND WATCH THE CRICKET...?
WITHOUT ANYONE ASKING US ANY QUESTIONS, YES.

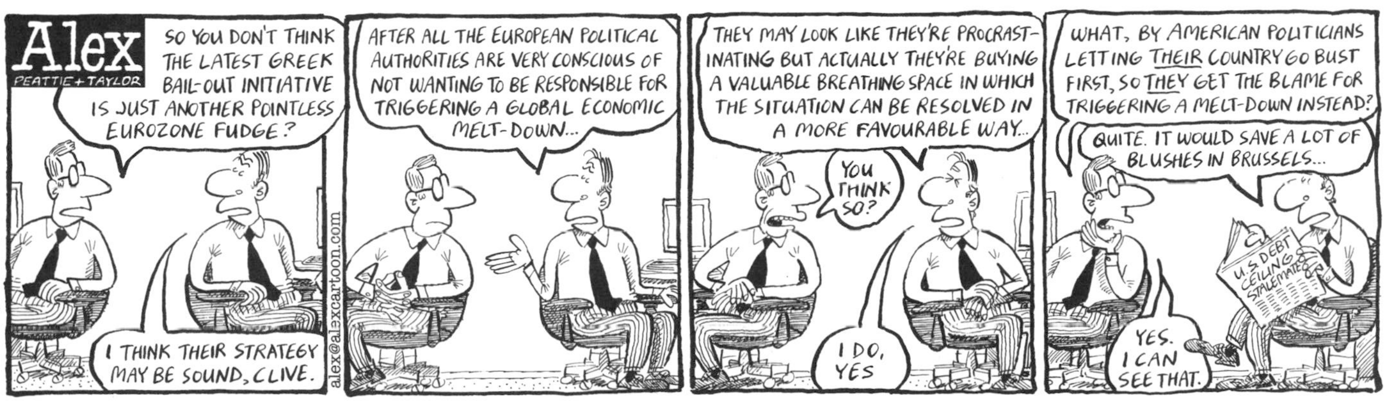
Alex
PEATTIE+TAYLOR
SO YOU DON'T THINK THE LATEST GREEK BAIL-OUT INITIATIVE IS JUST ANOTHER POINTLESS EUROZONE FUDGE?
I THINK THEIR STRATEGY MAY BE SOUND, CLIVE.
alex@alexcartoon.com
AFTER ALL THE EUROPEAN POLITICAL AUTHORITIES ARE VERY CONSCIOUS OF NOT WANTING TO BE RESPONSIBLE FOR TRIGGERING A GLOBAL ECONOMIC MELT-DOWN...
THEY MAY LOOK LIKE THEY'RE PROCRASTINATING BUT ACTUALLY THEY'RE BUYING A VALUABLE BREATHING SPACE IN WHICH THE SITUATION CAN BE RESOLVED IN A MORE FAVOURABLE WAY...
YOU THINK SO?
I DO, YES
WHAT, BY AMERICAN POLITICIANS LETTING THEIR COUNTRY GO BUST FIRST, SO THEY GET THE BLAME FOR TRIGGERING A MELT-DOWN INSTEAD?
QUITE. IT WOULD SAVE A LOT OF BLUSHES IN BRUSSELS...
U.S. DEBT CEILING STALEMATE
YES. I CAN SEE THAT.

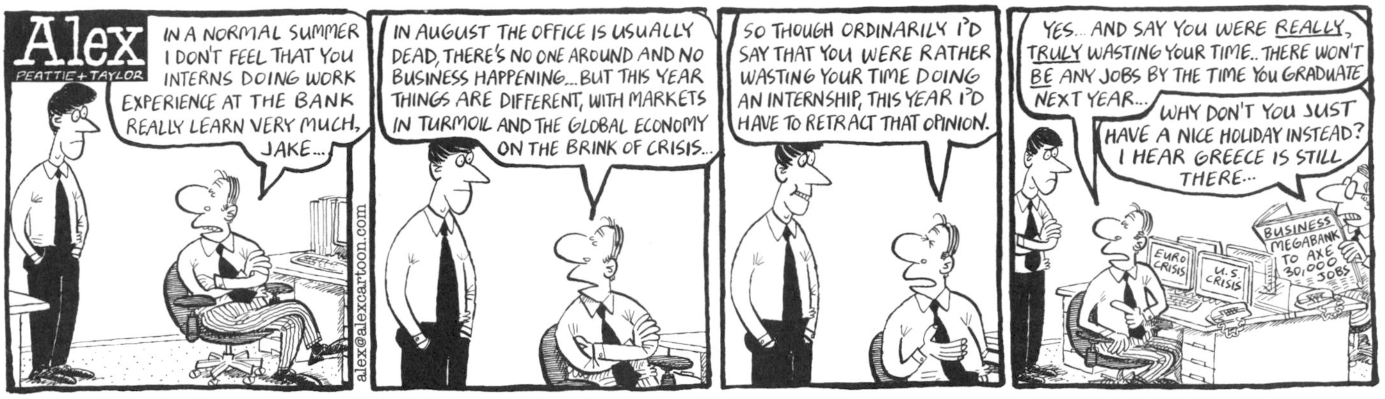
Alex
PEATTIE + TAYLOR
IN A NORMAL SUMMER I DON'T FEEL THAT YOU INTERNS DOING WORK EXPERIENCE AT THE BANK REALLY LEARN VERY MUCH, JAKE...
alex@alexcartoon.com
IN AUGUST THE OFFICE IS USUALLY DEAD, THERE'S NO ONE AROUND AND NO BUSINESS HAPPENING... BUT THIS YEAR THINGS ARE DIFFERENT, WITH MARKETS IN TURMOIL AND THE GLOBAL ECONOMY ON THE BRINK OF CRISIS...
SO THOUGH ORDINARILY I'D SAY THAT YOU WERE RATHER WASTING YOUR TIME DOING AN INTERNSHIP, THIS YEAR I'D HAVE TO RETRACT THAT OPINION.
YES... AND SAY YOU WERE REALLY, TRULY WASTING YOUR TIME.. THERE WON'T BE ANY JOBS BY THE TIME YOU GRADUATE NEXT YEAR...
WHY DON'T YOU JUST HAVE A NICE HOLIDAY INSTEAD? I HEAR GREECE IS STILL THERE...
EURO CRISIS
U.S. CRISIS
BUSINESS
MEGABANK TO AXE 30,000 JOBS

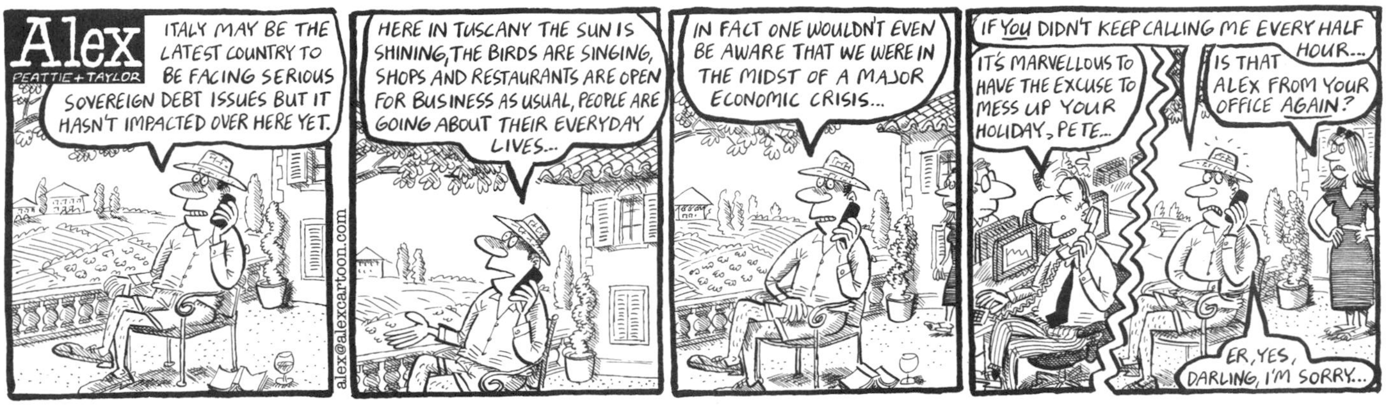
Alex
PEATTIE + TAYLOR
ITALY MAY BE THE LATEST COUNTRY TO BE FACING SERIOUS SOVEREIGN DEBT ISSUES BUT IT HASN'T IMPACTED OVER HERE YET.
alex@alexcartoon.com
HERE IN TUSCANY THE SUN IS SHINING, THE BIRDS ARE SINGING, SHOPS AND RESTAURANTS ARE OPEN FOR BUSINESS AS USUAL, PEOPLE ARE GOING ABOUT THEIR EVERYDAY LIVES...
IN FACT ONE WOULDN'T EVEN BE AWARE THAT WE WERE IN THE MIDST OF A MAJOR ECONOMIC CRISIS...
IF YOU DIDN'T KEEP CALLING ME EVERY HALF HOUR...
IT'S MARVELLOUS TO HAVE THE EXCUSE TO MESS UP YOUR HOLIDAY, PETE...
IS THAT ALEX FROM YOUR OFFICE AGAIN?
ER, YES, DARLING, I'M SORRY...

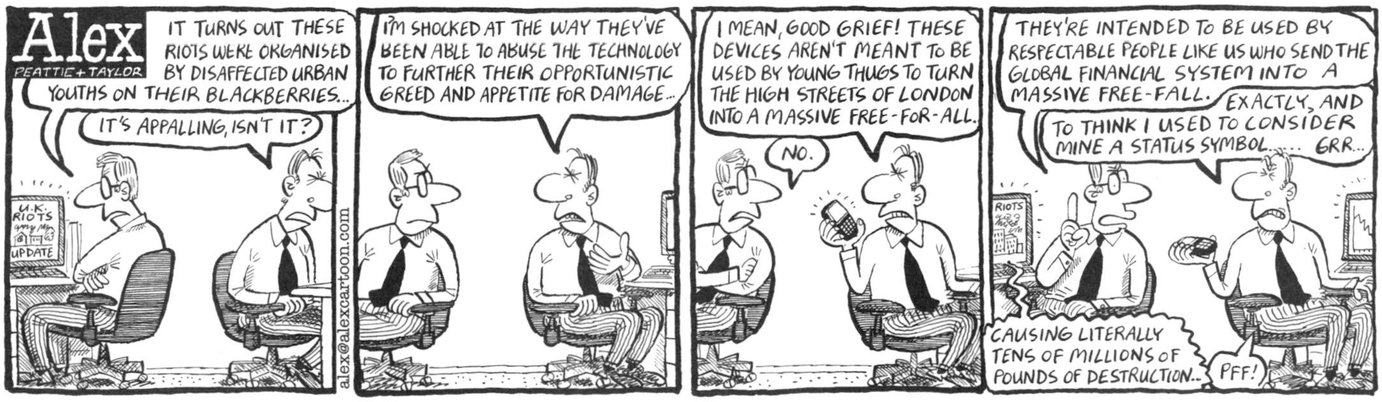
Alex
PEATTIE + TAYLOR
IT TURNS OUT THESE RIOTS WERE ORGANISED BY DISAFFECTED URBAN YOUTHS ON THEIR BLACKBERRIES...
IT'S APPALLING, ISN'T IT?
U.K. RIOTS UPDATE
alex@alexcartoon.com
I'M SHOCKED AT THE WAY THEY'VE BEEN ABLE TO ABUSE THE TECHNOLOGY TO FURTHER THEIR OPPORTUNISTIC GREED AND APPETITE FOR DAMAGE...
I MEAN, GOOD GRIEF! THESE DEVICES AREN'T MEANT TO BE USED BY YOUNG THUGS TO TURN THE HIGH STREETS OF LONDON INTO A MASSIVE FREE-FOR-ALL.
NO.
THEY'RE INTENDED TO BE USED BY RESPECTABLE PEOPLE LIKE US WHO SEND THE GLOBAL FINANCIAL SYSTEM INTO A MASSIVE FREE-FALL.
EXACTLY, AND TO THINK I USED TO CONSIDER MINE A STATUS SYMBOL..... GRR...
RIOTS
CAUSING LITERALLY TENS OF MILLIONS OF POUNDS OF DESTRUCTION...
PFF!

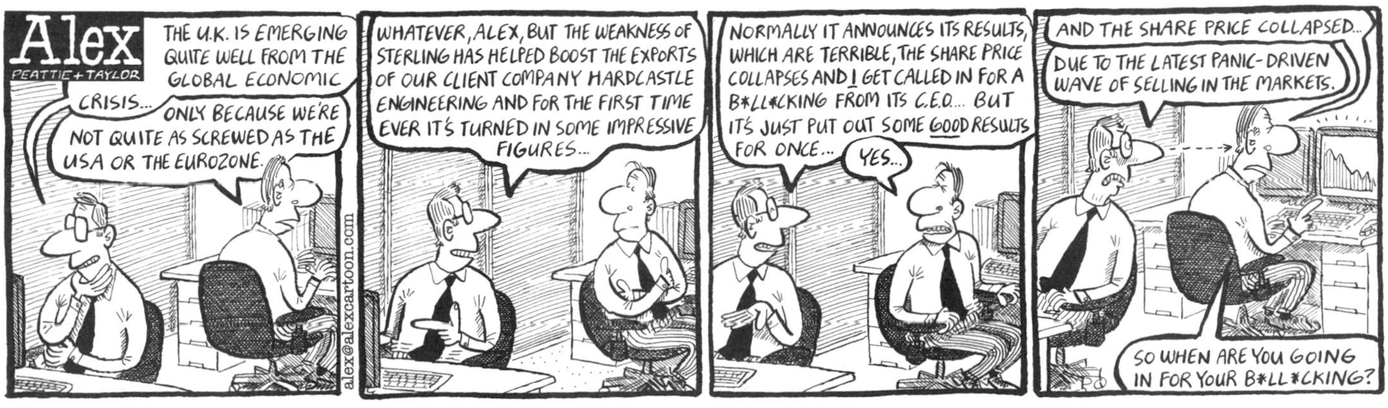
Alex
PEATTIE + TAYLOR
THE U.K. IS EMERGING QUITE WELL FROM THE GLOBAL ECONOMIC CRISIS...
ONLY BECAUSE WE'RE NOT QUITE AS SCREWED AS THE USA OR THE EUROZONE.
alex@alexcartoon.com
WHATEVER, ALEX, BUT THE WEAKNESS OF STERLING HAS HELPED BOOST THE EXPORTS OF OUR CLIENT COMPANY HARDCASTLE ENGINEERING AND FOR THE FIRST TIME EVER IT'S TURNED IN SOME IMPRESSIVE FIGURES...
NORMALLY IT ANNOUNCES ITS RESULTS, WHICH ARE TERRIBLE, THE SHARE PRICE COLLAPSES AND I GET CALLED IN FOR A B*LL*CKING FROM ITS C.E.O... BUT IT'S JUST PUT OUT SOME GOOD RESULTS FOR ONCE...
YES...
AND THE SHARE PRICE COLLAPSED...
DUE TO THE LATEST PANIC-DRIVEN WAVE OF SELLING IN THE MARKETS.
SO WHEN ARE YOU GOING IN FOR YOUR B*LL*CKING?

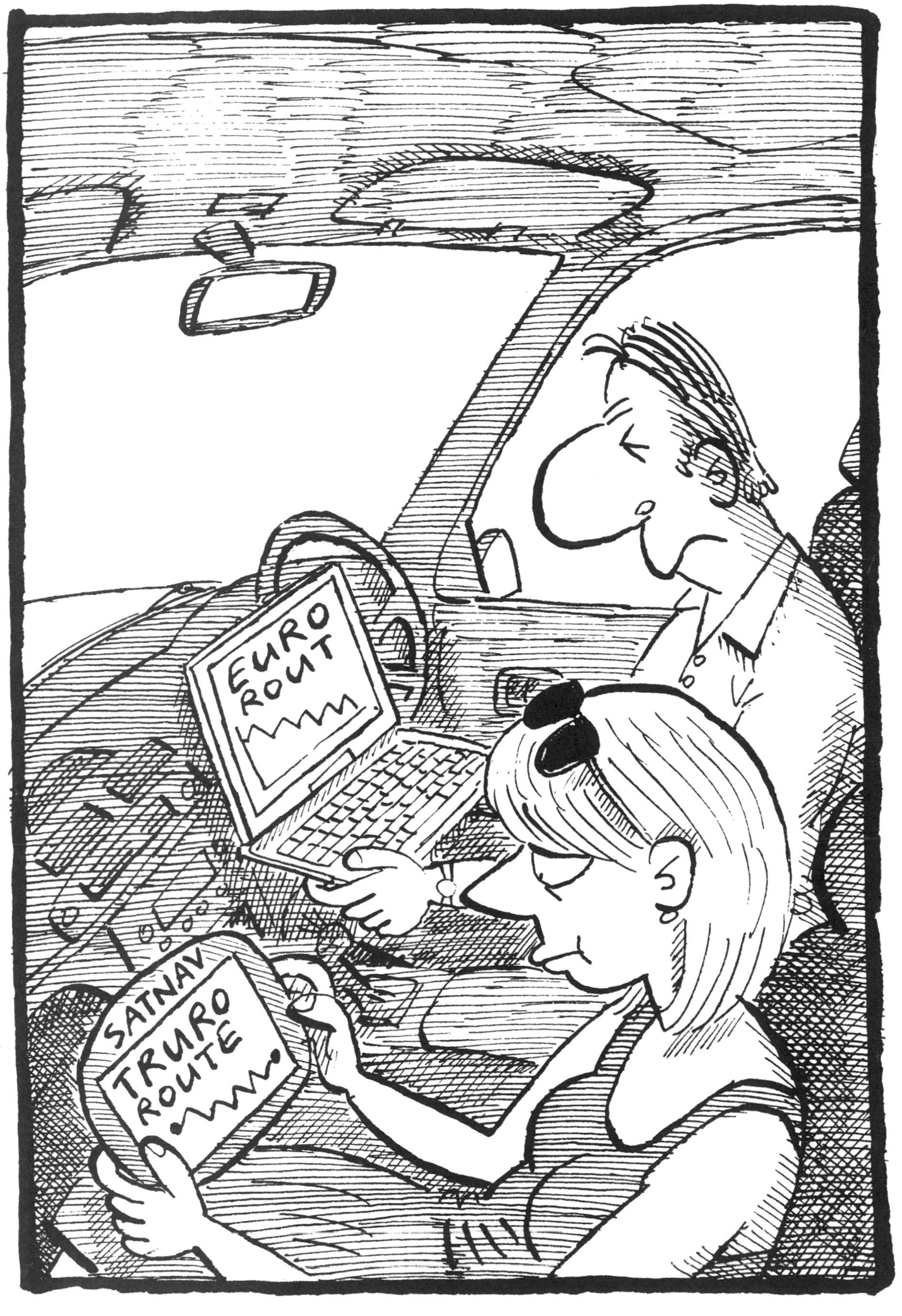
EURO
ROUT
SATNAV
TRURO
ROUTE

ALEX WENT ON HOLIDAY TO CORNWALL...

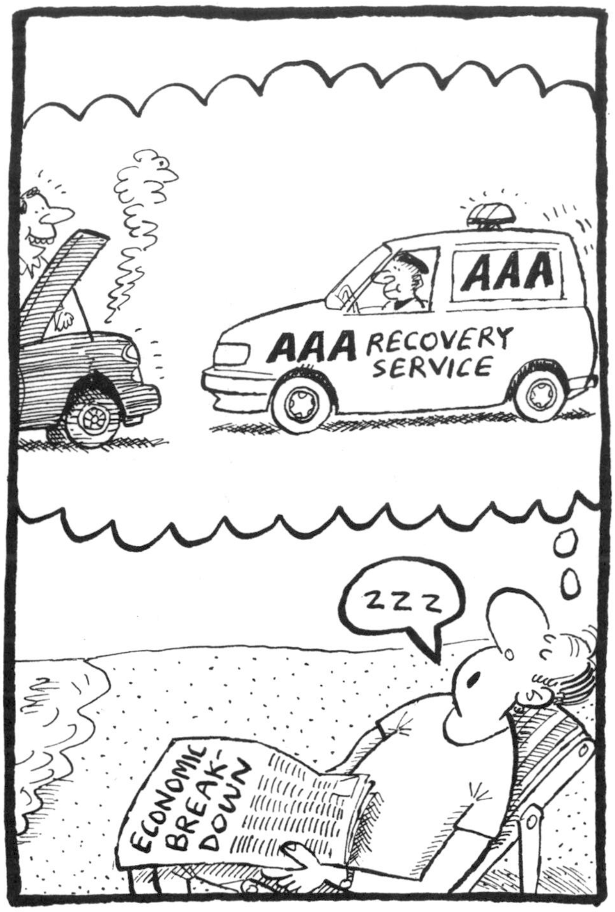
AAA
AAA RECOVERY SERVICE
ZZZ
ECONOMIC BREAK-DOWN

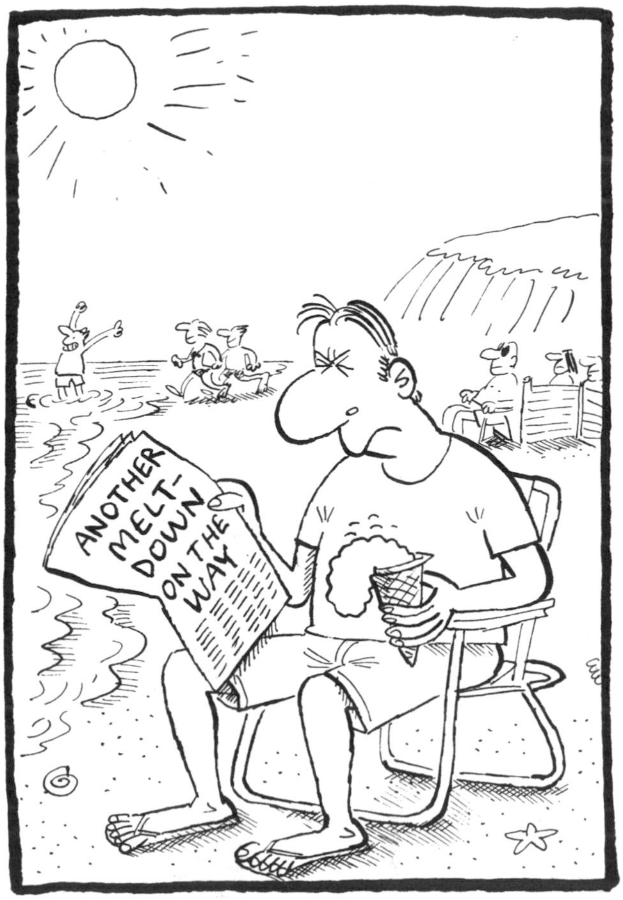
ANOTHER MELT-DOWN ON THE WAY

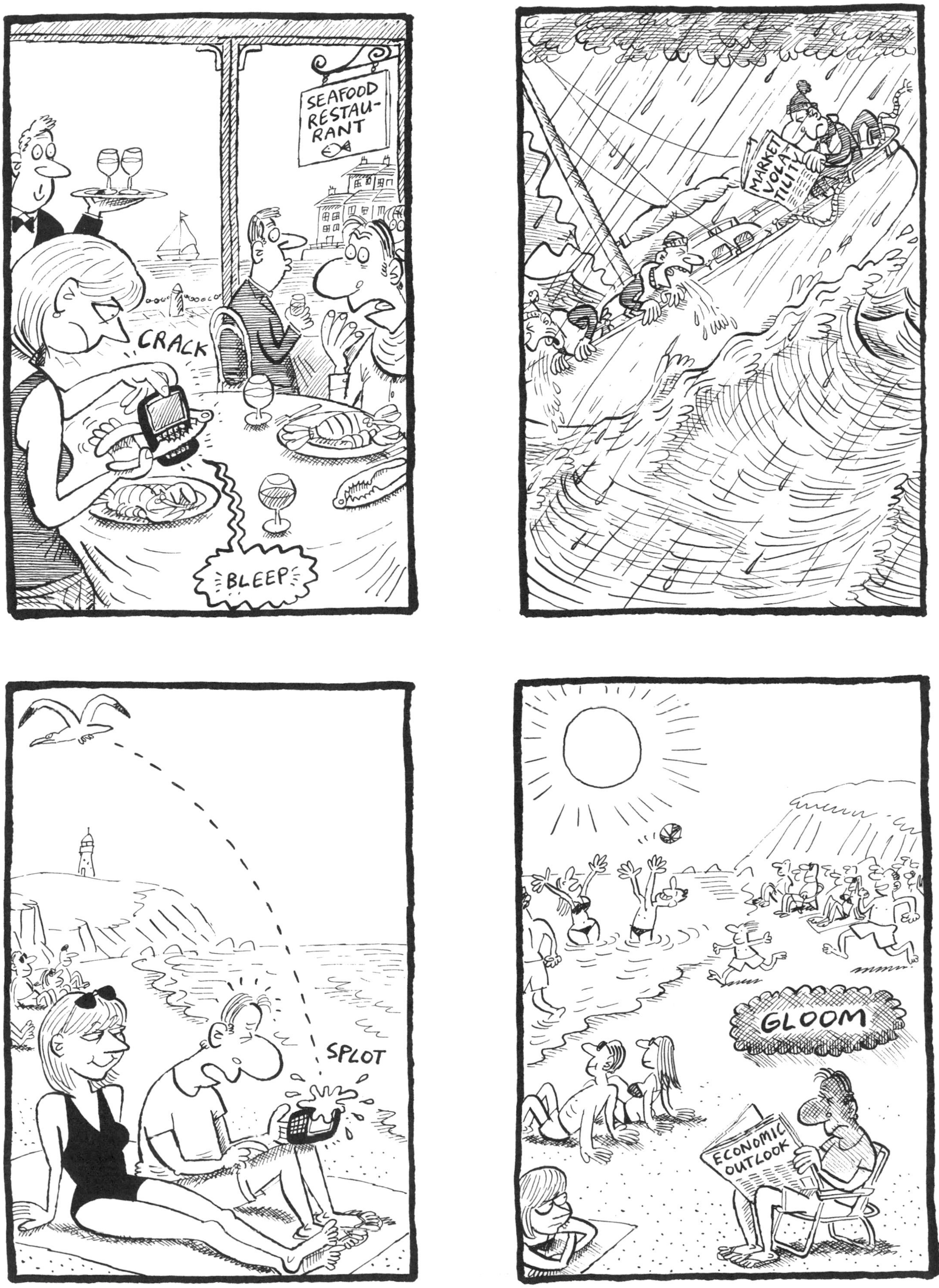
SEAFOOD RESTAU-RANT
CRACK
BLEEP
MARKET VOLA-TILITY
SPLOT
GLOOM
ECONOMIC OUTLOOK

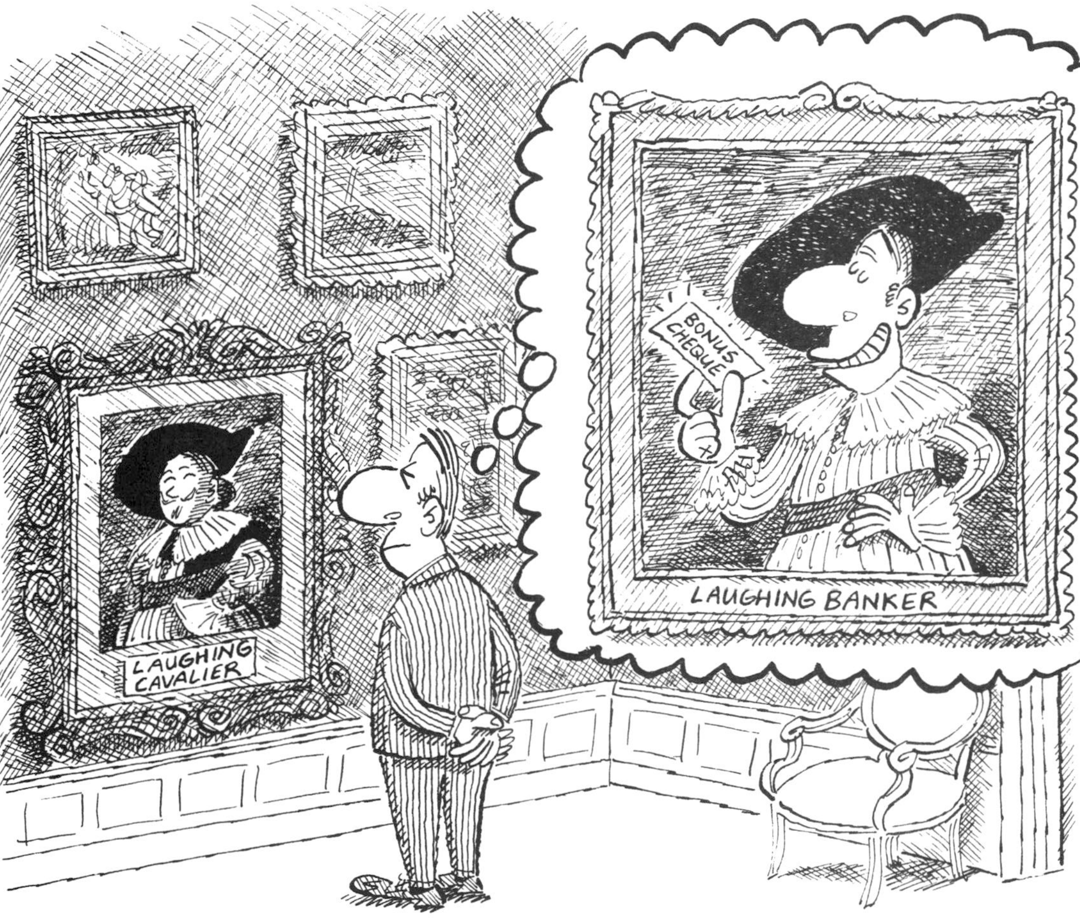
LAUGHING CAVALIER
BONUS CHEQUE
LAUGHING BANKER

Also available from Masterley Publishing

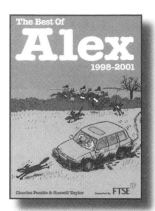

The Best Of
Alex
1998-2001
FTSE

The Best of Alex 1998 - 2001
Boom to bust via the dotcom bubble.

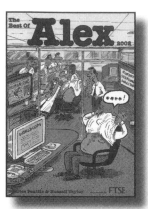

The Best of
Alex
2002
FTSE

The Best of Alex 2002
Scandals rock the corporate world.

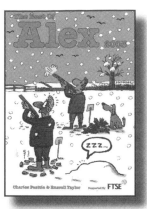

Alex
ZZZ...
FTSE

The Best of Alex 2003
Alex gets made redundant.

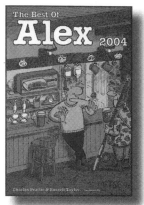

The Best Of
Alex
2004

The Best of Alex 2004
And gets his job back.

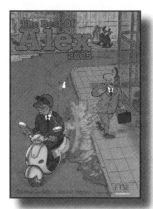

The Best Of
Alex
2005
FTSE

The Best of Alex 2005
Alex has problems with the French.

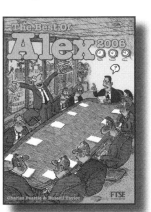

The Best Of
Alex
2006
Charles Peattie & Russell Taylor
FTSE

The Best of Alex 2006
Alex gets a new American boss.

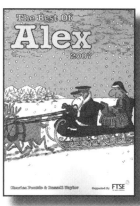

The Best Of
Alex
2007
FTSE

The Best of Alex 2007
Alex restructures Christmas.

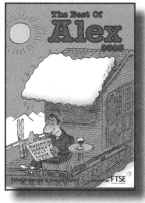

The Best Of
Alex
2008
BUSINESS
MARKET
MELT-
DOWN
FTSE

The Best of Alex 2008
The credit crunch bites.

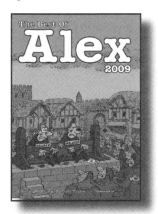

The Best Of
Alex
2009

The Best of Alex 2009
Global capitalism self-destructs.

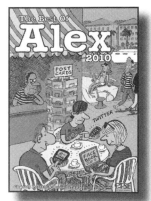

The Best Of
Alex
2010
POST
CARDS
TWITTER
FACE
BOOK

The Best of Alex 2010
But somehow lurches on.

Celeb
The Original Gary Bloke From
PRIVATE EYE
Charles Peattie and Mark Warren

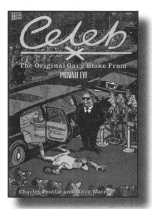

Celeb
Wrinkly rockstar Gary Bloke.

All books cost £9.99 plus p+p.
Cartoon originals and prints are also for sale.
They measure 4 x 14 inches and are signed by the creators.

For further details on prices:
Tel: 020 8374 1225
Email: alex@alexcartoon.com
Web: www.alexcartoon.com